Imm Mathilda
A Bethlehem Mother's Journal

By
Alison Jones Nassar
and
Fred Strickert

Kirk House Publishers
Minneapolis, Minnesota

Imm Mathilda
A Bethlehem Mother's Journal
By Alison Jones Nassar and Fred Strickert

The production of the first printing of this book was made possible in part by a gift from Bill Halverstadt of Hamel, Minnesota.

Library of Congress Cataloging in Publication data.
Nassar, Alison Jones, 1959-
    Imm Mathilda : A Bethlehem mother's journal / by Alison Jones Nassar and Fred Strickert.
        p. cm.
    ISBN 1-886513-92-9 (trade paper)
        1. Al-Aqsa Intifada, 2000—Personal narratives, American. 2. Nassar, Alison Jones, 1959-—Diaries. 3. Mothers and daughters—West Bank—Bethlehem—Diaries. 4. Military occupation. 5. Israel—Military policy. I. Title: A Bethlehm Mother's Journal. II. Strickert, Frederick M. III. Title.

    DS119.765.N37 2003
    956.9405'4—dc21

                                                2003047726

Kirk House Publishers, PO Box 390759, Minneapolis, MN 55439
Manufactured in the United States of America

Table of Contents

This book is dedicated to my husband, George,
whose love has been a gift to me
and whose courage has been an inspiration;

and to my three daughters, Mathilda, Nadine, and Phoebe,
who have given me so much light and love
in a world so full of darkness and hatred.

It is also dedicated to my mother, Nancy,
and my mother-in-law, Miladi,
whose strenghth got them through difficult circumstances
and whose love got me through some.

Surely we learn about God through our children,
Their arms and legs always about to burst into Flight,
their hair and skin about to catch fire . . .

Surely real prayers are made of children's laughter . . .

How precariously we have our children with us,
How grudgingly God gives them up!
Nothing in the world should ever be so precious,
So full of the possibility to loss!

Diana Abu-Jabar,
from the short story "Billets-Doux,"
published in *Story*, Spring 1994

Introduction

This book documents the daily experiences of an American woman living in Bethlehem, in the West Bank of the Occupied Territories of Israel. Alison Jones Nassar is neither a government diplomat, nor a church leader, nor a sacrificing charitable worker. She is not a person who would typically be labeled as a hero. She is not one who has grabbed news headlines nor whose face would be recognized. She is an ordinary person who lives in many ways what would be an ordinary life. She loves her husband dearly and is dedicated to raising her three daughters while going to work each day and trying to be a good neighbor.

What is unique about Alison is that she lives in Bethlehem, a town that has been ridden with violence over the past several years. Her ordinary life has turned into a maze of curfews, closures, and checkpoints where she is forced to share the road with Israeli tanks and where Apache helicopter gunships dominate the night sky.

Alison Jones grew up as a typical American girl in the United States. She did all the things common for children in the 1960s and 1970s. She was a rather good student and participated in drama and band. She attended Virginia Commonwealth University, majoring in math and reading education. What marked her character was a sense of adventure and a heart of compassion. Not every young American woman learns to fly an airplane. Not every young American woman joins the Peace Corps and volunteers to work among the poor of Senegal. However, like many Americans, Alison was fascinated with the Middle East and, as many dream, she volunteered to work on an archaeological dig in Israel. For five years she worked with the archaeology department at Hebrew Union

College. Later her artistic talents led to a position illustrating archaeological material at the Albright Archaeological Institute in Jerusalem. She also studied Hebrew on an Israeli kibbutz and Arabic at the Jerusalem YMCA.

Like many typical young women, even those with a knack for travel and adventure, at the age of thirty she fell in love. She came to Israel to work with Israelis, but what she least expected was that the man she would marry would be Palestinian. George Bishara Daher Nassar came from an old Bethlehem family. His father, who was ordained as an evangelist missionary, died in the 1970s, leaving his young widow to raise nine children, many of whom still live in the Bethlehem area. It was the ideal time for a budding romance. They married while the Madrid Conference was giving birth to a long awaited peace process between Israelis and Palestinians. Their first children were born amidst White House lawn ceremonies and the partial withdrawal of occupying armies. European and American investment in Bethlehem painted a promising economic future. Then the process fell apart. In July, 2000, the Camp David talks ended in failure. In late September, Ariel Sharon, prior to his election as Prime Minister, made a controversial visit to the Haram al-Sharif in Jerusalem, leading to the outbreak of the second Intifada. On October 22, Israeli tanks and American-made Apache helicopters began attacking the town of Beit Jala where Alison and George made their home.

I last saw Alison and George at Christmas in December 2000. Originally I had planned to bring a large choir to participate in the Gala Bethlehem 2000 celebrations in Manger Square. When that was canceled, Lutheran Pastor Mitri Raheb encouraged me to come on my own to offer encouragement to his congregation. We spent each night visiting the homes of congregation members, including a memorable evening with George's extended family. My wife, Gloria and a newspaper reporter were taken with the children. We had brought gifts, including art supplies to help the children express their feelings during these difficult times. The images they shared were rather sobering: scenes of their own neighborhood being bombarded by tank-fire and Apache helicopters marked "USA." "It's important for them to express their feelings," my wife encouraged them. "Perhaps we could send a copy of Harry Potter to give the girls an avenue for escape."

"And what about you, Alison?" I asked. "How do you cope? Perhaps you should put your thoughts into writing."

In the following months Alison occasionally sent us email messages concerning the situation and the happenings among the Nassar clan. She often forwarded articles from the Israeli *HaAretz* newspaper or from Jewish and Palestinian peace groups. Yet her own writing was quite good, and we told her so. So did others.

On August 6, 2001, Alison announced that she had been persuaded to write periodic updates that she would send by email to friends and relatives. By April 2002 it had become obvious that these reflections needed to be collected into a book. The only question concerned the parameters. It seemed natural to begin with the outbreak of the second Intifada in September, 2000 and continue until a resolution to the conflict had been found. Yet peace still remains elusive. The war in Iraq seems to offer a natural break. So the reflections in this book continue until April 2003. It is hoped that these reflections, plus the accompanying information, can contribute to understanding, especially among Alison's fellow Americans, and even help lead to a genuine peace between Israelis and Palestinians. If so, then the harrowing events she documents will not have been in vain.

Alison identifies herself in e-mail correspondence as Immmathilda. It is common among Palestinian women to refer to themselves using the name of their eldest son. Thus Imm (= Mother of) _____. Alison is the mother of three daughters, the oldest among them Mathilda. Her daughters define her existence. Her struggle is for them. Her commitment to record her experiences is ultimately their legacy.

In this book I have collected eighty reflections that she shared by email. They are filled with insight and spiritual depth. They are informative, but often very emotional, ranging from anger and despair to hope and determination. I have also included a number of short commentaries (printed in italics) to provide historical background.

The book is divided into two parts. The first speaks directly to the incursions of the Israeli army in Bethlehem. This includes the events surrounding the return of troops to Bethlehem in the fall of 2001 for the first time since Palestinian Autonomy under the Oslo Accords, Israel's Operation Defensive Shield and the Siege of the Church of the Nativity in the Spring of 2002, and the continued curfews and closures throughout the rest of 2002.

The second part includes reflections which speak particularly to various aspects of life under occupation: Reflections as Wife and Mother, The Land (holding on to the family farm), Suicide Bombers, Messages for Americans, Israeli Friends. Finally an appendix provides a timeline of events for this period.

Fred Strickert

PART ONE

Bethlehem Under Attack

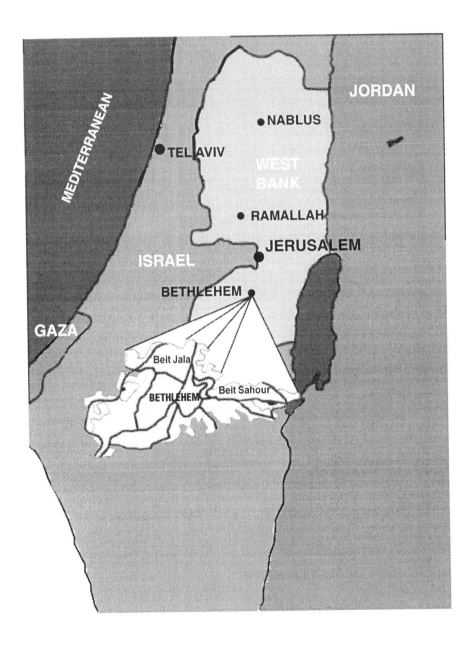

Alison's First Entry

6 August 2001 • Monday

My friend Dana suggested that I start sending weekly updates about our personal situation. Since I recently made a resolution to myself about trying to write more in order to increase awareness about the situation here, I decided I would try it.

But it won't be personal, except in the sense of describing what is going on around us. That is, I don't want to focus on us, in particular, because what's happening to us is also happening to everyone around us. We were able to improve our personal situation by moving out of harm's way to Beit Sahour, but plenty of people are still stuck up in Beit Jala, with nowhere to go and nothing to do but hope for the best. Those are the ones I want to focus on, and all the other people who just keep going and going because that is their only choice. But life for them these days is unimaginably hard, and I can't accurately describe the admiration I feel for them, or the sorrow, or the frustration on their behalf at the world's seeming indifference to all this.

When I got to work this morning at Bethlehem Bible College, there was a lady sitting on the ground by the front door. She's 78 years old, and she was wearing thick black glasses and a traditional embroidered robe, her teeth poking this way and that and her ankles swollen. I helped her up. She told me about her family's home up in Beit Jala, which had been damaged by shelling in the latest exchange last week, to the extent that they had had to move into a hotel. They didn't have money to pay for the hotel. No one in the family had managed to get to work in months. They don't have money for food. The children are hungry. This morning she fell on the steps of the hotel. She guided my hand to the spot, where I could feel a big lump. "Why are they," meaning the Israelis, "doing this to us?"

Phoebe, who's two, came home from daycare a few days ago, cocked her fingers like a gun, and with her baby smile said, "This is to shoot the Israelis."

In the space of a week, we have had three incidents of shelling and three horrendous assassinations. I leave the television on constantly so that I can see if a bulletin gets flashed up at the bottom of the screen. Not a day has gone by that there has not been a bulletin of some attack or other, some bombing, some shooting, some apache missile blast leaving another ten kids fatherless.

Yesterday the girls went to the Zaytooneh swimming pool in Beit Jala, directly across from the tunnel bridge and the tanks stationed there. At 1:30 I heard what I could have sworn was a shell exploding somewhere in the area. I called George, my heart hammering like crazy, and screamed at him to call the pool and find out if it was Beit Jala. He called back. There was nothing as far as anyone had heard. Everything was fine. Maybe I'm finally starting to go over the edge.

Mathilda told me, "If I was Harry Potter, I'd take my wand and wave all the tanks and soldiers away." Two nights ago, when the shelling was so fierce in Beit Jala that we could feel it through the floor at our house, I looked at the girls, whose faces were pinched as they sat listening, and said, "It's okay; we're safe now that we live here." Mathilda looked at me and said, "But what about the other people who are still there?"

She's right. How much can people be expected to take? Maybe if it had been my two kids killed up there in Nablus, I'd be on the next bus to the Tel Aviv station with as many explosives as I could pack.

Why can't they see that the logic and language they use to justify their attacks against us is just as legitimate and makes just as much sense from our perspective?

Can't it also be said that settlers are preparing to steal more land and perpetuate the apartheid policies against Palestinians, so they are legitimate targets for "liquidation"? Can't it also be said that Israeli leaders Sharon, Ben-Eliezer, and Mofaz are preparing to inflict more collective suffering (that is for sure!) on the Palestinians, so they are also legitimate targets for "liquidation"? Can't it also be said that soldiers are preparing to humiliate more working Palestinians (like George) at the checkpoints, so they also are legitimate targets? This madness will never end.

The Fall Incursion

*J*ust south of Jerusalem lie three Palestinian towns that played a significant role in Christian history. Best known of these is Bethlehem, the city of Jesus' birth, which has a population ratio of about 30% Christians to 70% Muslims. Nearby are two predominantly Christian villages that have grown to merge into the boundaries of the larger Bethlehem municipality. To the east is Beit Sahour, a community of about 10,000, that prides itself on high levels of education and historical roots related to the story of the Christmas shepherds. To the west is Beit Jala, a comfortable looking community nestled on a hillside overlooking the surrounding region. For more information see Mitri Raheb and Fred Strickert,* Bethlehem 2000: Past and Present *(Heidelberg: Palmyra, 1998).*

In many ways these communities share a link with Jerusalem, partly through religious connections and partly due to the economic interdependence resulting from the fact that many of their residents are employed in Jerusalem. In fact, in the 1947 UN partition plan, the Bethlehem area was taken out of the political realm and designated as part of greater Jerusalem, an international city to be controlled by neither Israelis nor Palestinians. Following the 1948 war, Bethlehem and East Jerusalem remained linked as part of Jordan. Then following the 1967 war, things began to change. While Bethlehem, Beit Jala, and Beit Sahour were designated to be included within the Occupied Territories known as the West Bank, East Jerusalem was annexed by Israel and the city boundaries were expanded to encroach upon the smaller communities to the south. Checkpoints were established which made travel progressively more difficult. Land was confiscated from Pales-

tinian owners for new Jewish communities within the reconfigured Jerusalem borders. Beit Jala residents lost farmland and grazing land for the establishment of Gilo, a community whose status is still debated as either an illegal settlement or a suburban Jerusalem neighborhood. Beit Sahour residents likewise lost a neighboring hillside known as Jabal Abu Ghneim that Israel has recently developed into a 6,000-occupant housing complex and renamed as Har Homa.

Bethlehem, Beit Jala, and Beit Sahour traditionally had a reputation for non-violence. During the first Intifada, Beit Sahour in particular led the way in such actions of civil disobedience as tax revolts and peaceful demonstrations. Its residents suffered retribution nonetheless. With the outbreak of the al-Aqsa Intifada, following the controversial visit by Ariel Sharon to the Haram al-Sharif in Jerusalem on September 28, 2000, things immediately turned violent. In the beginning, most confrontations were restricted to the area of the military installation located at the entrance to Bethlehem at Rachel's Tomb. Scores of rock-throwing youth were killed there by IDF fire in the first days. Eventually, however, gunfire from the edges of Beit Jala began targeting the community of Gilo. Two points are generally acknowledged. First, the gunmen were not residents of Beit Jala, but periodically came from outside the community at night where they positioned themselves for attack on the hillside. Second, the military response from Israel using tanks and Apache helicopter gunships far exceeded reasonable proportions and targeted the innocent residents of Beit Jala.

Alison and her family were among those residents of Beit Jala. It was normally a pleasant and convenient place to live. Alison was employed at Bethlehem Bible College located just down the street from Rachel's Tomb where the communities of Beit Jala and Bethlehem merge. The children attended the Lutheran Talitha Kumi School at the top of the hill. George's brothers Daher and Tony lived nearby in Beit Jala, and it was a short distance to George's mother's house near the Church of the Nativity in the center of Bethlehem. However, that comfortable life turned to terror when Israel began shelling Beit Jala on 22 October 2000. It touched home when a month later Harry Fisher was numbered among the victims. Like Alison, Harry was an expatriate who had married a Palestinian and chosen to settle in this area. Like Alison, Harry had first come out of humanitarian concern. He was a medical doctor, and when helicopter gunships fired upon a neighbor's house on the night of 15 November, Harry grabbed his medical satchel and ran to provide aid. Before he could reach his destination, Harry's body was blown to bits by a missile fired from an Apache helicopter. Harry's daughter and Alison's oldest daughter Mathilda were friends and classmates.

Over the following months, Mathilda responded by drawing pictures of her own once-comfortable community with helicopters hovering in terror above. Alison responded by recording her thoughts in the form of "updates" which she periodically shared by email. At times they included gallows humor, an example of which follows from a slightly earlier period.

Eventually George and Alison decided that they had to move out of the line of fire. They found an apartment in Beit Sahour which, although more expensive and less convenient, they thought would keep their children safe from further military attack.

18 April 2001

This is definitely getting worse. We are moving toward something, make no mistake. Last night was a whistling-through-the-air night. Out of all the many incidents, we've been able to develop a scale which goes something like this:

Distant shelling: you can hear it in the distance—from where we are it's probably Al-Khadr; turn on the TV—yep the Palestinian station confirms that; you think about the people there, knowing how they're feeling with it happening and hoping they're okay, you've got the luxury of feeling concern for others; it's not as abstract as reading an item in the paper but still, distant . . .

Local shelling: it's in the neighborhood but somehow still not so threatening that you bother to lower the newspaper or stop chopping the onions for dinner; the kids come in and stand beside you and you start to tell them something, anything to distract them, and they are willing to be distracted . . .

Very local: still not too threatening, but the girls want you to spread the quilt on the floor in your room in the small space between the bed and the computer so you do; they sit down on it and you bring them some papers and colors, or else you get Harry Potter and start reading to them, and it's okay; next thing you know they're bored and want to get up . . .

Ducking your heads: even though you're inside and down on the floor, it still sounds and feels so close that you're instinctively ducking your heads, and the window panes rattle every time a shell explodes; still, if the girls have already fallen asleep, then they stay asleep, and somehow it's still not loud enough to rouse them . . .

Whistling through the air: the shells are so close that you can hear the whistle, and then there's just a moment of absolute quiet before it hits and, even though you're bracing for the loudness of it, it sounds even louder and closer, loud enough to wake them if they're asleep, and if they're awake they're just barely controlling the panic; you have to sit with your arms around them and keep saying it's okay, even though they can feel you flinching so they know it's not really; plus whistling-through-the-air is usually accompanied by loss-of-electricity, and crouching in the dark is somehow even scarier, sort of dreamlike, and you know the usual rules aren't necessarily going to intervene . . .

Attack helicopters: these combined with the previous is the worst we have experienced so far; the volume alone seems enough to inflict injury and flatten houses, and the quiet which eventually follows seems oddly flat and still, like breath being held, which it probably in fact is. Waking up the next morning you feel sure stuff will look different; everyone has the same groggy expression which is only partly the result of a lack of sleep . . .

There is a difference between now and the end of last year. Last year you could hear the spaces between the shells. Now the incidents are relatively briefer but more intense by a factor of ten, twenty, a hundred, so that in the space of a half hour you will have heard hundreds of shells. Last night it took me a moment to realize it was starting—I just heard a roar and stupidly thought, a train? a plane? then realized it was shell after shell after shell producing one uninterrupted wall of roaring sound, something practically impossible in its intensity— and by the way, the shelling these days is *preceding* the shooting, not following it. This is not in retaliation, folks; this is to get the desired response, something to justify a "small military operation." Like reoccupying part of Gaza yesterday. Sorry, they didn't reoccupy it. They just went back in. For a bit. Just a couple of days or weeks. At most a couple of months. *Maximum 18 years* . . . and the hit on the Syrian base was a *complete coincidence.* Yeah. Everyone is in such denial it would be hilariously funny if it wasn't happening on my doorstep. . . And if I hear one more newscaster referring to "the efforts Prime Minister Sharon is making to ease the suffering of the innocent Palestinian civilians" I might just have to go and throw some rocks myself. . . .

10 August 2001 • Friday
The Nassars move to Beit Sahour

The other day George and I were driving up from Beit Sahour to Bethlehem, and he told me to look at the driver of the car behind us. The driver, George told me, is on Israel's wanted list for involvement with George Habash's PFLP (Popular Front for the Liberation of Palestine) group. "They say that he sleeps in a different place every other night," said George. "He drives yellow (Israeli) plates to decrease the likelihood that they'll blast his car with an Apache missile . . ."

I looked back. The guy was very benign-looking, the usual mustache and a cap on his head.

George told me, "He wears the cap all the time. The Israelis beat him so severely when he was in jail that his head is misshapen, with patches of hair gone and lumps and holes all over. He is always wearing the cap."

I looked back at him again and wondered if he was next on the "liquidation" list.

An article in today's *HaAretz* was entitled "Human Shields Protect Beit Jala Residents."

"The IDF says it is trying to find out exactly where the activists are staying for fear that wounding or killing any of them would create an international incident."

The implied message being that wounding or killing Palestinians does not arouse international anger and does therefore not have to be avoided.

I have started walking home from work a few times a week, so that the fatigue in my body can catch up with the fatigue in my mind and spirit. A few days ago I walked through Bethlehem up to Manger Square and on down to Beit Sahour, where we now live. Anyone visiting Manger Square now would be confronted with the sight of a huge banner depicting a dove flying against a backdrop of a Palestinian flag, a masked gunman, a body wrapped in a green Hamas shroud being carried for burial, and a pair of hands bound in chains, pleading. Some people would find that juxtaposition of images unsettling or even offensive. But I find that most people here do not differentiate between Hamas or Tanzim or George Habash and ordinary people. As I read recently, "Ordinary people do not see these assassinations as attacks specifically on Hamas or Tanzim. They see them as attacks on Palestinian citizens, in their homes and cars (and chicken coops)."

The Israelis have done their best to demonize these groups and individuals, but the fact is that Fatah leader Marwan Barghouti is a very ordinary person who is very good at articulating the Palestinian perspective for Palestinians. His remarks are very straightforward, and most Palestinians suspect that the crime that he is most guilty of as far as Israelis are concerned is speaking the truth in a way which is inescapable. Their methods may or may not be questionable, but their logic, as far as most Palestinians are concerned, is beyond reproach. I have found myself nodding in agreement as well, listening to speeches by Sheikh Hassan Nasralla (the spiritual leader of Hezbollah) and leaders of Hamas and Islamic Jihad. These guys may be many things, but they are not the demons Israel has made them out to be. Sharon, on the other hand. . . .

Anyway, my walk. I was surprised to run into so many people I knew, although it shouldn't really be surprising considering I have lived here for ten years in November. Ten years. I looked at faces as I walked. I saw lots of smiles, but also lots of hard life, and everyone who stopped to greet me had a comment to make about how the situation has been and continues to hurt them. But they just keep going. I really can't describe how much admiration I feel for these ordinary people, living in fear and enduring so much hardship. There is no lack of comments about what Palestinians do that they shouldn't do, or what they don't do that they should do. But how many have, or could, walk in their shoes down this endlessly long road of occupation? Their suffering needs to count for something.

6 September 2001 • Thursday

Looking over last Friday's edition of the Israeli newspaper *HaAretz*, I felt there were so many things which required a response. The experience of Beit Jala's reoccupation had the effect of making me hyper-vigilant of what people profess to know and understand about what is happening here and what they are getting away with saying and writing. Invariably, so much of it is only selectively true, if not completely false, according to the experiences of people who live here and endure this situation on a personal level every hour of every day. The question is whether or not we will allow these personal experiences to count.

I spent the last week arguing via e-mail with some anony-mous pro-Israel entity (I somehow got the impression that they lived in a West Bank settlement and the language they used suggested they may have been messianic Jews or Christian Zionists). I repeatedly tried to emphasize the unimaginable suffering of Palestinians throughout the West Bank and Gaza, some of which I have personally experienced and witnessed and which worsens by the day. People we know are standing in line to receive cards which entitle them to free bread. People we know are having to withdraw their kids from school because they no longer have the income to pay the tuition fees. People we know have had their houses and possessions completely destroyed by shelling. I have seen people walk into our office and start weeping out of sheer desperation and terror. Friday's paper had an article expressing grave concern about Israel's unemployment rate, which is currently 8.6%. The unemploy-ment rate among West Bank Palestinians is between 50 and 60%, higher still in Gaza, thanks to the 11-month (in 22 more days it will be a year) Israeli blockade of Palestinian towns and villages.

And yet these people, whomever they are, repeatedly dismissed all this with their neat arguments about how it is all "the Palestinians' own fault." They insisted on focusing on Arafat, whom they characterized in demonic terms and com-pared to Hitler, Saddam Hussein, and the devil himself. I, in turn, insisted that the demonization of Arafat is a deliberate strategy intended to redirect attention away from the unprec-edented humanitarian crisis taking place within Palestine, perpetrated by Israel toward a definite goal (making peoples' lives so miserable that they will finally surrender to "voluntary" transfer) and under the indifferent gaze of the United States of America.

In the end, this exchange left me exhausted and demoralized. It was the proverbial brick wall against which I banged my head until it was bloody. Do most people think this way? And if they do, what is the hope for these forsaken people? As the news of yet another suicide bomber came on Tuesday, I believed I could understand the depth of his pain, frustration, and exhaustion beyond all human comprehension. And I have only had to withstand all this for ten years. Think of them, decade after decade and generation after generation. And when I think of how easily this anonymous e-mail correspondent, in all his (or her) supreme ignorance and arrogance, passed his judgments of blame, and when I think of the waste and the suffering and the unbearable sorrow that must drive a young person to blow himself to bits, I could cry. Shame on everyone who sits in judgment of these people. Shame on everyone who stands silently by. Shame on everyone who perpetuates the lies that perpetuate their suffering. Shame on the hypocrisy of those who are comfortable and safe. Shame.

*O*n 21 December 1995, as part of the Oslo peace accords, the Israeli army withdrew from Bethlehem after 28 years
of military occupation. As a mark of self-rule, one of the first
buildings to go was the border police station at Manger Square.
Bethlehem, Beit Jala, and Beit Sahour were designated Area A,
meaning that the Palestinians had complete control. During the
first year of the second Intifada, Israel had reentered most of the
other areas of self-rule, but the Israeli army seemed to respect
something of the sacred character about Bethlehem.

Over the previous year tanks and helicopter gunships had
shelled both the communities of Beit Jala and Beit Sahour in
retaliation for sniper fire and sometimes without specific reason.
They also had carried out several assassination attacks. In
November, 2000, a Palestinian Tanzim leader was hit with a
missile while driving his jeep through Beit Sahour. Two older
women who had been out for a Saturday evening stroll were
killed because they were in the wrong place at the wrong time.
On 17 July, 2001, by guided missile, Israel assassinated four
Palestinians in a home not far from the center of Bethlehem.
They said they were targeting Omar Saarda, who they claimed
was a Hamas activist. Among those killed was Isaac Saarda,
his brother, who was a teacher at the Terra Santa School, a
peace activist working with Israeli educators, and a father of
eleven. Israel had struck from a distance, but that was quite
different from an all out invasion.

In late August, the Israeli paratroopers backed by tanks,
bulldozers, and helicopters moved into Beit Jala. They even
occupied the Lutheran Church, using the tower to shoot at
residents and holding 45 young boys in the orphanage hostage
as human shields. Only by the intervention of the Lutheran
Bishop through the American Consulate was the army pres-
sured to withdraw after four days.

On 18 October, when the Israeli army occupied Bethlehem
and the surrounding towns, this marked a major turning point
in the lives of the residents of the three linked communities.
The incursion came in response to the assassination by the
PFLP the previous day in Jerusalem of Israeli Tourism Minister
Rehavam Ze'evi. The minister had not been considered popular

in Israeli circles. He was considered extreme in his racist attitudes, advocating even that Palestinians should be transferred to the country of Jordan in order to open the West Bank for full settlement of Israelis. However, as the first Israeli government official to fall, his assassination became the cause for a massive onslaught against the Palestinians. There was no connection with Bethlehem, but the people of Bethlehem suffered.

The occupation of Bethlehem lasted from 18 to 28 October, leaving a trail of destruction and a significant number dead, both young and old. Perhaps the most striking thing, and a foretaste of things to come, was that the Israelis no longer restrained themselves from attacking the center of town including the Church of the Nativity. On Sunday, 21 October, worshippers at neighboring St. Catherines were even disrupted when Israeli snipers began shooting at the building. The previous evening, a seventeen-year old altar boy named Johnny Taljieh had been shot by Israeli sniper fire and killed after exiting the church from Saturday evening mass. For Alison and George, this hit close to home. George's sister Nahida had married into the Taljieh family and also lived within blocks of Manger Square. It could easily have been their own nephew, Isa.

19 October 2001

The assassination Thursday evening of the three Tanzim activists occurred within 500 meters of our front door. If I had left work 5 minutes earlier, the girls and I would've been driving down that hill either one car in front of or behind the booby-trapped jeep as it exploded. Or alternatively, if Mathilda and Nadine had spent the afternoon at Noor's house in Beit Jala as we'd planned, Phoebe and I would've been heading up that hill right about that time, between 5:45 and 6:00 p.m., to pick them up. As it was, instead of going to Noor's, they had gotten off the school bus at the college as usual. I had already left because I wasn't expecting them to come. Soon after getting home, they called me, so I took Phoebe and returned to Bethlehem. Once I got back to the college, the girls asked to watch a video ("Scooby Doo") in the guesthouse, so while they did, I went back to work at my desk. It was nearly dark around 5:25 as we left the college.

The girls had asked me to retrieve their scout uniforms from the old house in Beit Jala, so we drove up the hill to get those and a few other things. That took about 15 minutes. Then we drove back to the college, parking at the front gate as I tried to call George to find out if he was already heading back to Bethlehem in a taxi from his work in Jerusalem. I was thinking I could pick him up at the checkpoint before heading home. At first I couldn't get a line and had to retry three or four times before I could get through. He was still waiting for a taxi to fill up at Damascus Gate, so I told him I was going to take the girls on home.

Five minutes later, we reached the top of the hill which descends to our house. Pandemonium!! The road was jammed with cars whose drivers had simply leapt out and started run-ning. People were tearing in every direction, screaming and crying. I stopped a few people to ask what had happened. One told us two cars had collided at high speed. Another told us a helicopter had targeted a car with a missile. A third told us the car had exploded. I looked down the hill and saw thousands of people converging on the scene. Ambulances began arriving and I could neither go forward nor back up. A man ran up and pounded on our hood, telling us to clear the road for the medics. Others started directing cars that were attempting to back up. It took maybe 15 minutes to back up to a point where I could turn around. People running toward the scene kept cutting behind us, and I was afraid I would hit someone. Then the shooting began as people started to realize that this, in fact, was another assassination, the fourth in five days. I kept hearing the name Abayat and understood that the hit involved Tanzim. As soon as I could, I called George back. "They just assassinated somebody on the hill by our house, right near Imm Raja's house (our neighbor)! I can't get home, there's thousands of people! I'm driving back to Bethlehem!" As I drove back the way I had come, machine gunfire erupted on every side of us. I told the girls to get on the floor. Police cars and ambulances screamed past us, their sirens and horns blaring, heading for Hussein hospital in Beit Jala where thousands had already gathered upon hearing the news. I didn't know where to go. I called George back, and he was nearly to the checkpoint. I should go to Daher's in Beit Jala and wait for him there. It seemed like every corner we turned, we came upon jeepfuls of Palestinian police loading up or tearing off, their guns raised high.

We reached Daher's, and George arrived within minutes. The TV replayed the scenes of complete pandemonium we had just witnessed, scenes which have occurred countless times throughout the West Bank and Gaza over the past year. Coffee was prepared and we sat around muttering, "This is it! This is it!" An hour later we had made it home, helicopters hovering in the skies above us. I kept looking out our window at the scene, where people still milled around aimlessly, thinking, if we had left five minutes sooner.

Gunfire echoed throughout the night. This morning there are tanks everywhere, one parked at the entrance to the college, another in front of Daher's house, another on the other side of our hill, more in Beit Jala and Aida camp and Al-Cuba. The Paradise and Bethlehem hotels, the Intercontinental, the governor's offices, are all occupied. George went to the funeral gathering in Manger Square. Who knows when the Israelis will withdraw? By that time, there will surely be more bodies for burying. More and more and more.

An image keeps coming to my mind. A big muscular bully repeatedly pounding a scrawny kid, with hundreds of onlookers encircling them, gawking in silence. Every once in a while the kid gets a halfway decent punch in, momentarily stunning the muscleman who furiously pummels the kid flat. Amazingly, he keeps pulling himself up for another round.

How long will the people stand and watch?

21 October 2001

The last three days have been a blur of morgue shots and funeral marches. Sharon is not targeting ordinary civilians, no. That's why more than twenty of them have died since Thursday. Friday's death toll was the highest since the start of the Intifada. All to avenge the racist Knesset member Ze'evi. No matter what version is being invented in the media, the fact is that soldiers are shooting and killing indiscriminately. Snipers are positioned on all the high buildings that have been occupied throughout the downtown area. Soldiers are firing randomly and tanks are spraying machine gunfire into neighborhoods as they pass by (this was witnessed by American volunteers at the Bible College). Bullets have struck civilians in virtually every neighborhood in the Bethlehem area. Seventeen-year-old Johnny Taljieh (from George's sister's husband's family) was in Manger Square when he was struck in the chest. Seventeen-year-old Moussa Abu Eid (two doors down from our old house in Aida Camp) was shot in the head standing on his balcony in his pajamas. Twenty-two-year-old Rania Khouroufeh was buying milk from a neighborhood shop. She was the young mother of two babies and the footage of her wailing husband on the local channel was unbearable to see. A thirty-five-year-old woman from the village of Husan (about a quarter of an hour south of Bethlehem) went into labor and came to Bethlehem to deliver. The soldiers prevented her from entering, and she died trying to find a way to the hospital. A 25-year-old mother of five from Al-Khader, a 29-year-old father of seven from Azza camp, and the list goes on and on. Is the blood of these people so cheap? Is the pain of their loved ones so meaningless? Not only are the soldiers targeting civilians in their houses, but they are also targeting funerals and rescue efforts and shooting directly at the hospital compounds themselves. Both water and electricity have been cut in areas throughout Bethlehem, and people are running out of food. What this is is a controlled massacre.

And still it is the Palestinians who have to control the violence. It is the Palestinians who have to lay down their weapons. It is the Palestinians who have to answer for their "lawlessness."

What we are brought back to once again is the old double standard that says that the fifty-plus (I've lost count) assassinations which Israel has carried out over the past 13 months matter less than the single successful assassination of Ze'evi. That Palestinians should be held accountable for their murderers, but Israel should not be held accountable for theirs. That while Israel has "no choice" but to react strongly to Ze'evi's assassination, Palestinians are supposed to passively accept whatever unilateral actions Israel chooses to take. That Israel's daily aggressions should never be considered provocative, and that they never violate cease-fire agreements, whereas Palestinian actions are always aggressive and provocative, no matter the context. Miraculously, even as tanks patrol our residential neighborhoods and civilian deaths average one for every waking hour, our feeble attempts to defend ourselves are classified as "acts of terrorism."

There is something very, very wrong here, and our global sense of fair play is at stake. How can we establish global military coalitions and global economies and global rights commissions when we are not willing to enforce standardized definitions of what is and is not acceptable? This is why Durban failed. This is why September 11th happened. This is why Afghanistan is a farce and a tragedy. This is why the world and everything we claim to value is falling apart before our eyes. The double standard is at the very heart of the chaos, and the Palestinian problem epitomizes this double standard at its ugliest and most perverse. The First World is responsible for corrupting our sense of what is fair, and once that has been corrupted, nothing much remains. We are all witnesses to this.

5 November 2001

As bad as the ten days of the invasion were, last week was in a way worse. On Monday, as we were released from the imprisonment of our homes, we began to understand the true extent of the destruction and the slaughter. It seems to have touched, in one way or another, every single household in Bethlehem, and their stories, though they will for the most part never be known beyond the local community, are full of sorrow, helplessness, anger, and indignation.

Monday was spent exchanging greetings (*"Alhumdulilah Salamah"* meaning "Thank God you made it through the ordeal in peace") and stories and visiting the areas of destruction. As I walked through Manger Square on my way to work, I gazed at the hundreds of memorial posters that had been plastered throughout the old city to commemorate the dead. Groups of small boys gathered around pictures of the slain fighters. Images of recent victims mixed with others from months past, their posters ragged and blanched of color. I recognized many, including the little Jawarish boy killed last October while walking home from school, his backpack still on his back. George had attended that funeral. That was back before the Palestinians had started shooting back, back when the Israelis were still picking off twelve-year-old rock throwers and convincing Americans that it was their own parents who were to blame. What has all this death meant, and what has it accomplished? And when will it be enough?

The uncle of Mathilda's classmate Jihan was the one killed by a sniper as he drove to the central wholesale market. Her friend Samih's father, who was "detained" by the Israelis in the '80s, was taken from his house for "questioning," and for several hours the family did not know his whereabouts. He was beaten up, but allowed to return home. Nadine's classmate and best friend Majd lives just up the street from our old house in Beit Jala, and her house was damaged by both gunfire and tankfire, with the family inside at the time. For ten days they were without electricity or phone lines and they could not leave the house to bring food. Melvyn Barhoum's home next door (which had been evacuated), caught fire either from an exploding shell or from a pierced gas bottle. Rescue crews did not dare approach the area because of the tanks and snipers, and the house burned out of control all night and into the following day. Now it is uninhabitable.

On Tuesday I took the girls to a birthday party in Beit Jala and sat with one of the mothers while we waited for the party to finish. Twenty-two-year-old Rania Khouroufeh was their next door neighbor, and they had been to the house several times on condolence visits. She said the children (two and four) looked bewildered and scared by all the grief they had had to witness. The tanks had passed several times in front of their house and had been firing on downtown Bethlehem from a position just up the street. The sound was unearthly, and her youngest Sami (age 3) would literally blanch and hold his hands over his ears. The older girls (11 and 8) had started wetting the bed at night and refused to be left alone, even to go to the bathroom. Her husband had been in an Israeli jail in the '80s as well, and he was constantly in fear that they would find some pretext to "come for him again".

The house of Abu Samir, our old neighbor across the street in Beit Jala, had been occupied by 25 soldiers and the couple (both in their 50s) had been held hostage in one room for five days before the UN (with whom Abu Samir is employed) intervened. They told George that every hour or so, one soldier or another would step up to the window facing into the refugee camp and spray machine gunfire toward it (toward Majd's house on the next street up). They vandalized the furniture and furnishings, stole personal items including money (but fortunately no large amounts were in the house), and littered the floor with garbage and food. They knocked down the corner portion of the stone wall in the garden so as to position the tank facing the camp. Our neighbor Mazen and his extended family (five families plus the elderly parents, or a total of about 33 people) live in the house directly faced by the tank and were in the process of building an extension onto their house. They own a small grocery and a vegetable store. All of it was damaged by the tank fire and indiscriminate shooting, but *alhumdulilah salamah*, none of the people were injured. They also had no electricity, phone lines, or food supplies for ten days and did not dare step outside or even move toward the front of the house until the soldiers had withdrawn.

I stopped by to greet Abeer, who has a pharmacy by my mother-in-law's house. She lives in Al-Madbasa in downtown Bethlehem. They too had been imprisoned without electricity or phone lines in an area of some of the fiercest fighting. Much of the time had been spent in the bathroom at the rear of the house. As I stood talking to her about their experience, her three-year-old daughter was climbing on a stool. A car passed by and made a backfiring noise just as it passed the door. The little girl startled so badly at the sound that she lost her footing and fell off the stool, crying hysterically, not from injury but fear.

George's friend Imad lives in Azza camp, just across the street from the college. Or rather, he lived there. His house is now a blackened shell and looks as if an earthquake struck it. The four families occupying the house were huddled in a back bedroom when their gas bottle was struck by a bullet and exploded. Since Israeli snipers were positioned in a high building directly next door and had been shooting down on the camp from their seventh floor vantage point continuously since the beginning of the invasion, they could not evacuate immediately. One child's eyes were damaged by the toxic smoke and fumes coming from the fire, and his face is now wrapped in bandages in the hopes that he'll eventually recover his sight. George went to sit with Imad on Monday and said that not a single possession is left. They lost everything except what they were wearing. Imad had a garage at the side of the house and has often worked on the electrical wiring for our car; this too was damaged beyond repair. Next to the garage, his brother had a small shop for butchering chickens, also destroyed. Now they have nowhere to live and no source of income. And winter is coming.

On Wednesday I needed to change a few dollars, so I took the opportunity to stop by our moneychanger. He had the misfortune of being located across the street from the Paradise Hotel, where the worst destruction took place. On Thursday night, in anticipation of an imminent withdrawal (which did not take place), army bulldozers plowed into the shopfronts all along the street causing unbelievable damage. The wreckage along the Azza camp side of the street was by far the most appalling of Monday morning's sights, and many shops—a grocery, a watch repair shop, a pharmacy—were utterly destroyed. Our man the moneychanger was lucky. Although the metal door was bashed in and the entryway torn up, the counter at the back was not reduced to splinters, and on the day I stopped by he had pulled it out into the sunshine and was sitting casually behind it. I walked up, extended my hand and said, *alhumdulilah salamah*, and for just a moment I thought he would burst into tears. By then I had said *alhumdulilah salamah* enough times to expect a certain typical sort of response combining restraint (a Palestinian will always minimize his troubles), humble courage, and gentle humor. It took this man just a split-second before he could compose himself and respond with the standard reply, and the expression I saw on his face was pure unmasked pain. And he was one of the lucky ones.

My sister-in-law Nisreen was another lucky one. Unlike the pregnant woman from Husan who went into labor and died trying to get to the hospital in Bethlehem, Nisreen and her daughter (*alhumdulilah salamah*) survived the invasion. As soon as the tanks entered Beit Jala, she and her husband Tony fled to my mother-in-law's house in Bethlehem's old city, usually a safe location. This time it was the site of intense fighting, and they were forced on most days to descend to the basement. Nisreen's due date (20 October) came and went. Finally, early on Thursday morning 25 October, she went into labor. Nisreen had registered for delivery at the French hospital, but the French hospital had been hit by both tank and gunfire. So they cut through a thorny field leading from the basement down to the street below and took her to Doman clinic in Beit Sahour (where Phoebe was born). The baby (named Lubna, meaning "place deep inside the heart") was born at three that afternoon. That night I drove through the deserted streets distantly echoing with gunfire to say *alhumdulilah salamah* to mother and baby daughter. Upon discharge the following day, they could not go home; indeed, they could not even return to my mother-in-law's. They had to spend two nights in Beit Sahour. But they were grateful to be safe and alive and together.

This is what Palestinians have had to become accustomed to. The Israelis have taken so relentlessly that every small act of giving back is turned into a gesture of magnanimous generosity for which we must be grateful, even though none of it was ever theirs to take and it is not theirs to give back. They have taken so much land that we are supposed to feel thankful for the scrap which is left to us. They have appropriated so many of our basic civil and human rights that we are supposed to be grateful on that rare occasion when we are permitted to pass, unimpeded, to school or to work or to the doctor or to our land. They invade and batter us for ten days so we'll be thankful when they've gone, even though we find ourselves in the same miserable situation as before they came. Endless internal closure. Anxious of violent eruptions every minute of every day. Fifty percent unemployment. Every second household living below the poverty line.

It's a logical progression. Soon the only thing we'll have left to be grateful for is the fact that we have not yet been wiped out of existence. And when there is nothing at all left to take from us but our cheap lives, will it finally be enough?

The Siege of
the Church of the Nativity

Easter 2002

He is not here;
for He is risen, as He said.
Come, see the place where the Lord lay. *Matthew 28:6*

Easter greetings from the land of Christ. In this time, we remember His words: The Son of Man must be delivered into the hands of sinful men, and be crucified, and the third day rise again. Halleluia! We believe in the Living Lord, the Christ mission, a mission of challenge against the injustices of the oppressors, a mission of steadfastness against trials, a mission of martyrdom in the manner of Christ who redeemed us by His Holy Cross. Resurrection will remain the symbol of the coming victory and the rock will remain a symbol of the stones of justice.

Please pray for us as we celebrate Christ's resurrection under siege.

May God bless you all.

Happy Resurrection Day!

In Christ's love,

George Nassar and family

The celebration of Easter was muted this year by continued actions of the Israeli army in the West Bank. Two weeks earlier Alison had reflected on the images coming from other towns and villages.

15 March 2002

I watched the Hebrew news in English last night and I heard all their pretty justifications for what they are doing. They're "withholding the full extent of their military power." They're "acting with restraint out of concern for minimizing civilian casualties." They're "disabling weapons factories." They're "dismantling the terrorist infrastructure." Their purpose is "to establish a cease-fire and return to negotiations." Their "highest priority is peace." All this must sound so pacifying to the ears of the West. So proper. So civilized. So sterile. So believable from a distance. And then we switched the channel and came back to reality, up close and oh, so personal. As the local cameramen made their way from house to house, street to street, and camp to camp, we watched in horrified numbness. No words could possibly describe what the camera was showing us. The young woman with the baby on her hip just shook her head, speechless, gesturing to the rubble of the home behind her with tears slipping down her cheeks. The old man gazed uncomprehendingly at what remained of his home, his face seeming to collapse in on itself. The old woman, standing amid splinters of furniture, tore at her headscarf shouting, "What can I say? What should I say? What is there to say?"

What can and must be said is that heavily armed Israeli soldiers, accompanied by tanks, bulldozers, and helicopters, entered the miserable homes of some of the most impoverished and wretched souls on the face of this earth and vandalized everything in sight. They broke furniture, slashed clothing and bedding, shattered dishes and TVs, stole what money and valuables they could find, and then knocked down the walls themselves, leaving nothing. Leaving people who were already refugees homeless once again. They entered shops and vandalized the merchandise. They entered sewing workshops and vandalized the sewing machines. They entered computer clubs and vandalized the computers. They entered printing shops and vandalized the typesetting equipment. They entered a small appliance repair shop and what was left was not even recognizable. Words are truly inadequate to describe the destruction. It must be seen to be believed, and it must be believed because it is the ugly reality behind the pretty words.

Next we saw the hundreds of "captured terrorists," blindfolded, bound at the wrists, and squatting in the sun, being processed for arrest. Some wore only pajamas and slippers. Some were just a few years older than Mathilda. Some were the age of George. some we even knew. I looked at their faces, my heart thudding, wondering how I would feel to see my husband among them. And for the thousandth time in ten years, feeling thankful not to have sons.

The cameraman wandered among the "shabab," asking them to describe their capture:

> We were hiding in our bedroom, trying to keep the children calm. There was no shooting, no resistance. Just the sound of the tanks and bulldozers. People screaming and crying nearby. Suddenly the walls began to shake like an earthquake and our door fell in. Twenty or thirty soldiers came running in. Some surrounded us and some went to work smashing up the house with sledgehammers. They pointed to me and my brother and told us to put our hands up. I asked why. They told us we were 'wanted.' I said we hadn't done anything, we were only hiding from the tanks. They pointed their guns at our heads and said we had to go with them. When we left they were still tearing up the house. My mother and sisters and baby brother were hysterical. When we got here, we saw all of our neighbors, lined up and waiting to be arrested. None of us knows what will happen.

Those factories that were vandalized were not manufacturing rockets. Those men that were arrested are not gun-toting activists. Those families whose houses were destroyed were not terrorists. At least not yet. When my eyes and ears had had enough, I turned away and went to attend to my children's calls. Nadine looked into my face and said, Mom, are you crying? Yes, Nadine. Somebody has to.

On March 27, a Palestinian made a suicide bomb attack at a Passover Seder in Netanya, killing 19 and wounding 100. Two other suicide attacks followed in the next days in Tel Aviv and Haifa, killing another fourteen and wounding scores of Israelis. Prime Minister Sharon responded by unleashing a massive campaign against the Palestinian population with the interesting name "Operation Defensive Shield." In some ways, this was all a continuation of the March campaign in which the army had begun to go through refugee camps detaining young men by the hundreds. They were no longer content to go door to door, but even cut holes in walls from one house to the next. The holy week campaign began in the cities north of Jerusalem where all watched the events unfold on television. Everyone knew that the army was waiting for Easter to pass before invading the Christian city of Bethlehem. Tanks lined up on the roads leading to the city. As everyone expected, the invasion occurred on Easter Monday morning. As everyone feared, it was worse than anything they had seen yet. Even churches were not immune. Photos and reports immediately went round the world that the Lutheran Church in the city center had been entered and trashed by Israeli soldiers. The siege of the 1600-year-old Church of the Nativity began because a few militants had sought refuge there, along with priests and hundreds of residents. People living in the area of the church were confined to the homes where not even ambulances or medical care were permitted to bring aid. Hair-raising stories were widely circulated of dead bodies in the streets. Particularly gruesome was the story of the Abda family, confined in two small rooms of an apartment for 48 hours while two familiy members bled to death from gunfire penetrating their house from invading soldiers.

For much of the Bethlehem area there was silence. The army had destroyed a primary Palestinian internet provider so that even email messages were not going through. With Alison unable to travel to the Bible College for work, her regular email network was down. From the Nassar's April 1 Easter greeting until May 13 there would be no messages coming from Alison's keyboard.

This became a hardship for her growing network of friends and family who had become accustomed to regular messages. Even during previous incursions, she had been able to keep in contact to let people know that her family was all right. This time it was different. Close friends of Alison began to send messages to her email list, "Has anyone heard from Alison? Do you think they'll be okay?"

Alison's close friend Marita shared an ominous last message sent just hours prior to the invasion, in response to the question, "What will you do if the men are rounded up?":

> We have already decided that he (George) will go. If he doesn't and they start doing house-to-house searches and find him, it will be much worse. But so far, it seems quiet. Our corner store is open and the girls are playing out in the drive-way with their cousins, who are staying with us because their house is in Beit Jala. We are just waiting to see what will be.

Alison's words brought forth images of the hundreds of previous detainees stripped to their underwear, blindfolded with hands tied behind their backs, and forced to squat in the hot sun for hours on end. Still no newspapers reported house-to-house searches in Beit Sahour.

George and Alison do have a cell phone, yet repeated attempts to contact them brought no response. A word needs to be said about phones. The West Bank must be the cell phone capital of the world. Part of this goes back to the pre-Oslo days when Israeli phone companies simply would not come out to install phone lines for Palestinian houses. So cell phones then became a necessity, but today are a matter of convenience. The problem is that George and Alison live in a shielded valley in Beit Sahour where reception is very poor.

George's sister Nahida, who lives up the hill just a block from the Church of the Nativity, was able to report that Alison's family was fine for the time being. Through my wife's every-other-day phone calls to Nahida we were able to keep informed about the true situation of residents. Food was in short supply. There was concern for missing relatives. The soldiers were undertaking house to house searches moving from one area to the next. For Nahida, it was not once but twice. Fortunately her husband and sons had not been detained. From Daoud, George's younger brother who lives with his wife and infant daughter on the opposite side of Nativity Church, we were able to learn a more harrowing story. With constant gunfire outside their apartment, they had spent 48 hours cowering on the floor behind piled-up furniture. The situation in Bethlehem was not good. Yet the reports were that Alison and all of George's family were all okay, at least for now.

Even though Alison did not have access to email, she did continue to write. As if she were keeping a diary, she composed nine entries over the next three weeks to describe what it had been like for her family during this difficult time. On 13 May, as soon as the siege was lifted, Alison began emailing these messages two at a time to her family and friends.

1 April 2002 • Easter Monday

On Friday a friend from Israel called to see how we are. In the course of the conversation, she mentioned that her lovely teenage daughter had recently been coming to her at bedtime to express her fears about the situation. "Will there be another *pigua* (attack in Hebrew) tomorrow? How many will be killed tomorrow?" This is the legacy we are leaving to our children.

My own children, needless to say, have fears of their own. Will there be tank shelling tonight? F-16s? Apaches? Will there be another invasion? Will the class take tomorrow's math exam to the sound of machine gun fire? Will soldiers catch Dad as he's trying to get home from work? Will they put him in a prison?

During the last invasion, soldiers broke into the house of Mathilda's classmate Sophia and took her father and uncle at gunpoint. It's not hard to imagine what Sophia fears at bedtime. Nadine's classmate Miriam's grandfather died from dehydration because their neighborhood in Doha was under curfew and the soldiers wouldn't allow an ambulance through. Then they wouldn't allow the family to arrange a funeral, so he had to be buried at the entrance to the house. Last week, I spoke to the mother of Mathilda's best friend Noor on the phone. She told me how all the children had regressed to bedwetting at night and that the sound of the tank treads grinding up and down the street caused them to blanch with fear and shiver uncontrollably. In Palestine, as in Israel, the nightmares are not hard to come by.

But nightmares are for those who at least still have something to fear. What nightmare could the little girl in the black ski cap have that would be worse than what happened to her? And 14-year-old Nida, shot to death in the doorway of her home in Azza camp, does not dream anymore. Neither does Ayat Al-Akhras, the beautiful teenage girl from Deheishe who martyred herself at a Jerusalem supermarket on Friday. Her nightmares were the stuff of her daily life, until she decided that there are things even worse than death.

If these are the only dreams we have to offer these children, then we have let them down grievously, and in letting them down, we have betrayed the one and only thing that means anything in this world.

Three-year-old Phoebe, while playing with her two- and four-year-old cousins, had this conversation:

"I've got a very big gun to shoot the *jesh* (army soldiers)."

"Sharon has F-16s. Pretty soon he's going to destroy Bethlehem and kill all the Palestinians."

"I'm going to shoot Sharon then."

"Then George Bush will get mad at you."

"George Bush gives Sharon the tanks and helicopters so he can shoot at us."

"Then I'm going to shoot George Bush too. My gun is very, very big."

The conversations get more and more surreal. Tonight we had one as we were gathered around the television screen, that I participated in as if in a dream. Or a nightmare. Do we have enough food for an extended invasion? What if there's a curfew? What if one of the children needs a doctor? Where do we hide our money if the soldiers start going house-to-house? What will probably get vandalized (the computer, the sewing machine, the TV, the CD player . . .)? Should we open the door to them or stay hidden and allow it to be blown open? Should George hide or go to the square with the other men and boys? What he should wear? What he should take with him? When we will see him again? And his brothers? And his nephews?

Afterward the conversation evolved into memories of last year in Beit Jala, of the Gulf War, forty days of curfew, the first Intifada, Beirut, the war of 1967. . .

The dreams and nightmares of Palestine.

*O*n April 2, when Israeli forces moved in around *Manger Square, many Palestinians sought shelter in the Church of the Nativity along with members of the Palestinian police force. The Israeli army raised the charge that this number included some on Israel's "wanted list" and began a long siege at this the oldest church in Christianity. At first, media reports would claim over "two hundred armed gunmen" holding up inside the church and holding priests "hostage." Later these claims would prove unfounded.*

3 April 2002 • Wednesday

Eighteen tanks just thundered past at the top of our hill. Strangely, I suddenly feel like I am living in a grade Z techno-splatter flick, the kind that Hollywood churns out by the dozen. Invasion 4!: Ultimate Showdown, sequel to the box office blockbusters Invasion!, Invasion 2!: We're Back and We're Bad! And Invasion 3!: Rape of the Refugees.

We've got all the ingredients for yet another smash hit. The plot is third rate and predictable, true to the classic films of the genre. We've got your good guys—standing shoulder to shoulder and hip to hip just like *Men in Black*, zapping the scum of the universe with their state-of-the-art weaponry—and your bad guys, easily distinguishable by their dark skin, facial hair, and ominous-sounding language (translated incorrectly in the subtitles). The script is implausible and totally without depth or complexity, so as not to confuse the intellectually challenged audiences. The lines of the protagonists resound with hollow terms like "fighting against evil" and "protecting freedom" that we've heard a zillion times before, delivered with the same expressions of deadpan self-righteousness, which are meant to be profound and heroic but are nothing more than laughably pathetic. The supporting actors chime in on cue with their secondary plot developments, minor issues like moral corruption and human rights and the like, but, as we all know, Tommy Lee Jones never has to worry about that stuff. Everyone knows that, without the requisite ass-kicking with heavy weaponry, he has no reason to be. I blast, therefore I am. This is the spirit in which all the best wars are fought and won. The cast of extras gets mowed down by the thousands and you never even know their names. As characters they never get developed because, in the end, they don't matter. Their graphically violent and meaningless deaths provide the sole justification for the show, so they are tolerated briefly for the sake of dramatic effect before being smeared into oblivion. No one even thinks to cry for them.

The movie finishes, and the audience can walk away, without any interaction or reflection required. They can placidly await the next entertaining episode, knowing the ending in advance and feeling satisfaction in having had all their assumptions and convictions affirmed.

When it's not a cheap afternoon matinee, it's a Hieronymous Bosch painting, with dead bodies strewn throughout the streets and the wounded bleeding and groaning for assistance that does not come. Mass graves are being dug in hospital parking lots in Ramallah because the fridges are full to bursting and the soldiers are not permitting the bodies to be interred. Ambulance drivers are being detained at gunpoint while their patients die on the ground at their feet. Tanks are parked at hospital entrances to prevent treatment for the wounded. Thousands of families are without electricity or water and they cannot replenish their dwindling food supplies. If agencies like the UN were not created to intervene in situations like these, then I really have to wonder what their point is. We have watched day after day after day of useless discussions, elegant speeches, and blunt condemnations, and still no action is taken to stop this. In U.S. law, passive accessory to a crime is no less deserving of punishment than active commission of a crime. In international law, every possible violation has been committed, not once or twice but scores of times. History will judge those who failed to act.

Bad luck for Radovan Milosovic that he was not a good buddy of the U.S. president. Instead of being branded as a war criminal, he would have been recognized as a partner in the noble War on Terrorism. He would have gotten away with it all and been rewarded with aid and sympathy to boot.

The Palestinian Authority has been destroyed, for all intents and purposes, and so has most of the infrastructure which would have gone toward the establishment of a state. Peace will not be the thing that rises out of the ashes on the other side of all this. Sharon has condemned his people to years and years of guerilla attacks, and I sometimes have to admit that it is perhaps what they deserve after all. They elected him, freely and democratically. What did they think he would do for them? They only just extricated themselves from an eighteen-year war that he started. He has not just taken them back to Beirut in 1982, he has taken them all the way back to the beginning, fifty years ago, when every single country in the region hated them.

Just a couple of weeks ago, the Arab Summit offered a way forward—the only way forward, through full withdrawal—with full diplomatic relationships there on the table for the taking. Instead of going forward, Sharon chose to go back, dragging his people with him. I glimpsed a sign on the television. Another War. Then what? Our leaders may pretend that they do not know the answer to this, but we know. History has taught us this lesson, not once but many times, and we are either just too stupid to get it or too cynical to care.

Afterward, the international community will send money to rebuild all the destruction it passively allowed to happen. It will send wheelchairs for the people it helped to cripple and rice for the people it helped to make hungry and blankets for the people it helped to make homeless and funds for the children orphaned by its indifference.

Keep it all, keep it all. Now it means less than nothing.

I had a dream that tanks were rolling down Jaffa Road in Jerusalem, occupying the chic cafes of Emek Refaim and the expensive homes of Rehavia and Talbieh while F-16's destroyed "selective targets" in Tel Aviv, Herziliya, and Netanya. They smashed through the wall of the prime minister's compound, capturing him in one room along with his aides Peres, Ben-Eliezer, Mofaz, without electricity, food, or water. Half of the Knesset had already been assassinated. Soldiers stormed synagogues, bulldozers rampaged up Ben Yehuda, smashing shops and businesses. Channels One and Two were shelled.

Apache helicopters made in America fired machine guns down on residential areas. Families huddled inside their houses, under curfew, hiding their money and trying to keep their children from panicking. Arafat declares, on television, that Sharon is "the enemy" and Bush declares, from faraway Washington, that he has "a vision for peace." Of course, it was only a dream.

Mathilda wants to know, why does the whole world hate us?

5 April 2002 • Friday

Day Five: How we are

Every day since the invasion began we have been awakened by nearby tank fire. It begins around 6:30 or 7:00 in the morning and continues on into the night. When it's calm the blasts are half an hour apart. When it's worse, they average every five minutes or less, like labor pains. We have perhaps twenty tanks in the area at the top of our hill, and another twenty in the neighborhood over the next hill. More at the bottom of our wadi and more behind us at the YMCA and Jabal Abu Ghaneim. Snipers are in a building facing our front door from the direction of Manger Square. More snipers are on the opposite hill from us to the left and at night they sweep huge searchlights over the area. Tuesday and Wednesday morning Apache helicopters shot down on the area for several hours and they are the worst. The sound of them freezes the blood and shakes the viscera. We spent those mornings on the floor in the girl's room at the back, playing card games on the rug, Phoebe clutching tightly to me. Then the weather got worse and we have not seen the helicopters since. The sun finally came out this morning so we were able to open the windows, but we fear the return of the Apaches.

We are four adults (me, George, George's brother Daher and his wife Katie, who live in Beit Jala near Aida camp) and six children (our three girls and their three girls). We have not been outside since Monday, with the exception of yesterday when I took the garbage down to the bottom of our driveway. I told the girls to stand against the wall and wait for me, then I walked against the wall until the bottom, and quickly crossed the street, tossing the bags onto the pile, which was overflowing everywhere, and maybe 15 cats exploded out of the heap, scaring the wits out of me. I ran back up the driveway and when the girls saw me they started jumping up and down and cheering. Every kid knows the story of Rania Haroufah, who went out to buy her babies milk during the second invasion and didn't come back. The girls had their first glimpse of the tanks as they thundered past the top of our hill two days ago, roaring and snorting like huge beasts. Even at a distance they are terrifying. Since then, they have been worried. Can the tanks get up our driveway? Can they see us from there? Maybe they will hear us and come over here. They have been keeping quiet.

Katie has two boys, 10 and 13, who are staying with George's mom and sister Amal. During past invasions her street was generally considered safer, because it is right near Manger Square. This time, it is the worst place to be, and Katie cries daily about the safety of her sons. They are big for their age, and Bishara, the older one, already has a few hairs growing on his lip. She is afraid the soldiers will go house-to-house and detain them. We have stayed in contact over the phone, and yesterday my mother-in-law said they were hiding down in the basement, whose trapdoor is covered by a rug.

George has another sister, Nahida, who lives just on the other side of Manger Square at the Milk Grotto. There is a tunnel which goes under the Nativity Church and comes out right near her house, so the soldiers have been searching the houses in that area for escaped gunmen. Her house has been searched twice. Also, their car, parked on the street below, was run over by a tank. The husband of Nahida's husband's sister is a watchman at the bank in Manger Square. He has not been heard from in four days and does not answer his cell phone.

George's brother Daoud lives just behind Manger Square (the office that I use during invasions is on the floor below his apartment) and his street is full of tanks. They also ran over his car. It is from this position that they are preparing to besiege the church from the rear, so soldiers are sandbagging the road and building walls from behind which they will shoot any escapees.

Tony and Nisreen, over in Beit Jala, have been under curfew since Friday. The army invaded Beit Jala three days before coming into the rest of the area. Everyone is afraid of house-to-house searches, the vandalism, the theft of valuables, and the detention of the men.

Needless to say, none of us can get to a shop for food or supplies. With four adults and six kids in the house, stuff is going fast. We ran out of fresh milk and so have been making powdered Nido. Of fruits and veggies we only have a few withered carrots and some squishy tomatoes. Shampoo, pull-ups, and dish-washing soap are all running out. Katie and I both made bread yesterday and will make it again today. We have flour but things like margarine and eggs have run out. We have rice and pasta but nothing to put on it. We are lucky to still have electricity; without it luxuries like the oven, the fridge, the water boiler, the sewing machine, and the computer won't work. Many people stocked up on food in anticipation of the invasion, but in areas without electricity it is all going bad. We have been wearing layers of clothing so as not to light the heater in order to save the gas for the stove.

George's mom and Nahida have been without electricity for several days, so they have no news except from phone calls. We have the TV news on constantly. George saw footage of a high school friend of his, Sami, sitting cross-legged on the floor of his tiny house near Manger Square with the bodies of his brother and mother sprawled beside him. They were sprayed with gunfire while hiding inside, and he can't have the bodies removed. Ambulances are not being permitted to respond to calls, and people are prohibited from leaving their homes, even for emergencies. The wife of my boss Bishara's son is due to deliver her first baby this week, and I have no idea how they are coping. All the hospitals are under siege and there is no road to Jerusalem.

In footage of a demonstration in a neighboring Arab country (Egypt I think) we glimpsed a billboard showing Sharon and Bush giving each other a hearty handshake with the caption underneath, "Let's Kill, Kill, Kill!" In other footage shot by a news crew from Abu Dhabi, we saw the soldiers executing five gunmen who had surrendered. The Abu Dhabi crew was promptly deported from the country. Yesterday we saw footage of Americans being evacuated from a Bethlehem hotel. Local people, however, can wait another week or so as far as George Bush is concerned. Their safety is not a priority. As my brother-in-law remarked, he might as well have offered to send Powell next year. If I were Arafat, my response to Zinni's proposed visit would be, don't bother! Way too little, way too late. A mere withdrawal from area A is not the point at all. The only negotiations that should take place now are for full withdrawal. Period.

*O*n April 6, an Israeli army sniper shot an Armenian priest at the Church of the Nativity. In other parts of the West Bank, the onslaught continued.

7 April 2002 • Sunday

The spoiled child is rampaging out of control while the indulgent parent stands helplessly by, trying desperately to hide his embarrassment and his failure as a parent by inventing increasingly fantastic excuses for behavior that is, according to every conceivable standard, inexcusable. As usual, the blame is cast everywhere but where it obviously resides.

The latest orgy of devastation and bloodlust has entered the realm of the truly pathological, right under the nose of Zinni if not with his explicit cooperation, general-to-general. Sharon's legendary hubris combined with George Bush's phenomenal arrogance have created an apocalyptic atmosphere in which literally anything can be gotten away with, and the potential for escalation is unlimited. Sharon now considers himself, not simply chosen by God, but God Himself. He alone determines with whom Powell and Zinni will meet. He alone controls the decision to withhold food and water from Arafat.

An entire population is being held hostage at the mercy of his sadistic whims, and he is daring anyone to stop him. He is profoundly sick, deeply racist, and, needless to say, unquestionably dangerous. Nicknames like "The Bulldozer" and "The Butcher of Beirut" now seem to be vast under-exaggerations for what Sharon really is.

According to recent polls, half the population of Israel now supports Sharon's obscene policies and is in favor of ethnic cleansing. As if a democratic majority could render "transfer" morally acceptable in any context. Adolph Hitler was elected democratically, and his Final Solution could well have had support among the majority. So? In any case, "transfer" has already been in practice for some time, in its kinder and gentler form, also known as "making life unbearable." This is a large part of what the last 18 months have been all about. Every week a family emigrates from the Occupied Territories because they cannot take any more. Those who remain are holding on by their fingernails, living in misery and knowing it can and will get even worse. We are being forced to choose between two intolerable situations: staying and forfeiting even our most basic rights, or leaving and giving Israel the satisfaction of saying, "They left of their own volition." As for myself, I want to look them in the eyes as they put me on the cattle car. I won't do their dirty work for them.

Arafat has trumped their every card. They expected him to cower and grovel, they expected him to sell out, they expected to manipulate him like a puppet, but the reality is that he acted with integrity, strengthening his own leadership and revealing the savagery and corruption of theirs. Like his people, Arafat has been imprisoned and humiliated, and like his people, he has shown his willingness to be a martyr rather than to submit. What more can be done to him or to us?

Withdrawal and self-determination are still the lowest common denominators of this equation, and nothing they do can further dilute those two goals. Assassination, exile, transfer, massacre, starvation, suffocation have all been tried and have all failed. Neither will confiscation of arms alter the cause. Palestine was unarmed for all but the last six years and, miraculously, Palestinians only started turning their guns on their oppressors a little more than a year ago, after nearly 100 people had been shot dead. Without guns, we will go back to stones and shoes, or anything else that can be thrown. The point is still the same. Leave us alone. Stop interfering in every facet of our existence. Stop trying to dominate us. We will die, we will live in misery, but we will never surrender to domination. As long as there is occupation, there will be resistance. The choice is theirs.

11 April 2002 • Thursday

The images of Jenin are intensely painful and incredibly oppressive, and we see them over and over. The faces of the mothers with their children and their broken voices as they describe their ongoing nightmare are like knives in my heart. Bahrain, South Lebanon's Al-Manara, ANN (Arab News Network), Abu Dhabi (before they were thrown out), and the ubiquitous Al-Jezeera—the footage is all there and all familiar. Whoever has eyes to see, look. Whoever has ears to hear, listen. We have seen it before, in Dehesihe and Aida and Balata, in Gaza and Beit Jala and Tul Karm. And in Sabra and Shatilla. We have all lived it. We have all been down on the floor in the dark with our children, our hearts thudding as the Apache overhead rained down death and terror. It is a sound never to be forgotten, and a feeling never to be forgiven.

Meanwhile, on *Israel One* television, Knesset minister Limor Livnat exorts her weeping audience to "always remember the past." "We must always make the distinction between Good and Evil," she tells the people who have gathered to observe Holocaust Remembrance Day, while a few hundred kilometers away, the refugee camp of Jenin is laid to waste in a breathtaking military onslaught. I think about the concepts of Good and Evil, and whose privilege it is to make the distinction. And it occurs to me that land is not the only thing being stolen from the Palestinians. Israel's spin masters (on both sides of the Atlantic) are also doing everything they can to steal Palestinian collective memory, narrative, and experience and to transform it into something utterly detached from their reality.

On *Israel Two*, a popular talk-show host chatted with an American "journalist" from NBC (I think) whose name I did not catch. "We know what we will find when we are finally allowed to enter Jenin. We'll find destroyed houses, crying children and families. . . . We know that gunmen were shooting from these homes, and that once they are destroyed they will bring a family to say they were living there . . ." My blood ran cold at these smug remarks. What precisely does he think he knows, other than what he has read in military press releases and *Time* magazine? Sometimes I think I can endure everything but the killing cynicism of statements like these. "Israel is living September 11 every day!" he heartily assures his host, who heartily nods along with him. Conveniently failing to mention that Palestinians are living multiple September 11th's, every minute of every day. And he has the appalling audacity to speak about the fears of his wife and children. "I tell them I'm okay. I'm in a good place with good people." His wife and children have never lain on the floor in the dark with Apaches overhead and neither has he. He was never a refugee. He was never occupied. He was never forced to feed five children on $300. He never had to plead with a soldier to cross a checkpoint. He never had his house demolished. And he never had his history dismissed.

Has he ever bothered to seek out a Palestinian mother holding a terrorized toddler on her hip, to judge the truth of what she has to say? The terrible thing is that English speakers who hear his remarks will accept his version of reality over those of the people in the camp, the only ones who have access to the truth of what went on there. And these invented realities will become "The Reality" that people refer to in the future.

Is it merely ironic that while Holocaust survivors are marking the memory of their experience of atrocity, Palestinians are being denied the truth of theirs? Israeli bulldozers are scooping up the piles of bodies and burying them in mass unmarked graves so that Palestinian claims (up to 500) can be dismissed as exaggerations. Had this been done at Auschwitz, would it have changed the reality of what happened there? In many countries, Holocaust denial is a crime. The assault to the memory of atrocity is just as much an atrocity as the atrocity itself.

And yet there were no e-mail testimonials coming out of Auschwitz on a daily basis, no mobile phone calls, no live footage of the carnage of the ovens, and it has been convincingly argued that people really did not know, until the end. This cannot be said for Palestine. Palestinians, in addition to the experience of atrocity itself, are having to endure the additional atrocities of indifference to their typed and filmed and recorded cries, and the dismissal of these cries as mere "propaganda." It is an evil conspiracy of lies against truth and spin against experience. But all the lies and spin in the world will not change what happened here, and those creating the lies and circulating the spin are just as guilty of atrocity as those doing the killing and the destroying.

It is often said that history is written by the victors. In fact, the ultimate standards of victimization have also been determined by the victors as applied only to themselves, with the Holocaust and September 11 generally considered to be the unsurpassed measures of cruelty, inhumanity, and the suffering of the innocent. But authentic history can testify to countless events which are equal to and even transcend these standards. Palestine is one of them and its memory must triumph. No one can take that from us. We will remember.

18 April 2002 • Thursday
Day Seventeen

Last night, at the end of our sixteenth day of curfew, I sat in the darkness of our living room watching *Dead Man Walking* and I had a terrible realization. I realized that I sometimes hate Israelis, and this realization made me weep into the early hours of the morning. I went out onto our porch, in full view of the snipers, and over the hill I could see the glare of the spotlights shining on the Church of the Nativity. Every night we can hear the noise from the compound, where the army employs a variety of psychological techniques to break down the resistance of the people inside. Often they use a loudspeaker, cajoling or threatening them for hours to surrender. Sometimes they use percussion grenades or stink bombs or smoke bombs or tear gas. Sometimes a siren whines for hours. Every evening on Al-Mahed television, there are phone interviews with people inside, Mohammed Al Medini (the governor of Bethlehem) or one of the gunmen like Ibrahim Abayat or one of the priests. For sixteen days we have been forced to meditate on the awful circumstances of these trapped people, on the stupidity and futility and savagery of all this. We've been held hostage in our own homes, innocent of any crime save that of being Palestinian. And for sixteen days we have struggled with hate.

I think that perhaps it is a natural thing—or at any rate a human thing—to hate the people doing these things to us. It is certainly the easy thing. Simply the fact that we have been under round-the-clock curfew for seventeen days creates feelings of anger so intense that they sometimes seem to verge on madness, and much worse has been done. When soldiers enter a house and vandalize it needlessly, isn't it natural for its occupants to feel anger and even hatred? When a tank casually flattens a family car, isn't it natural for its owners to feel anger? When a child is shot, when a woman is forced to miscarry, when a worker is prevented from going to work or a patient is prevented from getting to the hospital, isn't hate the natural response? And when it happens not once but tens or hundreds or thousands of times, over months and years and decades, it would be almost unnatural not to hate, wouldn't it?

Watching the movie, I understood the honest and terrible truth that Israelis also have justification for hating. I have imagined George or one of the girls being killed in a bombing, and I knew that all the people who have lost loved ones in these attacks also feel the easy and natural and human response of hatred.

So what hope is there?

What should I teach my children? I despair at the possibility that they will grow up to hate, and I weep to think they are learning it from me. I want them to struggle with hate, and to know that this struggle is worthwhile because hate—we know this perhaps better than anyone else on the face of the planet—can only lead to death and only the struggle with hate gives hope for life, for a future. I want to teach them forgiveness, but forgiveness can only take place in the presence of honesty and humility and justice—or at least the hope of these things—and justice can only take place when we acknowledge the human frailty which characterizes us all and unites us all.

These are difficult days.

19 April 2002 • Friday
Day Eighteen

Every three or four days, the army lifts the closure for three or four hours so that people can get out for supplies. Sometimes they rotate neighborhoods. Sometimes the entire area gets lifted at once. It is never quite predictable. Yesterday we were "allowed" to leave our houses from 12 to 4:00 p.m. At five minutes to 12, we saw a car drive up the hill. Perhaps the clocks in their house were all fast, perhaps they figured that five minutes should not reasonably constitute a violation. But when they reached the top of the hill, the soldiers shot at them and they hastily turned back down the hill to wait for other cars to appear.

The girls prepared themselves as if we were going on an exciting trip. "It's twelve! We have to go!" they kept shouting. When you only have four hours, every minute lost feels significant. We composed lists of what we had to do and buy. First on the list was the pharmacy. My allergy had kicked in at the beginning of the week, and I had been desperately awaiting the lifting so I could buy an inhaler for my wheezing and something to help me sleep at night. For four days I sat wheezing and hacking on the couch, unable to sleep either horizontally or upright, exhausted and pissed off. There was no good reason for being made to wait. But buying medicine, like buying food or vegetables or supplies or going to the doctor or the dentist or doing any of the thousand things that human beings need to do in a day, were not "allowed" except when they decided to allow it, were not necessary unless they deemed it so. Earlier in the week, we watched an ambulance flying a white flag slowly approach the top of our hill, only to be shot at by the tanks positioned there. The senseless death of our neighbor, Attalah Al-Hayak, and the pitiful image of his wife shrieking hysterically on the floor of the clinic where he was pronounced dead, was all the example we needed. All that matters to these soldiers is their own sense of power over our lives. Their mission is to put us at their mercy, and we have no choice but to comply. Anything else constitutes terrorism.

At each pharmacy we were met by the same sight. Crowds of people jostled to purchase their needed medicines, and many were sent away empty-handed. Many shelves were bare, and fresh supplies were not being permitted to pass the checkpoints. Supplies of Nadine's heart medication, for example, had been completely exhausted. Fortunately, the day before the invasion, I suggested that George buy an extra box, and so we had enough for fifty days. Beyond that we dare not think. We had to go to several pharmacies before I was finally able to buy a Ventolin inhaler and a nighttime antihistamine. The other things on the list were the usual milk, bread, margarine, vegetables, and various odds and ends that are not essential, but help to maintain the illusion of normal life and human standards in a situation which is anything but normal or human. Shampoo and conditioner, dish-washing liquid and toilet paper. Most people never think of these things because most people are never in a position to have to. In the U.S. supplies are so plentiful that you can wander a single aisle in a supermarket for half an hour, contemplating nothing more than which brand of shampoo you will buy. And in many places you have the freedom to wander that aisle any time of the day or night. America is the land of 24-hour purchasing. God forbid anyone should ever limit what they can purchase or when. God forbid they should ever know what it is like to be us.

As we drove around town doing our errands, we passed scenes of random destruction. Numerous electrical poles had been knocked down by tanks. Countless cars had been squashed flat like cardboard boxes. Everywhere we went, the pavement betrayed the telltale gouges of tank treads. Here a section of stone wall knocked down. There a section of decorative tiles crushed. Here a length of sidewalk ground to bits.

There a decorative metal grill twisted arthritically back upon itself. Here a phone booth squashed. There a street sign mangled. We have to drive slowly, maneuvering around piles of stone rubble and heaps of metal and wiring. The vandalism is completely gratuitous, and therefore obscene, like the homes where they entered, smashing everything in sight. Just for the sheer pleasure of it, the sheer power of being able to get away with absolutely anything. They are drunk with it, and Uncle Sam, like the good bartender he is, keeps pushing the shots across the counter. Drink up.

I keep checking my watch. An hour and a half still to go. Forty minutes still to go. I look out the window and see people strolling just for the sake of strolling. The sight is incongruous and amazing. Suddenly I realize the sun is shining and the air is warm. On a normal day we would be enjoying this mild weather, the brief period between the cold winds of late winter and the suffocating heat of the coming summer. It is a beautiful day, but even this will be taken from us in another thirty minutes, as we rush back to our homes to pace and wait for the next lifting. I hate the sight of everyone scurrying around—the disgusting phrase drugged cockroaches in a bottle comes to my mind—and I think, I will not go out again. I won't precisely because they say that I can. I want to want nothing, neither medicine nor toilet paper nor sunny days. None of it is theirs to give.

*W*hen the siege was lifted on 10 May at the Church of the Nativity, life returned to normal in Bethlehem—that is if normal is a word that can be used for the ongoing struggle to survive under occupation. People began to pick up the pieces and those who could went back to work. During the following week and a half Alison was busy at the Bible College computer. Yet she wrote no long reflections. That seemed to be a common pattern. There was strength to write when the situation was darkest. Yet it was as if words could never sufficiently describe the return to the darkness that was there before.

Alison did send dozens of forwards, including articles on "The Truth about the Church of the Nativity" and the tragedy at Jenin. These are included below. Also, Alison was preoccupied with the fate of a friend, Nathan Musselman, who was imprisoned by the Israelis for his efforts to take food to the starving people trapped in the Church of the Nativity. For two weeks, until his eventual release and deportation to the United States, Alison forwarded emails from Nathan's parents and from the International Solidarity Movement appealing for intervention on Nathan's behalf. Those messages are too long to include here, so excerpts will have to suffice.

13 May 2002

This message is about a friend of ours, Nathan Musselman, who is on my mailing list. He was a volunteer here at the college for about a year, then went to Birzeit to study Arabic, and whenever he came to Bethlehem, he would sleep on our floor. The girls adore him, and he is like family to us. In his time here, he has been a very active participant in demonstrations and other events supporting human rights for Palestinians. His latest involvement was with the group of activists who entered the Church of the Nativity at the beginning of May. As you will see below, this resulted in his imprisonment along with three other activists, and they are all engaged in a hunger strike. I have received messages from his mother, and she is asking all of us to take some kind of action for his release. So please take a minute to read about him and to do something for him. The International Solidarity Movement has done great things for the Palestinians over the last year and a half, and they deserve our support in return.

While nine have been deported, these four young American men remain in Israeli prison and are on hunger strike (one of them, Trevor, is on his seventh day and the other three are on their fifth day):

> Trevor Baumgartner - Seattle, Washington
> Thomas Koutsoukos - Lake Forest, Illinois
> Nathan Mauger - Spokane, Washington
> Nathan Musselman - Roanoke, Virginia

Nathan and the others were never arrested by the Israeli authorities. They were dragged out of Palestinian territory (Bethlehem) by Israeli forces, held in detention and presented with deportation orders. For protesting this deportation and lack of due process, they remain prisoners—held without charge, hostages of the Israeli Authorities. The four men are asking to be allowed to go home, but of their own free will, for they will not accept the legitimacy of an occupation force to keep them from working with the Palestinian people, now and in the future.

14 May 2002

Here's some information I got this morning about Nathan (Trevor is being detained along with him and two others). It appears that the consulate and embassy folks are actually collaborating with the Israelis to delay their release. Why doesn't this surprise me?

Nathan has not been deported. He was told by the Embassy he would be deported two days ago. The Embassy demanded the four men's parents pay their tickets home. The four are still in prison. All four continue their hunger strike. They are not "free to go" as the Embassy continues to tell us. Please do take a minute or several to harass one or more elected officials in DC or Israel about this situation.

16 May 2002

There has been a very concerning development since this morning. We've been told that the four detained men offered to pay their own way to Amman and use their round trip tickets to go home. The Israeli officials have allowed three of them to do that . . . but they are detaining Nathan Musselman for questioning . . .

*D*ay after day Alison reported on her friend's plight, asking Americans to intervene with their government on his behalf. Finally after ten days of patient waiting, news came of Nathan's release and return to the States.

24 May 2002

An early morning call from the American Embassy in Israel said that all of the detainees wanted their parents to purchase tickets for them to leave from Tel Aviv. A second phone call by a more reliable source at the Embassy said that indeed the men had agreed to fly home from Tel Aviv. The flight leaves Tel Aviv at midnight on Sunday and Nathan should be in Roanoke sometime Monday.

*T*he Siege of the Church of the Nativity had made the cover of every major news magazine. Pope John Paul 2 had intervened, appealing to concern for the antiquity of the Bethlehem church. Still the entire situation was enshrouded in mystery. Cameron W. Barr expressed the dilemma in an April 9 Christian Science Monitor story: "Two Sides, Two Stories, One Church," and AP correspondent Ibrahim Hazboun reported, "The Israeli military prevented reporters from reaching the church to independently assess the rival claims." There were claims and counter claims. The story was spun in a way that once again ignored Bethlehem's own residents. Alison and others had lived through the ordeal and had a right to share their perspective.

14 May 2002
I know you guys are expecting me to write about the Church of the Nativity, what was true and what was not. I can't imagine the news you heard about it, but I can almost assure you that 99% of it was untrue. It was a big spinfest from day one, and just the thought of writing about it made me exhausted. But I did find this which I thought was pretty good and pretty thorough, and I might still add my comments later on . . . All I can say for the moment is that when the Taliban destroyed that Buddhist statue, the whole world went ape. But when Israel laid waste to the old (as in 4000 years old) city of Nablus nobody made a peep, and the Church of the Nativity, the site generally recognized worldwide as the birthplace of Christ . . . like this guy says, what can we say?

Father Labib Kobti has written *The Truth about the Church of the Nativity*. This is how Father Kobti reported the situation:

It was a war of misinformation and Public Relations. Israel felt herself in a very bad situation and needed to explain to the world why she besieged in the oldest Christian Church of the world. The Palestinians were morally justified in their resistance, even as that resistance led them to the Church of the Nativity.

Israel tried to tell the world that she did nothing wrong. That Israel entered a Palestinian town just to defend the future of the Israelis. That they deprived an entire population of food, water, and freedom so as to protect the security of the Israelis. And that all their behavior was not only ethical but just for the sake of peace. And that the snipers shooting on anything that moved in the church was legal and rightful. And they shot eight unarmed people, including a priest, as well hungry and thirsty people, in the dark, deprived of electricity. How many Israeli soldiers were killed by Palestinians inside or outside the Church? None. How can Israel claim that they were involved in battles with the Palestinians inside the Church? Israel's claims are dismissed as silly LIES and MISINFORMATION.

We do not understand why Israel is inundating the media with stories of how littered the Church was after the exit of the Palestinian resistance fighters? Surely Israel cannot think that the litter left behind by these fighters is worse than depriving people of food and water? Surely the litter is not worse than holding a people under domination and implementing a system of apartheid? Surely the litter is not as bad keeping entire towns under house arrest and curfew?

The Franciscans never complained about the behavior of the Palestinians inside the Church. The Franciscans knew that this would happen, and they stayed in the Church to ensure that Israel did not destroy the Church and to ensure that Israel did not slaughter the Palestinians inside . . . The Vatican neither complained of the Palestinians' presence nor wanted them to leave so as to be killed by the Israelis. The Vatican wanted a just solution for them and tried all its best to bring them out of the church unharmed.

While telling the world about the litter that was left behind, Israel never conveyed to the world that the Friars of the Franciscan Order, the Orthodox Priests and Armenian Priests preferred to stay with the Palestinians than to go free. In fact the Israelis told first the world that two hundred Palestinian terrorists invaded the Church of the Nativity and took the Priests hostage. Their lies started unraveling immediately as Priests with access to cell phones started calling people and telling them that they were there of their own free will. I place more value on reports from my Franciscan Friars who lived through the ordeal with the Palestinians.

*W*hile residents of Bethlehem were experiencing confinement during the Siege of the Church of the Nativity, Palestinians in Jenin were suffering a direct incursion which brought destruction and death on a grander scale.

16 May 2002

Here is a VERY good discussion of Jenin which I almost filed away without giving it my proper attention. We ourselves saw footage of the refrigerator trucks entering and leaving the camp and we heard many of the details corroborated again and again by civilians. I have no doubt that the death toll was in the hundreds. So again, it should be remembered that, if the truth is on your side, why try to manipulate it? The fact is that none of us knows what REALLY happened there, except for the camp residents themselves, which is the most compelling reason there is for an investigation.

"JENIN - THE PROPAGANDA WAR" by Tanya Reinhart, *Yediot Aharonot* Newspaper • April 21, 2002.

In Israel, Jenin is perceived mainly as a public relations problem (called in Hebrew 'hasbara'—explaining). It appears even that the army and the government believe that Israel is winning the propaganda battle. After all, all relevant principles of this battle have been strictly adhered to . . .

The first principle: No pictures or information in real time! The IDF (Israeli army) managed to fully prevent the media from entering Jenin during the events. Thus, all we were left with were 'conflicting reports'—a stream of horrible accounts coming from Palestinian witnesses who escaped the refugee camp—and the IDF's utter denial. In the meanwhile, the work of destruction could continue undisturbed for ten days . . .

The second principle of the propaganda battle: If you have full control over the local media, you can pass anything. These messages have been repeated since, again and again, not only by all politicians and Israeli spokesmen, but also by almost every reporter, weaved into the news reports, and by the analysts and columnists, disguised as spontaneous acts of expressing an educated opinion . . .

This line is pretty sophisticated. The word 'massacre' may bring to mind soldiers moving from house to house, shooting everyone they find—men, women and children (as in Sabra and Shatila). Such massacre clearly did not take place in Jenin. No Palestinian source ever described the facts this way. Still, HaAretz and everyone else insist on falsifying just this specific interpretation of the word.

What did clearly happen in Jenin is that the army simply ignored the fact that there were an unknown number of individuals and families in the areas which were bombarded day and night by missiles from 'Cobra' helicopters, or even in some of the houses erased by bulldozers to pave ways for the tanks. No one came to shoot them individually; they were just buried under their bombarded or bulldozed homes. Others died of their wounds in the alleys, or cried for days under the ruins, until their voices faded away.

Bit by bit, testimonies of reserve soldiers are filtering through the back pages of the Israeli media. . . For many, such descriptions are sufficient to make them shiver, and they don't really care whether the right word for this is 'massacre'. . . .

It may take a while before we (Israelis) start to digest what we did in Jenin. I don't have the words yet to speak about my shame, my horrible pain for the Palestinian people. Therefore I speak about what we did to ourselves. . . . We are turning the whole Muslim world against us."

*M*eanwhile in Bethlehem, life returns to "normal." Alison and her family try to fall back into a routine and search for meaning in the midst of chaos.

22 May 2002 • Wednesday

Maybe it's the book I'm reading now—*Best Travel Essays of 2001*—or maybe it's the fact that I'm going to be 43 tomorrow. Or, maybe it's just the natural consequence of spending 39 days under curfew. But this past week has been characterized by a sudden eerie awareness of the minutes ticking by. I look at Mathilda's leggy figure with astonishment and wonder, when did you grow up? During the curfew, certain moments were illuminated as if beams direct from heaven were shining down upon them, inviting me to pay strict attention. One day I stepped out the front door and felt the wind blowing across my skin, as if for the first time in my life. Another time Phoebe came crashing into my legs and said, I LOVE you, Mom! And I looked down at her, awestruck.

After nearly two weeks without any fresh fruits or vegetables, George managed to buy some apples, and I could not get over the amazement of biting through the crisp skin and chewing the sweet pulp. I took a shower and the warm water felt extraordinary, and the feeling of being clean felt even more extraordinary. And I doubt I will ever forget that afternoon when the girls and I spent an hour silently mesmerized by the sight of a spider building her web and catching ants in the bathroom. The loveliness of these suspended moments mercifully eclipsed other, darker thoughts and feelings, like what we will do for money next month and how many more invasions we can take. I knew I had to accept them for what they were, simple gifts for which I was and am inexpressibly thankful. Thank you, Sharon. Thank you, soldiers. Thank you, Occupation.

"Whatever your hand finds to do, do it with might, for there is no work nor device nor knowledge nor wisdom in the grave to which you are going." This is a truth that lodged in my cranium early on and drove me relentlessly forward. It's what made me enter the Peace Corps. It's what made me learn to fly a single-engine plane. It's what made me come to excavate in Israel, and work on the kibbutz, and study Hebrew. And Arabic. And even during the curfew, it was the thought which motivated me to sew like crazy, using the endless hours to create pleasing things (five patchwork pillows, four wall-hangings, two shoulder bags, and a cross-stitch), which in their own small way seemed to redeem the ugliness taking place all around us.

The essays suddenly reminded me of all the places I used to dream of seeing. I can distinctly remember sitting on my porch in the dark, watching fireflies and listening to my short-wave radio, floating hypnotized in a velvet sea of exotic languages. I've never been to Asia. Vietnam. Thailand. Nepal. India. Turkey. Alaska. Iceland. Antarctica. On my thirtieth birthday I walked up the length of the Dead Sea, sleeping in the shadow of the mountains and dreaming of cougars. After that, the idea of a Big Walk grew in my head and was resurrected in a thunderclap of yearning last week. I never imagined I'd find myself in a situation where I could not even walk down my driveway.

Without routines, we free-floated through the weeks, going to sleep late and waking up late, picking at food throughout the day without ever eating proper meals, pacing from window to window, the television always on. The cyclical nature of human activity can be both a burden and a source of redemption. The pointlessness of endless repetition—waking, eating, eating again, sleeping, waking again—magnified by the absence of even the illusion of purpose, can cause true existential despair, but in the wake of profound grief it can be the only consolation available to us. The sun also rises.

So much of life seems so meaningless, and the taking away of it feels meaningless too. The other night, the despair of this thought struck me with such force that I wept for an hour. And then Mathilda came and very gently placed her palm on my cheek, and I knew that if life means anything, it means exactly that, the simple gestures of human kindness and compassion that we extend to one another when they are needed. Or not.

And so the minutes slip past and the passage of each one echoes in my mind like the sighs of an expiring universe. For me, for George, for our kids, for everyone around us. The lives we are living are not Life at all, but some kind of semi-conscious state of non-Death, a numbness devoid of pleasure, devoid of ease, devoid of hope, devoid of meaning except for the sheer perverse determination to hang on as long as we can.

And the definition of "as long as we can" continues to be systematically degraded until we suddenly find ourselves confined to our homes, surrounded by tanks and snipers with the minutes turning into days and the days turning into weeks. And then I am suddenly breathless with terror at the thought that I have somehow sacrificed a whole decade to this, and that a decade is only a fraction of what people around me have sacrificed. And that it seems to mean nothing and to lead nowhere.

And I hate the thought of leaving.

And I dread the thought of staying.

And the minutes tick by.

Occupation without end.

Amen.

23 May 2002

Basically we are being confined to our own towns on a permanent basis. Bethlehem is now surrounded by a combination of trenches, razor wire, and walls currently being erected and, as was demonstrated yesterday, anyone trying to circumvent these barriers by foot will be shot on sight. Furthermore, permits are NOT being issued by the army or anyone else, for work or any other reason. George has been trying to get such a permit for a year and a half, and is not having any more luck now than he did half a year or a year ago. Also, taxi drivers are being punished for providing transportation between towns to West Bank residents by having their cars confiscated and being fined $5000 for any violation. So the situation is actually MUCH worse even than before the invasion.

*T*o outsiders the Siege of the Church of the Nativity was merely an interruption of the daily routine in Bethlehem. Perhaps time would heal the wounds. Perhaps residents would be able to put pieces back together. However, as Alison reflected upon the situation some six months later, it was clear that the siege had left permanent scars on the community. A decade of striving toward peace had suffered irreparable damage.

15 November 2002

Whenever I go to the Peace Center these days, I feel an overwhelming sadness for what we have been through and what we have lost in the last two years. The Peace Center was built at the site of the old Israeli police station flanking the Nativity Church compound in Manger Square, and after Bethlehem gained autonomy in December 1995, we were happy to see that ugly structure and all that it represented razed to the ground. The Peace Center rose up out of the ashes and expressed our hope that peace itself would rise up to redeem, at last, all the years of ugliness that had gone before it.

The Peace Center has been a beacon of progressive action and interaction, and before the Intifada erupted, it sponsored a whole variety of terrific activities that I was more than glad to support. I took the girls there on countless occasions for puppet shows, children's films, art workshops, clown performances, Palestinian heritage exhibitions, and countless other unique cultural events. Attendance at those events always carried with them a great sense of optimism because they lent to our lives the feelings of normalcy and participation that had been lacking for so long. People often consider the word "oppression" only as an abstract term in an abstract political lexicon, but the fact is that "oppression" very literally feels "oppressive." It has a suffocatingly visceral affect on daily life and these activities allowed us and our children to come up for air and breathe, however fleetingly, the liberating atmosphere of life as it is meant to be lived, with purpose, with choice, and with delight.

The year preceding the Jubilee Celebration was especially exciting for residents of Bethlehem. Money was being poured into the municipality for the purpose of renovating the historic Old City area surrounding Manger Square and the central market. Walls were being bleached white to remove graffiti from the first Intifada, archways and other unique architectural features were being restored, pedestrian pavements were being renovated, and classy little touches like ornamental street lanterns and street signs made of Armenian tile were added. It was truly beautiful, and we felt, for the first time in a very long time, that we lived in a good place with a good future.

The pedestrian walkway that led through Star Street to Manger Square had been transformed into a bustling tourist attraction, as had Manger Square in preparation for Christmas 1999 and the Millennium festivities. The rehabilitation of Manger Square was much more than your standard urban renewal project. Its objective was to revive the hope of a population that had virtually lost all hope—a steep ambition, but Palestinians are easily conned and it worked. Some of my best memories of Bethlehem are from Christmas and New Year 1999, standing in the packed square in front of the brightly-lit Peace Center in the pouring rain and the stinging cold, listening to the choirs performing on the Millennium stage and feeling insanely optimistic. Phoebe was strapped into a snugli on my chest and the girls, drenched but exhilarated, stood gazing up in wonder at the glittering lights. It was a time of pure magic.

Another of my best memories of Bethlehem is of the Norwegian cultural week, organized by the Peace Center just days prior to Sharon's visit to the Temple Mount in September 2000. The whole week was great fun, but the best part was the culminating event, a strange late night procession peculiar to Norwegian folk tradition which celebrates the autumn equinox. It was populated by a host of strange masked creatures on stilts that breathed fire and performed gymnastic tricks. Mathilda was positively mesmerized and wanted this to be her job when she grew up. We had never seen anything like it, but it seemed to form a natural extension to our horizon of hope, our continually, miraculously expanding horizon of hope. And we were so hungry, so grateful, for all of it.

This morning as I sat in the reception area of the Peace Center waiting for the girls to finish their art workshop, I looked out into the ruined square and recalled that crazy procession which, instead of exorcising our collective demons, seemed to have unleashed them in a savage flood. The events witnessed in this square since then, culminating with the unbelievable siege of the Nativity Church compound in April, have succeeded in surpassing our worst nightmares. Sadder still, they have extinguished not just our sense of optimism, but even the most remote possibility for optimism or trust for a very long time to come. In short, the foundation for peace no longer exists.

Even now, it is difficult to articulate the intimate sense of violation that accompanied the siege of the Nativity Church. From its first horrific days when unattended bodies lay decomposing in the streets to the final escorted departure of the militants, the forty-day siege was an assault which defied comprehension, much less expression. I somehow think it would not have been so bad had it not taken place precisely where it did, in the very spot where our hopes succeeded in transcending so many years of oppression and despair. The conclusion is inescapable: the siege was about a lot more than capturing Bethlehem's "wanted men."

The staff of the Peace Center can certainly testify to this. During the siege, the Israeli army occupied the Peace Center and used it as both a center of operations and as the location for the negotiations over the fate of the militants. Because the first-floor area in which the negotiations were conducted (in fact the reception area in which I was seated this morning) was the focus of intense media attention for the duration of the siege, its appearance was maintained. It was only after the withdrawal of the army from the town that the full extent of the damage to the building was revealed. I must share the news bulletin which reported on this:

> The director of the Bethlehem Peace Center entered the premises of the Bethlehem Peace Center the evening of Friday, 10 May 2002, while the IDF was still evacuating town from the back of the building. Within the hour, diplomats of the Swedish Consulate General in Jerusalem joined him. What they encountered was a scene of utter devas-

tation, inexplicable and inexcusable even under the circumstance of a military occupation. This is certainly not the hallmark of a civilized army. While the structure of the building itself was left largely intact, the inside of the building was defiled in every possible way imaginable. This Bethlehem Peace Center, which had been a gift of Sweden to Bethlehem and is dedicated to the promotion of peace, democracy, religious tolerance and cultural diversity, was coated in a mixture of dirt, beer, wine, urine, eggs, rotting food, spilt coffee and tea from wall to wall, room to room and floor to floor. The bathrooms had feces and vomit in the toilets, on the floors and on the walls. The entire furniture of the building was rearranged to meet the need of the military administration, with not a single desk or chair remaining in its original place. In fact, chairs have been found scattered in the municipality and in the street behind the Peace Center. Those chairs that were still in the Peace Center were, without exception, soiled, torn, ripped or cut to pieces. Doors and drawers have been forced open, a number of them having been blasted with dynamite. Hundreds of keys were strewn throughout the building, including under various toilet seats. All cash boxes were compromised. The kitchen, which was recently installed and has never been used, has been soiled beyond recognition, knee deep in oil and grit and grime, with egg yolks dripping from the walls and spread across the kitchen floor. The store of food purchased with humanitarian donations and intended for distribution to the needy was entirely looted. Rotting food and drinks were everywhere—on the tables, on the floor, on the walls and on the ceilings. The galleries were apparently used for shooting and partying. There was evidence of heavy drinking of beer and wine, and at least one instance of takeaway pizza. A veritable mountain of empty bullet casings on the floor of the gallery facing the Church of the Nativity tells its own story. Photographs from an exhibit on Palestinian architecture were used to cover the windows to protect the soldiers from incoming bullets. Joseph from the exhibit of a Crèche from Hong Kong served as a dummy in a window and lost his head. The elevator was destroyed. More than 25 cars parked in the garage of the Bethlehem Peace Center seeking shelter from the invading army were destroyed and taken to a scrap heap near the Bethlehem checkpoint. As for theft, it has been extensive. The list includes at least seven computers and printers, fax machines, a heavy-duty photocopier, ALL the telephones in the building, a laminator, two scanners, a video projector, a DVD, a VCR, two televisions, two slide projectors, two sound mixers, CD players, microphones and a digital camera. From the stores they stole tools and spare parts. Many official files and scores of personal items, including private family photographs, were taken. The children were also not spared, as soldiers used and soiled the mattresses used for their activities and even destroyed the instruments used for the course in Music Appreciation for Toddlers, including drums, xylophones, and the teacher's electric organ. The price-tag for restoring the Peace Center to how it was on 1 April 2002 is in the vicinity of USD 200,000 and will take weeks, if not months, to complete. This does not include the cars in the garage. To this day, Israel insists that its operation was aimed at rooting out terrorists and the terrorist infrastructure in the Palestinian territories. Reports of looting and vandalism are explained as single and isolated incidents perpetrated by individual and exceptional criminal elements in the army. It is argued that theft and vandalism is neither the intent nor the interest of the IDF. The case of the outrageous defilement of the Bethlehem Peace Center, a cultural center of the highest order in Palestine, dedicated entirely to aesthetic and cultural pursuits, would prove quite the opposite to be true. While it is not the only civic institution to suffer this fate during the Israeli incursions into Palestinian-controlled areas, the mere extent of the devastation, and the fact that the Bethlehem Peace Center served as the IDF's headquarters for 38 days, belies Israel's denials of intent. The defilement of the Bethlehem Peace Center proves beyond the shadow of a doubt that the destruction of Palestinian civil society and the looting was not only tolerated by the military, but was orchestrated by the IDF at the highest level and was, indeed, one of the objectives of Operation Defensive Shield."

Today is the tenth day of Ramadan and the second Friday of this month of fasting. It is also the day designated for the observance of Palestinian "Independence" Day. "Independence" never had so much meaning for us, and it has never been so far away.

The square is packed with fasting worshippers facing Mecca, their backs turned toward me as they bend and bow in perfect unison through the stages of the midday prayer. As the children emerge from the art room clutching their projects and chattering excitedly, the feelings of sadness and loss drench me like the rain on that faraway Christmas Eve. The vandalism to Bethlehem will eventually be fixed, the grounds of the Peace Center have already been restored, but something much more fundamental has been crushed beyond repair. We could have had coexistence, we could have had peace, we could have had a future. How did it all go so horribly wrong?

Life Under Curfew

*P*eople in Bethlehem often talk of the forty days of curfew during the Gulf War. People were imprisoned in their own homes, only allowed periodically to buy groceries and other necessities. Those were the days of full occupation. The border patrol was a constant presence in Bethlehem with a major post at Manger Square. Soldiers in riot gear were constantly patrolling the streets. The army had absolute rule, arresting whomever it wished, shooting tear gas and rubber bullets whenever it wished, making life unbearable. That was the reason the Oslo peace agreements came about.

In the Biblical tradition, forty days simply meant a very long time. It is impossible for an outsider to imagine how long when it comes to curfew. Forty is also considered a complete number, so that someone condemned for punishment was never inflicted with forty lashes. That would be the same as the death penalty. Thus forty lashes less one. The April/ May occupation of Bethlehem included 39 days of curfew. It nearly broke the backs of its residents.

It also signaled that life had returned to the pre-Oslo days when military rule was continuous. While U. S. media reported that the Church of the Nativity standoff had been resolved and that tanks were withdrawing from Bethlehem, the inhabitants of Bethlehem, Beit Jala, and Beit Sahour knew that there would be no return to normality. First, they tried to pick up the pieces. Yet, the occupation army was there to stay. On 25 May, only fiften days after the army had withdrawn, a one-week curfew was back in place. On 19 June, it once again imposed curfew on these three towns. Five days of curfew. Twelve. Fifteen. Twenty-eight. Thirty-Five. Forty-two.

31 May 2002

I remember a day—I think it was in November of 2000 when the tank shelling in Beit Jala was becoming surreally intense—when we visited the family of a friend of George who lived in upper Beit Jala, right in the area that was taking the brunt of the worst assaults. Sitting on their fragrant outdoor veranda, I could look all around and see the scars of war: chipped tiles and bullet-riddled cars, shattered windows and punctured water tanks. Where we lived seemed bad enough, but this house was the classic image of "life in the war zone." As we were served little cups of Arabic coffee and listened to their hair-raising tales of missiles shaking the foundations of the house while they crouched on the floor inside, I remember feeling astonished that they still had the capacity to laugh and be hospitable, and I felt proud of their heroic ability to endure the nightmarish nightly assaults. I felt very privileged to be among them, and I still feel that way.

At one point, the mother of the household turned to me and said, "Let them do whatever they have to do to us at night, but in the morning I need to go to work." And this remark neatly summarized the perverse trade-off being made available at that time. Yes, the checkpoint was still relatively "easy," at least in comparison to the life-threatening excursion it is in these days. But the price was fierce nightly military assaults. I can remember how utterly bizarre it seemed to be shot at by Apache helicopters in the night and then to wake up in the morning, send the kids off to school, and prepare for the day's work. The only thing more bizarre is how we have come to consider that an improvement over our present state of stark survival.

For Palestinians, life has become nothing more than a continuous erosion of the threshold of what we think we can tolerate, and the remark of that woman on that day is a perfect illustration of this principle. Because, looking back after a horrendous year and a half, I realize that we were lucky that our worst concerns were merely the nightly assaults. Now, not only do we live under the constant threat of these military assaults in the even more intimate form of tank invasion, curfew, snipers, and house-to-house searches, we are also facing serious threats to our few remaining options for working, earning income, and supporting our families. Not only is getting to work in Jerusalem nearly impossible, but getting to work in Ramallah or Hebron or any other Palestinian center is also a very tricky proposition. In fact, the installation of razor-wire fences, trenches, and walls has made it virtually impossible to leave Bethlehem for any reason whatsoever. And those whose jobs are in town are not necessarily any better off, because the restrictions on the movement of materials and clients between towns, not to mention the massive destruction and vandalism to so many workplaces and public spaces, has brought most forms of commercial activity to a complete standstill.

But the true nightmare is that it doesn't stop there.

The message of the last several months is crystal clear, though it seems we are the only ones who truly "get it." Those who continue to stay on in Palestine, do so literally at their own risk. Their very presence constitutes a threat, an act of Terrorism, according to the post-9/11 lexicon, which justifies any and all forms of "response." Not only are the ordinary luxuries—the family trips, the strolls by the beach, the mundane pleasures of eating in a restaurant or taking the children for ice cream on warm summer evening—not only are these things that most people take for granted far out of the question for us because of the lack of money, because of the constant threat of invasion, because of the siege mentality to which we have all succumbed. It's not the mere deprivation of this or that routine or activity, or the degree of legitimacy or indulgence in question. It is the very assumption that personal freedom exists for us at all, on any level. Anytime. Anywhere. For any reason. It is Israel that dictates the terms.

The events of last Saturday evening provide a perfect illustration of this. The daughter of a relative of George's was having an engagement party. I didn't want to attend, so George took the girls, who have a Palestinian love for such occasions. It was their first outing in a long while. The earlier part of the evening was blissfully calm for me. Having taken a leisurely shower, I was sitting out on our porch in the warm night air, listening to Schubert's *The Trout* and feeling vaguely optimistic, when around 8:45 p.m. there was the sound of some sort of explosion nearby. Immediately alert, I started itemizing the options in my mind: An assassination? An unexploded device found by some unfortunate kid? A "work accident?" A tank shell? Suddenly a fleet of attack helicopters moved into the area and my low-level sense of panic shifted into high gear. I turned on the local station, shocked to learn that a tank invasion was under way. At nine o'clock on a Saturday night. Curfew had been imposed in Beit Jala. Tanks had reached Al-Madbasa, the town center. They were heading up to Beit Sahour from Jabal Abu Ghaneim and also to Jabal Al-Hindasi, the neighborhood just over the hill from us. I had no way of reaching George, and he had no way of reaching me. I could only wonder where they were, if they could even get back home, how scared the girls must be. In the forty-five minute interval before they finally reached home, I thought I might really lose my mind. A few hours later, the army withdrew having accomplished exactly nothing. The next night, they invaded again and stayed for the duration of the week, though we are no more privy to their plans for withdrawal than we are to those for their arrival.

Invasion and the threat of imminent invasion. This is the miserable selection available to us now, and the bad thing is that, in my gut, I feel it is only a matter of time, a matter of conducive circumstances, before it becomes much much worse. As Robert Fisk states at the conclusion of his most recent article, we wake these days to a sense of profound foreboding. And the new trade-off is this: the firestorm of true atrocity versus the mere desperate nightmare of daily survival, in which even the most fundamental of activities—supporting ourselves, sending our kids to school, seeking medical treatment, giving birth, doing what we must simply to get from one day to the next—are risks fraught with unimaginable danger. We never could have imagined that life could get this bad, but then in Palestine, imagination at its most perverse doesn't stand a ghost of a chance against the mundane brutality of real life. Whenever will it end?

On June 5, a car bomb killed 16 Israelis, including 13 soldiers. Islamic Jihad claimed responsibility. Israeli helicopters attacked Jenin, and Israeli infantry attacked Yasser Arafat's Ramallah headquarters, killing six. The Bush administration publicly announced that Israel had a right to defend itself.

5 June 2002 • Wednesday

My workplace has been the scene of near-riots since the beginning of the week, a fact I'll bet never made any headline. Today's bombing, on the other hand, no doubt made front-page news all over the world, though it's not really possible to make sense of today without knowing about yesterday and all the days that preceded it. For the last three days I have arrived at work to find restless crowds of people milling around the entrance of the college, waiting. By 8 a.m. they already look exhausted. Some are toting small children, many are dressed in grubby clothes, a few are obviously infirm, limping slowly down the driveway on twisted limbs with a gait that expresses not just physical disability, but also enormous emotional exhaustion. Virtually all of them are clutching documents of one kind or another: prescriptions for unaffordable medicines, x-rays or laboratory analyses indicating the need for treatment of one kind or another, again too expensive under the circumstances, electrical bills, water bills, phone bills, non-payment warnings from school accounting offices. Their destination is the Shepherd Society, a charitable organization established half a decade ago by the administration of the college to respond to the humanitarian needs of the local community, which are now rapidly multiplying beyond human imagination.

Both the college and the Shepherd Society are small institutions, operating on modest budgets and facilitating modest relief projects. Faced with the need which is now being manifested in the town, what they can offer is a drop in the proverbial bucket. These folks have had a very bad year and a half, and that would have been enough in and of itself. But the fact is that there is no end in sight and the raw truth of this is sinking in big-time. Razor wire and trenches tend to have that affect. If anything, the only thing visible on the horizon for any of us is a significant worsening of an already nearly unbearable situation and people are scared like never before. I know because I walk around day and night with a barely contained sense of dread and anxiety, and we are better off than many. A thousand lifetimes ago (during college) I worked in an inner-city pediatric emergency room and the chronic poverty I encountered there was nothing in comparison to what we are witnessing here. Compared to this, that was a picnic in the park on a dazzling summer day. Here, the darkness is about to overcome us all.

So they come clutching their children and their bills and hope that they will receive something, anything in the way of assistance. They crowd around the door in the heat of the June morning, and as the hour advances from nine to ten and then eleven, their annoyance and frustration and fear just erupt. Palestinians are generally polite to a fault, and so such displays are not at all a common thing to witness. Yesterday people were pushing and screaming and pounding so loudly on the door that the windows of our office directly above it rattled. Today people forced their way in through secondary entrances, squatting on stairs and refusing to leave until something could be done for them. "What are we supposed to do," one woman fiercely asked me, "just die?"

The irony is that assistance—the benign euphemism for charity—is the last thing they really want. Culturally, it is a source of great shame ("*aeb*" in Arabic, one of the first vocabulary words I ever learned) to be in a position to have to ask for such help, and I have seen many people burst into tears in front of the office staff, or hang their heads simply unable to meet the gazes of the people from whom they have been forced to request help. God knows there isn't a family in Bethlehem that doesn't need it, a fact which eases the shame somewhat by acknowledging it for what it is, a comprehensive social phenomenon affecting all classes and walks of life without distinction. Still, that doesn't change the fact that people don't really want bags of rice or used clothes or grocery coupons or tuition

stipends. They want to work. They want to support themselves, as they have always done. They want this endless
closure to end. They want the razor wire and the trenches to go
away. They want the Occupation, which never ever should
have gotten to this desperate point, to be stopped once and for
all by those who have the means and the decency to stop it.
Theoretically at least, it makes sense that this task should fall
to the biggest, richest, most powerful, and most self-righteously
Christian nation in the world. Instead, it is a fact that this
country, which can remain nameless because we all know
exactly which one I mean, is the principal reason all those
people are streaming to my workplace, having chosen to stand
passively by while the situation moves inexorably to a state of
full-blown crisis. Or worse.

Now stop for a minute to consider the connection between
today's headlines and yesterday's non-event.

Each household copes in its own way. Lately we have
been discussing things which I never in all my ten years here
thought would come about. Some of them, though they may
seem relatively insignificant, constitute real Red Lines for us.
Like getting rid of our yellow-plated Renault Express. Half
passenger car and half service van, we bought it used on the
eve of Barak's election and the psychological difference it
made in our lives was tremendous. The whole idea was that we
could throw an unlimited amount of stuff in the back and go,
and for a year or so we did just that, right through the checkpoint and to the nearest beach or countryside. I remember
aimless drives through the hills, stopping at monasteries for
picnics and wine purchases. Unbelievably, the seashore is only
45 minutes from us, and going for a day has been on countless
occasions an opportunity for deep emotional renewal for all of
us, completely disproportionate to the place itself. As a matter
of fact, where we go doesn't even matter as much as the fact of
being able to go, to get out if only for just an afternoon, to
escape the confines of the prison our town has become and
pretend that everything is going to be okay, even when we
know deep down it is not.

But now of course, we never go anywhere, and the car is
nothing but a needless expense that we can no longer afford or

justify. I am one of the lucky few that collects a paycheck whether I work or not, but George hasn't seen a full paycheck in more than five months, and he hasn't been to work more than a handful of times in the last three. In practical terms, this means our income is half of what it was last year (a quarter of what it was in George's casino days). So the new arrangement is for him to sleep at his workplace two or three nights a week, working twelve or more hours a day and keeping in touch, when able, by phone (which is why getting a line installed last week was such a big deal). He's there now and we spoke to him just a few minutes ago. It is a dramatic new development for all of us, another Red Line, although there are families who have been living in this fragmented state for years. The irony, of course, is that Bethlehem is only 15 minutes' drive from the center of Jerusalem, though we might as well live in Gaza or on a distant planet, for that matter. It requires some physical and mental adjustments, but for most Palestinians, the continuous need to adjust to increasingly abnormal circumstances is all they have ever known. It's what constitutes, for us, Life.

Tonight the older girls have been crying hysterically, afraid of the prospect of yet another invasion during the night. It's not anything we haven't experienced before, but this time the difference is that Daddy's not here. I keep trying to comfort them with the consolation that, at least, he's working and so we will have enough money for the coming month. But for little girls who live in fear of Apache helicopters, rumbling tanks, and soldiers with guns entering the house, such assurances don't mean much. And so we sit embracing each other on the couch, silently awaiting whatever will come. I have never felt so helpless or hopeless in my life.

For us, the question is not, why do these bombings continue to happen, for the answer to that is horrifically obvious. We only want to know how long this inferno called Palestine will be allowed to continue burning before it consumes everything and everyone. The key to all this is what's not in the headline.

*O*n 18 June, a Hamas bus bombing killed the bomber
and 18 others, including one child, and injured 54 near a
Jerusalem settlement. The previous day Israel had assassinated
Walid Sbeh near Bethlehem. In response, Israeli troops put
several West Bank cities under 24-hour curfew including the
Bethlehem area. The following week's curfew, was expanded
to all West Bank cities, virtually placing two million Palestinians on house arrest. Several days later, President Bush made
a historic speech calling for a change in Palestinian leadership
that would lead to a provisional state.

5 July 2002 • Day Fifteen

Yesterday morning at 8 o'clock there was a soft knock at
our door. I had barely been awake a few minutes and had only
just switched on the local station. According to the announcement, there would be no lifting of the curfew this day. It was
already hot enough to turn on the fan. Who was at the door? I
opened it, and before me stood a young-old woman in a
headscarf holding several plastic bags full of vegetables. Would
I buy some? We didn't really need any, but I went to get my
wallet. Sweat was sprinkled across her forehead and I asked
where she was coming from. Her village, Al-Abadiyyeh, is
down below Beit Sahour along the road to Abu Dis. She must
have walked several kilometers at least, hauling her sacks of
faqous, a locally-bred cross between a cucumber and a zuc-
chini. I asked her if she knew the curfew was in force. The
streets were absolutely quiet and still. She shrugged her shoulders and mumbled something about eight children and a husband stuck at home. The look on her face summed up all the
helplessness and misery of the last two years. And yet, her
eyes were kind and a small smile lit across her face as she
thanked me and went on her way.

As I closed the door the phone rang. It was George in
faraway Jerusalem.

The day begins. When there is no lifting, we sit at home and think of things to do. A day doesn't go by that the girls don't gather together on the floor with the photo album of our U.S. vacation from the summer of 2000. Phoebe calls me over to look at a picture, and I realize with shock that the date is almost exactly two years ago. Here we are swimming at grandma's big fancy pool with the curlicue slide. Here we are eating hot dogs with Terri, Kaylie, and Terri's mom at a wooden picnic table. Here's a picture of the girls getting their faces painted with Helen at the Science Museum. And all these are, of course, from the day we went to King's Dominion. For a long time afterward, the girls declared, "that was the funnest day in my whole life!" Looking at the photos, I can recall sights and smells, as if it all just happened yesterday. The heavy feel of the air as a storm approached. The smell of the pool chlorine. The muffled sound of feet tearing down the carpeted length of the Barnes and Noble bookstore toward the kids' section. I cannot believe what we have been through since, what we are going through now.

There is a commercial on Israel's Channel Two for Spring Fruit Drink. "I'm free . . ." The girls dissolve into giggles on the couch and I look curiously at them. What's so funny? They look at each other and break into their own version of the song, crooning, "I'm not free. . ." Curfew humor. They have inherited their dad's weird sense of *Comedy Under Occupation*. I feel too numb to discern whether I am relieved or concerned.

The Shawshank Redemption is not a good movie to watch under curfew, because the themes it explores—the meaning of freedom, the extraordinary waste of human potential among incarcerated populations, the mentality of institutionalized imprisonment, the human need for hope—are best left unexamined when tanks are prowling the streets of your neighborhood. Neither George nor I was familiar with the film, and we left it on for lack of anything better to watch. By the end we were both open-mouthed and glassy-eyed. It said too much about our predicament, too much about the oppressive feeling in our chests as we submit once again to what, according to all predictions, will be yet another prolonged invasion. Submit . . . I am haunted by the spooky feeling that the entire town is being held hostage by the same three vehicles—a jeep, a tank, and an armored personnel carrier—which circulate end-lessly, creating the illusion that the town is swarming with them.

Our/my passivity makes me cringe. Helpless and hope-less. The phrase "drugged cockroaches in a bottle" keeps thumping in my head. If we are passive, then they disdain us for our passivity. And if we act, then they demonize us for those acts. It was no drugged cockroach that killed Rehavim Ze'evi or blew up that bus in Gilo. At the end of the movie *The Mission*, Robert De Niro renounces his monastic vow of obedi-ence to take up arms in defense of the mission and the people he loves. Jeremy Irons takes up the cross, surrendering him-self and his congregation to divine justice and protection. Both are mowed down. More and more, I think that it just doesn't matter what we do or don't do. Either way we are doomed. The natives are getting restless and uppity. The children fly kites and imitate their soccer heroes in the dusty gouged streets, scattering only when the tanks rumble into view.

I remember looking at the *HaAretz* breaking news one morning. "Four Palestinians killed in gunfire exchanges" was immediately followed by "Score at half-time between Senegal and Turkey is zero-zero." Why do I get the feeling this is all some great big game, fixed from the start? The players are getting creamed, and they never even had a chance. Mind games. The Israeli army is playing mind games with us. They make high-profile announcements on a daily basis about lifting the curfew "to ease the plight of the suffering Palestinians" and then leave us locked in all day. Or they announce in the evening that the curfew will be lifted the following day from 10 to 2:00, then change the hours the next morning. Don't plan for the future, is the message, because you don't have one. You only have what we will give you, and it's not going to be much. Not much at all.

The other morning we listened awestruck as a news commentator announced that permits would be issued for travel between Palestinian towns to "persons over 40." That is, persons under 40 would not qualify for permits. I was sure I had heard wrong. Does that actually mean that people under 40 can't leave their areas, ever, for any reason? Incredibly, this is what it seems to mean. I had a sudden vision of vast graveyards, young people by the thousands suffocated to death, the potential and the hope squashed out of them and their humanity extinguished like fireflies blinking out inside airless glass jars. In *The Shawshank Redemption*, Tim Robbins plays a selection of opera over the prison P.A. system, and the inmates stare motionless and open-mouthed at the speakers. "We need to be reminded that there's a place they can never touch." How much brutality can people take before that place closes over and becomes impenetrable? And think what they would be capable of once that happens . . .

Travel Essays of 2001, again. An essay entitled "Something Wild in the Blood" whispered to me in that vulnerable place, and I sat on the couch in the late-night silence of curfew mourning for my children and for the children of the woman from Al-Abadiyyeh and for my sister-in-law's newborn daughter and for everyone who will grow up in this collective insanity, never knowing how much they have to give, only knowing how much has been taken.

There's a place they can never touch, girls.

No matter what happens, don't ever forget that.

17 July 2002 • Day Twenty-Eight

There is a great temptation these days to give in to whatever it is we are supposed to give in to, to wake up late and sit around half-comatose in our smelly pajamas, drifting through rooms and not even having the motivation to brush our teeth. I wake up before six to check the TV, hoping against hope to see the blue-and-white announcement for the curfew lifting, and when it is not there, what I feel is something I don't know how to put into words. Or else I am afraid to put it into words because articulating it would be the first step toward surrendering to its seductive power. The day stretches out before us, blank and hollow, and I go back to bed struggling under the unbearable weight of the empty hours ahead. Whoever wrote the *Book of Ecclesiastics* understood what it is to feel true despair. "Let thy garments be always white, and let thy head lack no ointment." And later, "Truly the light is sweet, and a pleasant thing it is for the eyes to behold the sun." When you don't have a reason for living, go through the motions. I cling desperately to these reminders as we drag ourselves through the endless days.

In the beginning, it was easier somehow. It was a novelty, a challenge. It was kind of exciting, in a perverse, state-of-emergency sort of way, preparing for curfew, making sure you had everything you needed. There was a strange schizophrenia that characterized those earlier invasions, obliging us on the one hand to think ahead as far as we could, trying to foresee and prepare for all kinds of unlikely possibilities in advance. On the other hand, the enforced inactivity collapsed whole weeks into a continuous sense of "right now" and we learned never to think beyond "today." Fast forward, pause. Fast forward, pause. A month or so ago, numbness was a condition we would sink into on occasion, but shrugging it off was easy enough. We were still alive enough and awake enough to apprehend beauty, the weather, the taste of food. Now numbness is a condition we only occasionally manage to transcend, and then only to find we are better off under full anesthesia. The alternative-awareness is too excruciating, too maddening, too masochistic. I feel that with one more month of it, I will be a goner.

Maybe I should line the girls up on the bed and execute them, saving the last bullet for myself. Who would give a damn, just so long as I don't take any Israelis with me? That many fewer Palestinians plaguing the world with our unreasonable demands and inconvenient insistence on rights. I think of that woman in Texas, and although I do not pretend to understand what kind of hell she had to have been going through, I also know she never had to go through this particular hell. Maybe we should all commit mass suicide Jim Jones-style and save everyone the trouble and expense of all these cumbersome military operations and distasteful moral compromises. Surely they wouldn't have too much difficulty explaining it away as just another variation on the theme of "voluntary transfer." Or finding some way to pin it on Arafat. Neat, tidy, conclusive. And it would spare us all the hilarious joke of "negotiations."

In a recent phone conversation with my mom, I ranted for a while about all my woes, and then she said, well, you just need to go sit somewhere and think about all the good things in your life. For a split second I thought, easy for you to say, but after I hung up I knew it was true, so I did go and sit and think about all the good things. And I do try to do that every day. On a good day, it is enough to sit with my arms around the girls and to think of George, far away but alive and well.

Annie Lamott is a good curfew read, because she's not afraid to admit how down-and-out she's been or to acknowledge how much help she has needed at various stages in her car-wreck of a life. She's the one whose sense of spirituality comes closest to mine, and she's also one of very few writers capable of making me laugh right out loud. I've been rereading *Operating Instructions* with a great sense of recognition ("I'm probably just as good a mother as the next repressed, obsessive-compulsive paranoiac"), but I also can't help continually wondering how she would or wouldn't manage under curfew. She's always talking about being rescued from one of her blue funks by a visiting friend bearing treats, or else fleeing the house in a black mood to go to the ocean or a restaurant or just to take a walk around the neighborhood. None of these escape valves are available to us, and in fact, our range of mental health options is so slim as to be virtually nonexistent. How many hours can we possibly fill putting on nail polish (fingers and toes), braiding hair, looking at photographs, reading stories, swimming in the bathtub, baking bread, napping, eating, talking on the phone, watching *Spacetoon* and *The Bold and the Beautiful*, playing computer games, playing Barbies, coloring pictures, sewing. . . . And yet we do get through, one day, sometimes one hour at a time, and in the evening we sit on the porch in the merciful breeze and feel thankful.

Today I decided to try driving over to the clinic in Beit Sahour to have my mammogram done. I have been meaning to do it for several months, but we have been under curfew on and off (more on than off) since my birthday in May, and it seemed I could just never coordinate the appointments. On days when the curfew is lifted, the clinic is swamped with patients, and my gynecologist, who participates in the village clinic program, is often not around. Yesterday I spoke to the technician, who told me many of the medical personnel are driven to work on curfew days using ambulances, and that if I could get over there, she could do it fairly quickly. So I decided to give it a try. The clinic is only a five-minute drive from our house. At 2 o'clock in the afternoon, the temperature was topping 35 degrees Celsius, and the streets were stunningly still and quiet. I have never gone out on a curfew day, so the look of utter desertion was a shock, even though I knew in theory what to expect. I drove very slowly, my heart hammering, rounding every curve expecting to run head on into a tank or foot patrol and imagining what I would do in that event. The killing of our neighbor Attalah Al-Hayak had taught us all the protocol of getting out of the car with our hands raised. I was hoping my foreigner appearance and yellow plates would save me. In the end, I made it there and back within an hour and without seeing anyone. And I felt a small sense of rebellious triumph, having finally decided they would not control my decision to do this thing which needed to be done. But it was a risk others have died taking.

*O*n 22 July, after five weeks under strict curfew and closures, an agreement was reached between Tanzim and Hamas to discontinue suicide bombing against Israeli civilians. There was a glimmer of hope for Palestinians. That night an Israeli F-16 assassinated Hamas leader Salah Shehadeh in Gaza, killing 14 others, including nine children, and wounding 150.

24 July 2002 • Day Thirty-Five

I recently read that the best way to induce psychosis in lab rats is to be inconsistent with them. Well, we are quickly learning to hate lifting days even more, if that is possible, than curfew days. At least on curfew days, everything is clear and unambiguous. We're stuck, period, and as much as that sucks, it's better than the mind games. Lifting days are supposed to give us some relief from our confinement. They are supposed to "Ease the Suffering of the Palestinian People." However, the last few liftings have allowed us to understand that the point is really just to inflict another kind of hardship, a kind which is utterly perverse in its gratuitousness and utterly obscene in its malice. Four words that summarize pretty well what I think of Israel's "Man of Peace" (plus a few more that I will refrain from using here).

On Tuesday the 16th, the curfew was lifted briefly (originally from 9:00 to 1, and then at 1:00 they extended it to 2, although everyone had already rushed home by then, so the extra hour meant very little), and then for the next three days we were under collective house arrest. Then another lifting was announced for Saturday the 20th, although no one could really figure out the hours. On our local channel the announcement indicated 9 a.m. to 5 p.m. Wow, eight whole hours! How kind, how generous! But on the radio the announcement indicated 7 a.m. to 5 p.m. and on the other local channel the hours of 8 a.m. to 5 p.m. were given. I erred on the side of caution and aimed for leaving the house by 9 o'clock. Driving around is an exceedingly unpleasant business these days, because the traffic is awful. Not only are people leaving the house all at the same time, the driving is also significantly more aggressive because of the time limitations and the cooped-up craziness factor. In addition, the streets in many places have been reduced to piles of rubble. Wreckage and dust are everywhere, and there is no one to fix anything because the P.A. has been liquidated and Israel couldn't give less of a damn about the people formerly under its authority. So it is distressing and depressing to have to go anywhere, but when you only get to leave your house one day in four, you're not left with much of a choice.

Anyway, we had major plans for that day. George would be coming home after being stuck in Jerusalem for ten days (because on the previous Saturday the lifting was announced for 9 to 5 and then abruptly changed at 2:00 in the afternoon from 9 to 5 p.m. to 9 to 3 p.m.). Phoebe would be going to daycare. The older girls had arranged a play day with Mathilda's best friend from school, Noor, who lives in upper Beit Jala and whose birthday had been the day before. And I, of course, would be going to work to slog through the (as of today) 487 messages in my inbox and try to add another couple of coherent sentences to one of the dozens of overdue reports for the previous academic year. I was also planning to schedule a long-awaited doctor's appointment after 2 o'clock. By 1:30, George was back in town and at 2 we both went to pick up Phoebe. Then he dropped me at the clinic in Beit Sahour and went off with Phoebe to do errands and see family members whom we never get a chance to see anymore because we are always rushing around. In the morning I had told the girls that one of us would pick them up around four, unless something changed.

Down at the clinic, I was seated in the waiting room discussing how to arrange an appointment with my gynecologist (you try doing it when you only get to leave the house every third, fourth, or fifth day for from between four to eight hours, never knowing in advance when and for how long or if it will change) when someone burst in saying he had just been at the bank up on the main road and had seen columns of tanks rumbling up the road announcing *"Mamnuah tejawal"* (Movement is forbidden). It was just after two in the afternoon. I rushed home in a panic and called George's mom right away, hoping to find him there. He had just left to get the girls and was aware of what was happening. I held my breath waiting for them to come. His sister Mary was at her mom's house, and she was a bit upset. She had arrived in Bethlehem just before 2:00 from Jerusalem, where she lives, to visit her mother, thinking she'd have plenty of time to get back across the checkpoint before five. Now she was stuck, and it was anybody's guess for how many days. Everyone I spoke to had similar stories of being stuck (again), of being afraid (again), of being played with (again), of being angry (again).

Hate washes over me in waves, hate it never even occurred to me to feel before, with intensity I would never have thought possible. I hate them for making my kids miserable. I hate them for forcing my husband to spend most of the week away from us. I hate them for making me a size heavier than I was last year at this time. And then I hate them for making me to feel so much hatred. I struggle against it almost constantly and then I wonder why it is always us who must contain our rage and control our frustration. The USA is full of marginal nutcases who blow each other away by the thousands each day for nothing more than spare change or a cigarette, and they don't have to endure a tenth of what we do. A couple of weeks of this—God forbid!—would be enough to send them all over the edge.

So spare me the Christian exhortations. I noticed that turning the other cheek wasn't an option after September 11. And "Death to the Arabs" and "Forced Transfer" are understandable expressions of the understandable feelings of anger and frustration that Israelis are understandably experiencing in the wake of each bombing. They can go to work, but they feel fear. They can go to school, but they feel fear. They go out for coffee and movies and shopping in the evening, but they feel fear. They swim and travel and do whatever the hell they want, but the fear they feel is enough to justify ANYTHING they do to us. And, of course, their polite refusal on Monday night of Hamas' unprecedented offer to end all suicide bombings in exchange for withdrawal—what more could they possibly want, for God's sake?—is cause for even greater fear. Well. You don't treat human beings like lab rats without expecting to get bitten back.

Somebody, somewhere, please explain to me the logic of deliberately driving an entire population insane, of causing them to feel such overwhelming hatred and despair. All this time we were supposed to believe that the point was security. Is there anybody anywhere stupid enough (George Bush excepted) to still believe that? As the Gush Shalom statement observed, anyone even remotely concerned with the security of his own citizens would have, at the very least, taken the Hamas offer into serious consideration. But Sharon doesn't care about the lives of his people any more than Sheikh Ahmad Yassin. He wants the bombings, and he's ready to sacrifice as many civilians as necessary to justify what he has already been planning to do for decades: provoke a full-scale confrontation and get rid of us so he can realize his mad dream of "Greater Israel." He's a sadistic warmongering megalomaniac, and anyone who thinks otherwise is delusional (G.B. included).

I recently read a book called *Seventy Times Seven: The Power of Forgiveness.* It is a powerful book that holds a lot of meaning for me, and not a day goes by that I do not meditate on its message and its implications for our situation. But in truth, the most meaningful part comes at the end, in the postscript written by Mumia Abu-Jamal, an African-American who spent sixteen years on death row for a murder that the book's author believes he did not commit. "The book ignores the inherent imbalance between the personal and the political—and therefore seems to be a spiritual indulgence for the powerful. . . . In my mind, I cannot imagine myself ever asking the oppressed . . . to forgive their oppressors. Who can dare?. . . It's easy for folks who live in a virtual paradise, who have enough to eat, farms, land, nice homes, businesses, etc., to preach about forgiveness. But is it really fair to say that to people who live in hellholes—jobless, threatened by imminent death by starvation—people who are, as Franz Fanon put it, 'the wretched of the earth?' Are they to forgive the fat, well-fed millions who voted for their starvation? Who voted for war? Who voted for prisons? Who voted for their perpetual repression? Who wish, in their heart-of-hearts, that they were never born? Should they forgive them for the repression to come? For the genocide that is to come? . . . It is for this reason that my heart has been called to political action: to change hellish realities, and to try to transform this world from the hell it is for billions of her inhabitants. Change those conditions, and then perhaps forgiveness can be born."

Don't ask us not to hate, not until you've walked a mile in our shoes.

Take away our reasons for hating.

Before it is too late.

*T*he problem of home demolitions is so great that Israeli peace and human rights advocates have organized "The Israeli Committee Against House Demolitions" (www.icahd.org). The coordinator, Jeff Halper, originally from Minnesota, is a Professor of Anthropology who has lived in Israel since 1973.

Home demolitions are not new. ICAHD has documented some 10,000 demolitions in the Occupied Territories since 1967, which have left some 50,000 residents homeless. It notes that such a policy is contrary to the fourth Geneva Convention, which prohibits collective punishment (article 33) and the forced transfer of the local population (articles 35 and 49). During the first Intifada, some 449 homes were demolished as punishment, according to B'Tselem, The Israeli Information Center for Human Rights in the Occupied Territories. In 1997 Israel discontinued this practice. In October of 2001, however, when Israel invaded territory under the control of the Palestinian Authority, the policy was renewed. During the next two months, the Israeli army demolished eight West Bank homes of individuals suspected of attacks on Israel. Then in 2002, the number increased to 174 homes, more than any previous year.

As Jeff Halper has noted, "The vast majority of demolitions. . . have nothing to do with terrorism." He estimates that 94% "were simply houses of ordinary people that were in Israel's way." So why does Israel pursue a policy that would only alienate Palestinians? Halper gives several reasons:

> First, the policy of home demolition confines Palestinians to tiny overcrowded and non-viable islands of land, allowing Israel to control the entire West Bank and Gaza through its expansive system of settlements. Second, Israel knows that homes are sacred to Palestinians, the core of their extended family life. By demolishing Israel hopes to break the Palestinians' will to resist the Occupation and accept life in a truncated bantustan. And third, house demolitions are a key mechanism to the process of displacement, of Israel's exclusive claim to the entire country.

8 August 2002 • Day Fifty

This morning I was awakened for the third time in a week by a house demolition. The sound was God-awful and I leapt straight from the bed to the window, heart hammering, hands shaking, and breath caught in my chest, to see an enormous cloud of smoke billowing up from somewhere up the hill in Aida refugee camp. It was seven o'clock exactly, a beautiful sunny morning. In the ringing silence which immediately followed the explosion, another sound could be heard gaining pitch. The hysterical wailing of perhaps hundreds of nearby children wrenched from sleep by the sound of the world coming to an end.

A week ago, at precisely two o'clock in the morning, the army demolished the house of Masjed Atta, the 17-year-old who had blown himself up prematurely two days before at a falafel stand in Jerusalem, lightly injuring five Israelis. That morning's *HaAretz* had blandly reported the "early morning" demolition of a suicide bomber's home. A single sterile phrase. I stood at the dark window of my apartment at the college watching the same huge cloud of smoke mushrooming up into the night sky and feeling the same slammed sense of shock, wondering whose perverted idea it was to schedule the demolition for 2 a.m. Just a few short days before, a bomb dropped from an F-16 had ripped through a downtown Gaza apartment building at midnight, raining down chaos and death. I can still recall the blank expressions of deep shock on the sleep-rumpled faces of the small children being wheeled into emergency. That, supposedly, was a "mistake." Are these late-night and early morning house demolitions also mere "mistakes?" Or are we in fact dealing with something much more demented and hateful?

The house demolished this morning belonged to the Al-A'an clan, a large extended family of first, second, and third generation refugees. It was a two-story building housing four families. This evening as we watched family members and neighbors being interviewed on Al-Mahed, I counted scores of people newly homeless, at least fourteen of them kids. They were interviewed under the shade of a large tree. That's where they spent the day, and that's where they would spend this night and countless more nights to come. Their pitiful handful of remaining possessions was spread out over the dusty ground. According to their testimonies, they were first awakened by platoons of armed soldiers at 2 a.m. in search of a family member "wanted for terrorist activity." They stormed through the house for several hours inflicting random vandalism and interrogating the people present, and when they failed to accomplish their mission (or was it all premeditated?) they gave the families 25 minutes to remove their belongings while they finished rigging the house. One small boy with the high tender voice of a five-year-old was asked if he had been able to remove anything before the demolition. His poignant reply was classically Palestinian: he rescued his school backpack.

A young woman wearing a head scarf claimed to have asked a soldier if he did not fear God. His smug answer to her was, "We are God."

Neighbors joined the families under the tree, out of sympathy, but also for another reason. Aida is a densely packed camp, and many houses are separated by nothing more than narrow alleyways. It doesn't take much imagination to realize that an explosion capable of razing a two-story house in a single instant will inflict one hell of a lot of collateral damage.

Following footage of the ruined home itself (reminiscent of the sight of Arafat's Bethlehem compound following three nights of F-16 assaults) we toured others nearby, whose roofs had been partially removed by the blast, whose windows had been blown out, whose furnishings in certain rooms had been reduced to splinters. The only crime these neighboring families had committed was living nearby. These days, that seems to be justification enough. In any case, does anybody care?

A young man of perhaps twenty-eight or -nine stood under the tree facing the camera and holding a sleeping infant, his chin stubbled and his forehead arched into an expression of fierce rage. His voice snagged with emotion as he quietly said, "When they do this they say it is to stop the violence. Look at all this. Look at all of us. Look at the children." The camera did. It panned slowly and in silence across the faces, the many angry, exhausted, and sorrowful faces. "What are we supposed to do? They took away our home. They took away everything." He turned his face from the camera for an instant, then turned back. "They only increase it. They increase it more and more and more. That must be what they really want."

9 August 2002

Time is short today, and everything is such a mess! We only have time to rush around, but we never really get anything done and everything gets further and further behind. . . . I am going to blitz you guys quickly with a handful of messages I think are worth being forwarded.

No time for more today. Curfew's back on at three. How is it to live like this? To live for days shut up at home and to go out only when "allowed"? In most cases, it is not a matter of one big important or life threatening event (although sometimes it is), but more often an accumulation of many, many small things. During every curfew lifting there is a rash of weddings. Think how it would be to have such an event take place under such circumstances. We watched footage of the Fourth of July celebrations, and we watch Israeli TV channels with all their ads for pools and beaches and travel and summer festivals—the film festival!—and think, just so long as the Americans and the Israelis can enjoy themselves, no one really else matters. My three take turns swimming in the bathtub, and our only other entertainment is watching the tanks and jeeps stomp around the neighborhood. It's not really such a big deal not to be able to swim or go to a summer camp. But if Americans or Israelis were in our position, it WOULD be a big deal after all, wouldn't it?

PART TWO

Life Under Occupation

Reflections As Wife and Mother

*T*he reflections recorded above directly speak to the concerns of Palestinians under occupation and particularly during a period of intensive Israeli military activity the Bethlehem area: The fall 2001 incursions into the city reversing Oslo agreements, the Siege of the Church of the Nativity in the spring of 2002, and continued curfews and closures over the summer and fall of 2002.

The reflections which follow specifically address Alison's role as wife and mother over that same period. They show her concern for her husband George's safety crossing checkpoints to work in Jerusalem and his own well-being when he is no longer able to support his family as in the past. They show her concern for three daughters attending school, getting proper health care, and growing up with attitudes of respect for Israelis and Palestinians alike.

In the fall of 2001, Nadine and Mathilda were ready for grades two and four at the Talitha Kumi Lutheran School in Beit Jala. The Nassars had moved to Beit Sahour from Beit Jala because of the frequent shelling by the Israeli army. What did this mean for the girls? What did it mean for their mother with typical motherly concerns?

27 August 2001 • Monday evening

Today was the first day of school for Mathilda and Nadine. Last night I spent a long time tucking them in and reminding them of how much they like school and the teachers, how fun it is to be with their friends. I made a point of doing this because they have been obsessing lately about the possibility of shooting and shelling occurring during school hours. They even declared that they don't want to go back to school at Talitha Kumi. "What will happen to us? How will you know how to find us?" Mathilda wanted to know. I often ask myself the same exact questions, but I'd rather not admit that to them, just because I know that would not be a good strategy for alleviating their anxiety. At the same time, I try not to spin fairy tales for them that I myself don't believe. I don't tell them a shot won't hurt when I know it will, and I know they know that I know. So, as I tucked them in, I reminded them that this has been going on since the beginning of the previous school year (yes, indeed) and nothing ever happened during school (not strictly true, there was at least one occasion during the final weeks of the spring semester). And anyway, I reminded them, Arafat and Sharon promised not to fight anymore in Beit Jala. Of course, as I was sitting there telling them all this, we suddenly heard the roar of machine gunfire very close by. Five minutes later the television confirmed that heavy gunfire exchanges were taking place between Jabal Abu Ghneim and Beit Sahour, on the other side of the hill from us.

Sweet dreams, girls.

To my relief, they went off this morning, excited and ready, and I thought to myself that, who knows, maybe it really would be better this year. By midday, we had the news that the Israelis had pulled off their most audacious assassination to date. As the full significance of the "operation" dawned over us, the girls got off the bus and burst into the office, eager to tell me how fun grades two and four were going to be! I looked at them and wondered how the parents of Ramallah must have felt around 11:00 a.m., with the Israelis conducting Apache strikes in midtown during school hours.

Today was a long day and the sense of foreboding is very heavy. As I write this, intense gunfire exchanges are again taking place in Beit Sahour. Fighter jets are thundering over-head, flares are lighting up the sky, and tanks are moving in on all sides. When I finished work at 4:30 and walked outside, the streets were deserted. A policeman I passed waved and said, How can we calm people when the Israelis keep doing these things? I met George at his mother's house and sat watching TV with them. Scenes of the destruction in Ramallah. Scenes of the dead man's wailing relatives. Scenes of agitated spokes-men, vowing revenge. At about 6 p.m., we started for home and ran smack into a massive demonstration heading for Manger Square. Hundreds of masked gunmen toting machine guns and chants of "We will redeem the martyr!" Mathilda and Nadine saw classmates from school marching along. Shots were being fired into the air and people crouched instinctively at the sound. Just like on TV.

What would Israel's course of action be if its governmental leaders, Knesset members, and political activists were being picked off one by one in violent operations using heavy weap-onry? How would Israelis behave if their towns were sur-rounded and they were being besieged daily and nightly with helicopter and fighter jet and tank attacks? How would Ameri-cans behave? And what exactly is expected of Palestinians if shooting and bombing are unacceptable, but so are rocks and demonstrations and negotiations and cease fires and "propa-ganda stunts" and UN resolutions? What are Palestinians supposed to do?

School is cancelled for tomorrow, and possibly the next day. Work is cancelled. People are hunkered down in front of their televisions, waiting for what will happen next. Whatever it is, it won't be good. And whether it happens tonight, or tomor-row, or tomorrow night, it feels inevitable.

A new start to a new year.

*O*n 19 October , the Israeli army invaded Bethlehem, reversing Oslo decisions of Autonomy that went into affect in December, 1995.

22 October 2001

I finished the wall hanging this weekend and called it by its name: Al-Aqsa Intifada. If at first it seems an incongruous title for something so colorful and hopeful, then consider its subtitle, "Dream for a Better World," which is also the subtitle for the Intifada itself. In the center panel is a multi-colored sun against an electric blue sky background. In each corner is a multi-colored house. And linking hands between the four houses are rows of alternating boys and girls in bright outfits. Only three of the children are white-skinned. The rest (16 in all) come in a variety of tones of red, yellow, brown, and black.

I have vivid memories of creating this quilt, started back when the Israelis first began shelling Beit Jala. So, as Americans commemorate the one-month anniversary of the attacks in Washington and NYC with missile and attack helicopter strikes on Afghanistan, we have our own anniversary to commemorate. 22 October 2000, the day we first found out what it feels like to be on the receiving end of those assaults. I never thought the quilt would take this long, but then, I never imagined the Intifada would go on this long either.

I can remember hand-piecing the blocks in our front veranda, to the rumble of exploding tank shells and the menacing puncture of machine-gunfire, the drone of hovering helicopters and the whistle of missiles flying overhead. I would sit on the couch and force my hands still, making myself place the needle precisely and pulling it out if it didn't align properly.

On several occasions when the power was cut, I sat hunched beside a candle. I'd look up and see red tracer bullets flying past the front window and tank shells exploding against the buildings across the wadi in upper Beit Jala. If the kids woke and wanted me to be with them, I'd sit on the edge of the bed and stitch as I talked, telling them stories or going over the next day's homework or remembering with them our visit to America a thousand years ago. On the nights we were able to get out and spend the night on the floor of George's mom's, I'd take it with me and stitch while we all sat around the television watching the onslaught. I finally began to feel an inordinate anxiety about the project and started carrying it around with me everywhere I went. I'm not sure if I was using it as a mechanism to redirect all the fear I was feeling for us, or if I felt it was the only thing getting me through these surreal episodes and enabling me to get the girls through. Maybe it became a kind of talisman for me, a superstitious form of protection of the kind people typically develop in the face of complete help-lessness and powerlessness. Maybe all of the above.

Once all the blocks were done and I began to assemble them, the girls would watch intently and make their comments. Mathilda once said, "I wish we lived there." I asked why, al-ready knowing what she was going to say. "Because there's no tanks or helicopters or soldiers. And the kids are happy." Each of the girls chose a kid block to represent them, and other blocks became classmates and friends. Mathilda would ask if brown people had tanks shooting at them in their countries and we had discussions, gazing at maps, about all the places in the world with wars. And in one memorable discussion we talked about how, if I stitched a block for every Palestinian kid shot or injured during the Intifada and sewed them all together, it would probably cover the entire wall. If projections regarding the duration of this conflict are correct (standard predictions are for two more years), I'll still have plenty of time to complete an-other project. Maybe I'll call it "Wall of Tears." Dedicated to Mathilda, Nadine, and Phoebe of course.

15 December 2001
Waiting for the ax to fall

At 6 a.m. the alarm goes off, and I wake up groggy. Typically I get up two or three times during the night to check the local channel for emergency bulletins: explosions, inva-sions, assassinations, Arafat's "death by irrelevancy," the *Haram Al-Sharif* consumed in an apocalypse. The imagination can conjure up many possibilities these days. As soon as I wake up I check again, then turn on the *Voice of Jerusalem* and wait for the morning news. I wake the girls and help them get ready for school, reminding them on a daily basis that "if anything 'strange' happens (like sudden violent gunfire exchanges), if the kids get let out early 'for any reason' (like military mayhem), or there's any kind of 'emergency' (like a tank or helicopter assault), stay together and call me with the phone card and we'll decide what to do."

I have been over this drill many times with them though it's hard to do without making them nervous. Traumatized classmates of theirs routinely freak out in class, reacting to slammed doors or leaping up in the middle of math class to declare that "the Israelis are going to attack tonight." I kiss them as they head out the door, wondering if today will be the day all hell breaks loose.

We get Phoebe ready and drink our coffee while watching Al-Jazeera. George shaves to maximize his chances of getting through the checkpoint and minimize his chances of being stopped once in Jerusalem. Whether or not he can pass or has to sneak in depends on a combination of obscure factors, including but not restricted to: the events of the past day or so and whether Jews were attacked, the time of day, the mood of the soldiers, the language of communication (Hebrew, Arabic, English, Russian, Ethiopian . . .), pure chance. Seven times out of ten, he is rudely refused entry to Jerusalem and is obliged to sneak in on foot. I always ask him to call me when he arrives at work, because the soldiers and police are becoming more and more aggressive. Numerous Palestinian workers have been fired upon at checkpoints in recent weeks, and Arab transport vans are vigorously harassed by the police en route. I try to imagine George forced to stand facing a wall in a line of male passengers, guns trained on their backs. Or sprawled on the ground in a pool of his own blood. These images haunt my imagination from the time he walks out of the house in the morning until he returns at night. Every day.

Meanwhile, I walk to work through Manger Square, greeting people I know and observing the morning traffic. One morning I see a crowd gathering to receive UN relief packages. Another morning, a pack of boys surrounds the poster of a martyr, all of them clutching handmade toy guns. Another morning, an old woman in traditional dress walks with a walking stick at a brisk clip ahead of me. Although her face is lined and her back is bent, I can't catch up with her.

I arrive at work at Bethlehem Bible College and open my computer. People trickle into the office and greet each other. My colleagues coming from Jerusalem often don't make it in until mid-morning. Brenda spends an hour waiting at the checkpoint to enter Bethlehem. Salim spends an hour and fifteen minutes. Shafiqa spends fifty minutes waiting and is told she cannot enter. Some students have to sneak in along the same route George uses to sneak out. I check the Internet news: *HaAretz*, BBC, CNN. Gaza strafed during the night, police stations in Ramallah destroyed, Jenin reoccupied, Nablus pounded by tank fire.

I get to work, muttering about how much more obvious it has to be before people start to GET IT. What can be said that hasn't already been said hundreds of times? I feel speechless with anger and frustration and turn my attention to the mail. Patricia Smith's Palestine Monitor—forward. Gush Shalom—forward. Mazen Qumsiyeh—forward. Too numb to write myself, I depend on others to say what needs to be said. I read the Martin Luther King quote taped to my computer for the thousandth time: "How long? Not long, because no lie can live forever . . . the arm of the moral universe is long but it bends toward justice . . ." Every hour or so I check the breaking news. More Palestinians dead. More buildings bombed. More roads closed to Palestinian traffic. More tanks deployed in Area A. Punctuated by the occasional uncomprehending commentary of some uncomprehending American spokesman. How many "envoys" have to troop in and out of here chanting about cease-fires before someone realizes a different approach is required, a fundamental shift in thinking, in language, in emphasis?

The phone rings—George at work. Something loosens imperceptibly in my chest.

Bishara tells me he may not be able to travel to the U.S. for Christmas. The airport is closed to Palestinians and so is Allenby bridge, and the American Consulate is suddenly refusing to assist Palestinians with American citizenship to secure travel permits.

The girls wander into the office close to noon and my chest loosens again. They made it.

I ask Brenda to pick some things up for me in Jerusalem because I can't face the hassle of the checkpoint, and I hate the feeling of guilt if I actually succeed in getting out. Our post box only gets checked once or twice a month, and I haven't visited my friends in ages. We have learned that we can mostly do without Jerusalem.

We pick up Phoebe at daycare and head home. I check the Bethlehem station as soon as we arrive and leave it on for the rest of the afternoon, in case there is any news that will affect George's return journey. At five, I start holding my breath. At six Mathilda says, what if something happened? At 6:15 p.m., a feeling of low-level panic fluttering in my stomach, I call. If there's no answer because his battery has already run out, the feeling increases a notch and my anxiety causes me to snap at the girls. At 6:20 or 6:30 George arrives at the check-point and is told he cannot enter Bethlehem, even though Bethlehem is indicated as his place of residence on his ID. This is how they punish the ones sneaking out. He is forced to walk around, which adds another 15 minutes to his arrival. At 6:45 he walks in the door, tired and annoyed. He made it.

Evening. Dinner. Homework. News. Harry Potter. Coffee. The streets are quiet and still. Al-Jazeera summarizes the day. The number of deaths. The amount of destruction. The useless phrases. The next step in escalation. I am too tired and disgusted to do anything but read and fall asleep. Another restless night. The feeling of amorphous dread never leaves.

Goodnight girls, I love you.

Goodnight George, I worry about you.

Tomorrow is another day.

30 January 2002

George had gone to work in Jerusalem and was caught by Israeli soldiers. For his "crime," they beat him to death. The commanding officer was happy to admit this to me, in private. But publicly, of course, his cause of death was attributed to some "accident" unrelated to them. They refused to return his body to me, knowing it would implicate them, so they buried it and would not tell me where. I was crying. A friend came to me and said, "I can't imagine how you must feel, knowing they did it and knowing they will never be held accountable for it." I woke up, full of terrible grief and sadness.

For me it was just a nightmare. Completely within the realm of possibility, but a dream nonetheless, which ended when I woke. For so many others, it is a reality they must live with. It does not end and they don't wake up. Imagine what it must be like to live with that.

We recently watched a program on Al-Mahed TV, "The Martyr From My Hometown." One by one, ordinary people spoke of the deaths of their loved ones. The sister whose brother was on his way home from work. The mother whose son was walking to school. The son whose father was taken in the dead of night. The boy whose classmate was throwing stones. The wife whose husband, a policeman, was manning his post. The father whose son, a university student, was sleeping in his bed. The mother of the mother of six. The parents of the baby whose birth was obstructed by a check-point until it was too late. I can barely stand to listen to their voices, to look in their eyes. They will never be able to cry enough, their hearts will never heal.

These survivors are the people who must ultimately find it in their hearts to live in peace. The process of "making peace" is something entirely different, and in a way, so much easier to do, because it's an impersonal thing taking place at a level far removed from the lives of ordinary people. If it ever happens, it will take place at a great height and hopefully filter down. In effect, it will be imposed. But ultimately, it will have to some-how penetrate these hearts full to bursting with terrible grief and sadness. How will they ever be able to just let it all go?

As someone recently wrote, this has been a year that will live for a very long time in the Palestinian collective conscious-ness. And there is nothing abstract about that. It consists of all these faces, slick with tears, pinched with pain, struggling to live with something which cannot be lived with. Last week we got an e-mail about the 9/11 survivors. The writer wrote of his many encounters with people who were simply unable to move beyond that tragedy, the shock of that day. Palestine is a nation full of people just like that, although this is something that is hardly ever acknowledged. They're just ordinary people, they're just human beings, and they have had to endure so very much. Who will one day look upon them with ordinary human compassion and say, enough?

I keep thinking of the process of "making peace" and how it will finally penetrate all the pain and all the stories. I cannot imagine it taking place without some sort of truth and reconciliation commission. The reconciliation will never happen unless the truth-telling precedes it. And there are plenty of stories waiting to be told. Told and acknowledged and recognized for what they are, genuine narratives full of needless loss and unspeakable cruelty. There is no way around them. Who is ready to listen?

22 February 2002

Last night, George came back from work late and approached the checkpoint on foot after dark (around 7:15 p.m.). He said there are soldiers now training machine guns on anything that moves, with light beams that track peoples' movement. He said his heart was hammering until he made it safely back inside. He could have been shot, and they would have just said he was attempting to attack them, end of story. Another widow, more fatherless children, another mother burying another son. And no questions asked. Today (and until Monday, they say) the checkpoint is closed to all traffic, walking or driving, foreign or local. There has been sporadic shooting all day. We are all afraid of what is coming.

*M*ilitary checkpoints have become one of the major points of contention for Palestinians. Israelis say they are necessary to prevent suicide bombers from entering Israel. Palestinians say that they are not effective since bombers continue to get through. The ones who are affected directly are ordinary Palestinians who are simply trying to make a living.

Like many Bethlehemites, George has had a long history of work in Jerusalem, previously as a goundskeeper at the Jerusalem Zoo and now at the Dormition Abbey south of the old city. Occasionally, the army set up checkpoints to monitor those traveling to Jerusalem. However, one of the ironies of the peace process is that the checkpoints were established near Rachel's Tomb as a permanent fixture as Oslo was unfolding in 1992. George's brother Daher is an example of a laborer who lost his job when closures kept him from entering Jerusalem during that period. Later his Jewish boss pleaded for him to return to work since he was reliable and hardworking. Yet even the most reliable individual cannot get through when the checkpoints are a hindrance.

The Oslo peace accords were based on the principle of economic interdependence between Israelis and Palestinians. It is in Israel's best interest that the high-quality work force provided by Bethlehem residents be part of its economy and vice versa. Likewise, education and health care requires travel. Nevertheless, when self-rule was granted to Bethlehem in 1995, the closures increased so that travel to Jerusalem was hindered rather than facilitated. Today the move is toward separation, which will cripple the economics of Bethlehem and make life difficult for laborers like George.

1 March 2002

I was going to start this with the sentence, "A couple of weeks ago we went to Jerusalem . . ." but the implications of that simple statement were so amazing that I had to stop and wonder.

If someone had told me ten years ago that things would get to the point where I only went to Jerusalem once or twice a month, I doubt I would have believed it. When George and I first got married in 1991, there were no formal checkpoints in Bethlehem, and we had a choice of seven or eight roads in and out of town (three of which were in Beit Jala where we lived). Occasionally some big shot like James Baker would come to the region to "discuss peace" and temporary checkpoints would be erected. But experience taught us to be patient, that every period of restricted passage would be followed by a relaxation sooner or later. Back then it was usually sooner. And back then the utter arbitrariness of it made it seem almost like a game, certainly in comparison to the deadly gamble it has become. Back then you could be refused passage at 9:30 a.m. but allowed through by the same guy at 10:00. Or refused by one guy and allowed through by the guy standing next to him. Or you could argue for a while until the guy changed his mind. Or you could apply for a permit and actually hope to get it, in which case you'd be entitled to walk through just like the white folks.

The permit legally entitled you to be in Jerusalem between 5:30 a.m. and 8:30 p.m., and you didn't have to sneak around or fear being stopped in the street or in a van. In any case, the soldiers never really had to take themselves seriously because they knew there were other roads we could get out through. And perhaps they could tell themselves that what they were doing was harmless because no one was really locked in. Not like today. Whoever could have imagined that this apartheid system would actually be an improvement over what we now face?

I remember: On the day I gave birth to Mathilda, I was in Jerusalem. I had just finished work and was walking toward a movie theater downtown (Woody Allen) when my water broke. I found a phone and George came to get me, driving our yellow-plated Peugeot all the way down Hebron Road from Bethlehem right up to the front door of the central post office on Jaffa Road. This might seem like a nonevent, but these days it would be unthinkable.

I remember: When Mathilda and Nadine were babies, I drove to Jerusalem numerous times each week. Occasionally I went for a reason, like buying groceries, but usually I went just to go, because getting out helped me to cope with the kids. Going for walks and visiting friends were the activities that kept me sane and connected, and I frankly can't contemplate having to do now what I had to do then without the benefit of those basic pleasures. And even though I have pretty much passed out of that mother-of-young-children phase and so probably wouldn't be doing so much walking or visiting these days in any case, the point is that it is not my decision, but one that someone else has arbitrarily imposed on me.

I remember: Mathilda's first daycare was on the Mount of Olives, and I used to drive her to Jerusalem first thing in the morning, five mornings a week. Sometimes I drove back home and drove back a second time to pick her up at midday. It truly amazes me to recall this because, again, in these days it would be not just unthinkable but impossible, not to mention insane.

I remember: At the time of Nadine's birth, there was no cardiologist in Bethlehem, and she had to be taken frequently to Al-Mukassed hospital on the Mount of Olives for her echocardiographs and other tests. Speaking from experience, I can testify that serious illnesses are quite stressful enough without having to worry about whether or not you are going to have to argue with an 18-year-old about the legitimacy of your reason for wanting to pass. When seventeen-month-old Nadine's open-heart surgery was scheduled in Beer Sheva, we tried to play the game according to the rules by applying to the regional military office for the needed permit for George to be in Beer Sheva for the surgery. It was refused. He went any-way, of course. The point is that Palestinians lose either way. By going, he was at risk of being caught without a permit. By not being present at his own daughter's surgery, he would have been forfeiting some of the humanity it is presumed he in any case does not possess.

It is impossible to identify the exact moment at which the checkpoints made the irreversible transition from temporary structures to permanent entities. But at some point they did. Lately I tend to think of the last ten years in terms of phases, and these phases are necessarily related to the character of the checkpoints, because the checkpoints are an intimate factor in our lives. How could they be otherwise? In 1991 and '92, we were childless and took transportation each morning to our respective jobs in Jerusalem. 1992-96 were the small-child years, when I drove back and forth with great frequency. The period 1996-2000 was characterized by the election of Netanyahu and the opening of the tunnel below the *Haram Al-Sharif*, and there was a fundamental shift in the atmosphere. The checkpoints became by imperceptible increments uglier and more oppressive, and this ugliness ascended to new heights, needless to say, with the eruption of the *Al-Aqsa Intifada* in September of 2000. And the latest phase brings me back to the beginning.

A couple of weeks ago we went to Jerusalem. It was early afternoon and raining, so it didn't take long to get through. Perhaps fifteen minutes. Our turn came and I rolled down the window to pass our documents to the young soldier. He ducked his head down to look at the girls in the back, then waved us through. I flapped the documents at him. Don't you want to take a look at these? "You look okay to me. Have a nice day!" he told us and we looked at each other and drove through. We "look" okay. What he means is "we don't look Palestinian." George doesn't have a mustache. I don't wear a headscarf. The girls have straight American hair. In contrast, when George tries to pass on foot in the mornings, he doesn't look "okay" even though he looks exactly the way he did sitting next to me in the car. And he never gets told to have a nice day. They grunt at him in rude monosyllables. "*Tazrich* (per-mit)!" "*Lech* (Go home)!" "*Feesh* (No way)!" More often than not, he has to sneak around and risk getting caught or shot. It's still a game, but a deadly one now.

So we went into Jerusalem and did our little errands, though we didn't get any enjoyment out of doing them. I was preoccupied the entire time with how difficult it would be to get back in. Sure enough, when we approached the Gilo intersection leading into Bethlehem at 6 p.m., a line of cars which didn't seem to be moving snaked back from the checkpoint. We took our place, no longer having the choice to drive around through Beit Jala or Al-Khader. Those roads have been block-aded with huge mounds of earth for months. Imagine. One road in, one road out. We are at their mercy, and they know it.

It took us an hour and a half to move perhaps 500 meters. The girls were hungry and thirsty and tired. They had to go to the bathroom. They bickered in frustration. The car over-heated. People kept getting out of their cars to look. And this is what they saw. One thing we could all see was that the soldiers had obviously been instructed to take as long as they could to process the traffic. There were two lanes leading back into Bethlehem, but only one was open. The other had a plastic barricade across it. The two lanes have to feed into one, and the cars approached the frontier one at a time. There was a soldier standing outside the booth and another lounging inside. The one outside strolled back and forth to the booth continuously, chatting to his comrade, showing him documents, asking questions, or simply shooting the breeze. I have seen soldiers reading newspapers. I have seen them talking on their mobile phones.   I have seen them conduct conversations, making the drivers wait until they have concluded their discus-sions. Sometimes they circle the car, looking for who-knows-what. Sometimes they insist that the trunk be opened. They examine bags and boxes. One driver in front of us was asked to step out of the car, and when he did so they frisked him. They make others (Palestinians from Jerusalem or Israel, Bethlehem residents without permits, foreigners) get out and return in the direction of Jerusalem, not being "authorized" somehow to enter Bethlehem.

On the other hand, religious Jews wanting to pray at Rachel's Tomb are always authorized to enter, and on our right we could see a parade of cars with Israeli flags flapping and bumper stickers stating "(Meir) Kahane was right" (Meir Kahane was an outspoken advocate of forcible transfer) back-ing down the outgoing lane so that they wouldn't have to wait in line with the rest of us, and parking beside the army encamp-

ment. Now, I probably don't have to tell you what would happen to any Palestinians who tried that trick. At the very least
they would be screamed at to take their car and go to the back
of the line. Or they could be forced to stand or squat facing a
wall for a few hours. Their car would probably be blown up or
confiscated as a "suspicious object". But never would they be
allowed to park and walk through the checkpoint, as I could see
entire families being permitted to walk through toward their
destination while our cars overheated and our kids screamed
for a bathroom. Then I realized that traffic was actually being
deliberately blocked to enable these people to walk "unmo-
lested" to Rachel's Tomb. So if anyone was doubtful before
about the racist nature of the checkpoints, this should assure
you beyond question. They are the living symbol of Israeli
apartheid at its ugliest and most belligerent.

At 7:30 p.m. we reached the booth, and I practically threw
our documents at the soldier. I said, "Can you give me a good
reason for making my kids wait for an hour and a half to go
home?" and he said, "I only understand Hebrew, so if you want
to speak to me, speak in Hebrew." He went away to the booth
for a few minutes, then came back, gave us our documents,
and allowed us to go through.

A few days later, a checkpoint between Modi'in and
Ramallah was attacked by two armed Palestinians, killing six of
the seven soldiers on duty. I won't deny that we both felt a
measure of satisfaction, although—as with Ze'evi's assassination—we knew that we would be made to pay dearly. But it was
completely appropriate and undeniably legitimate from the
Palestinian perspective, and I don't feel inclined to seem apologetic. If you don't live with it everyday, you're not in a position
to judge. Period.

George and I have been married ten years, and for ten
years we have been living with checkpoints in some form or
other, him more than me. In stark numbers, we can calculate it
thus: if George has gone to work in Jerusalem an average of
four times a week, those four multiplied by 52 weeks is 208
times a year, multiplied by ten years is 2080 times. Two thousand and eighty times he has had to justify himself to 18-year-
old soldiers. Two thousand and eighty times he has been at

their mercy. Two thousand and eighty times he has endured their rudeness. Two thousand and eighty times he has had to choose between his work and his personal safety. If you really want to know the source of Palestinian "terrorism," this is where it begins and ends. Now ask yourself the best way to get rid of Palestinian "terrorism". . .

In the spring of 2002, Israel launched Operation Defensive Shield with regular incursions into the West Bank.

6 March 2002

George knows how to keep cool. Over the years, he has developed a variety of mechanisms for dealing with the unpredictability, the frustration, the anger, the hate, the madness, and the fear. His most common response is to act as if it is all a hilarious joke. He laughs frequently, and the worse the situation is, the more hysterical he sounds. This is how I know it is bothering him: it has a sharp edge. Last Thursday when I called him in Jerusalem to say that people in Bethlehem were preparing for a big confrontation, his laughter shook the phone line. The more I tried to impress upon him the potential seriousness of the situation, the more he laughed.

In the last two nights, though, he did not react with laughter. When the F-16's started blasting across the dark skies of Bethlehem, his face blanched, and he turned to me. "I was Mathilda's age during the Six-Day War. I remember this sound, the sound of the planes bombing Bethlehem. They bombed everything. People hid in the churches, and they bombed the churches."

Since last Thursday, my kids have been sent home early from school four times in anticipation of "something happening." Since last Thursday, my kids have gone to sleep with that old "Bet Jala" look on their faces, the pinch of fear, the recollection of Apache missiles whistling overhead. Last night Nadine came to sit on my lap, wanting to say something. I waited. "Right mom, they couldn't bomb this house because someone lives on top of us? Right, we don't live up high like we used to?" Mathilda said that when shooting exchanges erupted yesterday morning in Al-Khader, just down the road from the school, the children in the class started to cry. Most of these children are Beit Jala residents and so are already very traumatized. By the time they were sent home, tanks were poised at the entrances to Al-Khader and Beit Jala (on either side of the school grounds). I don't imagine they have gotten much studying done. I haven't been able to get much done myself, and George, needless to say, has been homebound since the weekend. A bomb exploded in a school in Sur Baher just after the girls went off in their bus. Even though I knew that school was far away from Talitha, I hugged my girls tight when they finally arrived at noon, so glad they were safe.

A friend whose husband is Lebanese recently wrote this: "I spoke with Tony's mom this morning, and I remembered one of the daughters of his cousin, El-ham, whose hair turned white at seven years old from the fear, the fear of the bombs falling and the war all around her. . . . Tony's mom tells me that now she is a beautiful, tall teenager who has dyed her hair red. I guess one can cover the color, but I don't know if she may ever be able to 'cover' those deeply grained experiences."

They say that human beings can become accustomed to just about anything. Isn't this one lesson of the Holocaust? We can become accustomed to doing evil as well as enduring it. Surely the last seventeen months are a testament to this phenomenon, for both sides. I remember the sense of surprise I felt when I realized I had become used to the sound of afternoon gunfire. Our range of possibilities has expanded since then, with gunfire being the least of them. I must say that nothing prepared me for what I saw today when we went to inspect the site of the F-16 attacks of the last two nights. The devastation was stunningly complete, like nothing I had ever seen before. It made the machine guns and tank shells and Apache missiles and car detonations of our previous experience seem almost like nothing. But it is really just another notch further along on the continuum, another line crossed. And deep in our guts, although we may say we don't know, we do know where this continuum will lead us.

I can only imagine that Israeli soldiers have also experienced some sense of surprise, especially in recent weeks. Surely it must be a surprise to realize that you are capable of shooting a little kid in the head, or a pregnant woman in the back. Or that you shelled a car with a family inside, or that you deliberately targeted an ambulance. Or that you stood with your foot poised on a dead body like a trophy while a comrade snapped your picture. But these things also, it seems, can be gotten used to, and even seem almost like nothing. And in that way you become capable of committing ever-greater acts of barbarity. And eventually your humanity is unrecognizable, even to yourself. And so the riddle of the Holocaust is being solved—through reenactment—by the very people who struggled so hard for so long to understand its meaning. The answer to the question, "How could the Germans do what they did?" is the same as the answer to the question we are asking ourselves now. Unarmed civilians, innocent bystanders, families, school children, infants, women in labor, the elderly, the sick and handicapped, medical personnel. Every conceivable line of human decency has been crossed since September 2000, not once or twice, but tens and hundreds of times. And tomorrow another line will be crossed, and the day after that another line.

Never again. Wasn't that another lesson of the Holocaust? Growing up, I naively understood that to apply to everyone. And now what I'm waiting for is confirmation that it really does.

When Mathilda is forty-five, will she turn to someone and say, I remember the bombing of Bethlehem? Will she tell her children, never again, or will they still be enduring the same nightmare that she endured, and her father, and her grandmother? Will she recall the trauma of the F-16's, or will there be something worse for her to recall? Or will she be a faceless statistic in a history book, whose lessons we will have once *again* failed to absorb?

21 March 2002

Mother's Day is approaching in Palestine where we have been meditating a lot these days about the meaning of motherhood, especially because of the killing of the mother of five in the Aida Refugee Camp. It is difficult today for me to put feelings into words. So I'll let the Israeli writer Israel Shamir speak for me from his "Our Lady of Sorrow:"

Quietude of the West should frighten us well beyond the Middle Eastern context, as it possibly means our civilization is dead.

In the Upper Church of Annunciation in Nazareth, there is a striking collection of images, homage of artists to Mary—a dainty Virgin in colorful kimono holding her child dressed in ceremonial Japanese royal robes among blue and golden flowers, a naïve Gothic face of Madonna transferred from French Cluniac illuminations, the Chinese Queen of Heaven cut in precious wood by Formosa devotees, the richly inlaid Cuban statue of Madonna of Guadelupe, the Polish Black Madonna, the tender face of the Byzantine Mother of God, a modernist steely Madonna from the United States—look from the walls of the church, uniting us in one human family. There is hardly an image in the world as universal and poignant as that of the Virgin and the Child.

Wherever you go, from Santiago de Compostella in the far west of Spain to the golden domes of Russia, from frozen Uppsala in Sweden to Hagia Sophia in Constantinople, you will find this adorable face. Best artists depicted her compassionate features, her love to her child and her sorrow. Botticelli painted her with a pomegranate and among the Kings of the East; Michelangelo and Rafael, Cimabue and Titian, van der Weyden and Fra Filippo Lippi were inspired by her image. This unique mix of a young girl and mother, of vulnerability and protection, of admiration and love formed the spiritual and inspirational base of our civilization.

This week in Bethlehem, an Israeli shelled the Virgin. A Jewish soldier in the formidable tank Merkava-3 constructed according to the U.S. technology at the U.S. taxpayer's expense fired a shell at fifty yards at the statue of Madonna on top of The Holy Family church in the Nativity town.

The Virgin lost an arm, and her pretty face was disfigured. She became one of a hundred Palestinian women shot by the Jews in the present outburst of war. This seemingly unnecessary act of vandalism could not be an accidental shot. No terrorist hid behind her gentle figure on the pinnacle of the hospital church. At fifty yards, you make no mistake. It could be orders; it could be a spontaneous expression of feelings by a Jewish fanatic.

Whatever it was meant to be, the shrapnel shot became the last check of the mind control system: will this sacrilege become widely known? And will it stir the hearts of Christendom? . . . The current Israeli invasion of Ramallah and Bethlehem was covered under the heading 'Sharon looks for peace'. The UN resolution equalized the aggressors and their victims in *sotto voce*. The Western mainstream media drew the blanket of silence over the cries from the Holy Land.

This quietude of the West should frighten us well beyond the Middle Eastern context, as it possibly means our civilization is dead.

24 March 2002 • Sunday

A little over a year ago, two-year-old Phoebe was admitted to Caritas hospital in Bethlehem with double pneumonia. The woman whose infant was in the next bed was from Beit Fajjar, a small village near Hebron. Although I have forgotten her name, I have never forgotten her tired smile, her brisk and friendly manner, or the warmth in her eyes.

Because she was breastfeeding her newborn and had young children at home, she was obliged to shuttle back and forth between the hospital and her village twice a day. Even though Beit Fajjar is only about 15 minutes south of Bethlehem by car, it could take the woman two hours or more to reach the hospital because of the numerous army checkpoints, dirt barriers, detours along rocky back roads, and the constant harassment of the transport vans by the border police. I can recall her bursting into the ward, breathlessly lugging packages of diapers and apologizing deferentially to the nun on duty. Phoebe adored her and would sit on her lap when I wasn't around, comforted by her gentle nature.

It was around that time that the Israelis were mounting their massive spin campaign to convince the international community that uncaring Palestinian parents were deliberately sending their children to become martyrs at the checkpoints, but I knew that the reality was much more accurately and lovingly reflected by this nameless Palestinian mother. I have often thought of and feared for her in these intervening months, whenever Beit Fajjar has appeared in the news. She will never know how much admiration I have for her and for all the mothers she represents. They are truly the ordinary heroes of Palestine.

There is a familiar and mournful song for martyrs which goes like this: "No, my mother, no, don't cry for us. No, my mother, no, God will take care of us." Contrary to what the Israeli spin masters would have us believe, Palestinian mothers do cry for their lost children, and this was painfully evident in the Mother's Day program broadcast on Al-Mahed TV last night. Young or old, smiling or weeping, the suffering and grief of these women were visible for all to see. It is no wonder these images are rarely shown or acknowledged in Israel and abroad, for they speak volumes about what Palestinians have endured. But, in addition to the pain, other things were evident as well, and I imagine that these are the things that strike true terror in the hearts of the oppressors.

Things like faith and strength and righteousness, being bravely proclaimed from battered couches in humble living rooms across the West Bank and Gaza. Truly it must freeze the blood in the already chilled veins of those who believed they could be silenced and dominated with military might. As one woman declared through streaming tears, "Justice is with us, and the strength in our hearts from knowing this makes us stronger than all the tanks and all the helicopters and all the F-16's on the planet. They can never defeat us because we have justice on our side. And we know justice will be done. *Enshallah.* God-willing."

Mothers of activists and mothers of school children, mothers of detainees and mothers of refugees, mothers who are daughters and wives and sisters—their tears of suffering unite them, yes, but so do their courage and their determination, their strength and their conviction. And the sight of this is a gift of appalling beauty. It is their gift to us this Mother's Day, the thing which will enable all of us to carry on. The sacrifice for what is right. The hope for a future.

Perhaps nowhere was Palestinian motherhood more bravely or beautifully manifested than in the absence of the mother from Aida camp, whose little daughter sat facing the camera with shy resolve, clutching her mother's photograph and wearing the same black ski cap in which she appeared in the dreadful Channel Two footage, her face a mask of agony. "Why do you think we have Mother's Day?" the interviewer gently asked.

And in her high lovely child's voice with her lovely child's face shining like the full moon, she answered, "So we can thank them for loving us and for everything they do for us." She bites her lip and looks down at the photo. "My mother loved us a lot and she did a lot for us. She did everything. She loved us and we loved her. I think of this . . ."

Precious little daughter, Palestine is full of mothers who have lost children and children who have lost mothers. Your tears and your sorrows have drenched the land, but your strength will redeem it. Together, in beauty and in terror, you will lead Palestine to freedom. *Enshallah.*

*W*hen the Easter incursions of Operation Defensive Shield developed into the Siege of the Church of the Nativity, the entire Bethlehem area felt besieged as never before. For husbands used to the roles of provider and protector, it was a time of humiliation. Alison describes what it was like for George to be kept at home day after day.

# 13 April 2002 • Saturday
Day Twelve

All across the West Bank there are men just like my husband, loving spouses and responsible fathers, being driven to the very edge of despair. It has been more than a month since he went to work. He sits on the couch or moves restlessly around the house, unable to step out the front door because of the snipers positioned on the hills above us.

Yesterday our neighbor Attalah Al-Hayak was shot to death in his car as he returned from the market down at the bottom of Beit Sahour, a trip George made just the day before. The area was under curfew according to the soldiers, though for us it is a guessing game. We don't always know because it is not always announced. People look out their windows and see children playing beside their front doors. The neighborhood is quiet and you think, nothing will happen, I'll just quickly run down the street. Attalah Al-Hayak is now dead, leaving a grieving wife and a young son. His death makes no sense at all, and no one gives a damn.

George sits on the couch and recalls every little humiliation that he has experienced at the hands of the Israelis, and his memories go all the way back as far as he can remember. He mutters about all the rude young soldiers who screamed at him at the checkpoint. The arrogant settlers who casually pointed their guns at him, his mother, and his siblings as they were farming their own land. The disdainful military judge who dismissed the legitimacy of their ownership documents for the farm. He recalls the soldier who grabbed his younger brother by the neck during the first Intifada. The soldier who pulled him from the car and kicked him in the legs once when we were on our way to Jerusalem. The captain who refused to give him permission to go to Beer Sheva for Nadine's open-heart surgery. The clerk who repeatedly "lost" the paperwork for my residency permit. He remembers forty days of curfew during the Gulf War, pacing from window to window like a caged animal.

He worries about where the money for next month's food and water and electricity will come from. He worries about whether the Israelis will finally succeed in confiscating the land his grandfather and father farmed. He worries about how he and his siblings will pay the lawyer who is trying to prevent the confiscation from succeeding. He worries about school fees and rent, about snipers and arrest.

The relentless television broadcasts are profoundly disturbing and yet, we have to know. In Jenin they are pulling the bodies of women and young children out from the rubble of houses that were shelled. Families are drinking water gushing from damaged pipes because their supply has been shut off for ten days. Parents are frantically searching for children lost in the chaos of the non-stop military siege. Patients ill with diabetes and kidney disease and heart conditions are all going without treatment. Ambulances are shot at. Hospitals have no supplies and no medicines, no electricity and no water. Prisoners are being used as human shields. We all stare wordlessly at the awful images of senseless suffering, shaking our heads, imagining ourselves and our families and our children going through what these poor people are going through. Ten times a day tears spring to my eyes. Oh, God help them. Somebody do something. It just goes on and on.

We switch to something else to relieve the monotony. American wrestling, attended by thousands. This is what concerns them, this theater of absurdity. The Oscar presentations. *AllyMcBeal. Survivor.* I find it all so obscene. Kofi Annan making his billionth plea for a cease-fire. Another suicide bombing. The depth of despair is so palpable we are suffocating. It goes on and on.

As a matter of fact, I can't think of a single good reason why each and every one of us should not go out strapped with explosives and kill ourselves and everyone around us. Show me one faint flicker of hope for a future different from the hell we have been living for the last 18 months, the last ten years, the last thirty-five years, the last fifty-four years. When I think of enduring another year like this past one, I want to rip my hair out. Convince the young people of Palestine that they have something to look forward to besides unemployment, disrupted classes, checkpoints, permits, imprisonment, random destruction, and death all around. Convince people like my husband that this is the last invasion, that he will be allowed to go to his work like anyone, without subjecting himself to daily humiliations and dangers, that his farm will not be taken in order to expand a settlement. Convince the refugees that they will not be squashed like bugs because they are a political inconvenience, that they will not be massacred on live TV while the viewers yawn and search for something more entertaining, like *Survivor.*

George jumps up and begins yelling at the television screen. "We cry too! We bleed too! See how you like it! Where is our security? Leave us alone! Go away! Give me my land back! Not in two years or five years or ten years! Now! Let them understand! They are not the boss! Let them ask permission from me! They are all liars! They don't want peace! Sharon will destroy half the world before he agrees to give us anything!"

It pours out in a torrent of helplessness, frustration, bitterness, and fury. Somewhere a "ticking bomb" activates. Somewhere the abyss draws closer.

17 April 2002 • Wednesday

When Nadine was a sick newborn and the doctors were not predicting her survival, I came across this passage and have carried it around in my wallet ever since:

> Surely we learn about God through our children,
> Their arms and legs always about to burst into
> Flight, their hair and skin about to catch fire.
> Surely real prayers are made of children's laughter.
> How precariously we have our children with us,
> How grudgingly God gives them up!
> Nothing in the world should ever be so precious,
> So full of the possibility of loss!

It was written by a Palestinian-American author who grew up in Lebanon's Ein Al-Hilweh refugee camp, and her voice seems to sum up not just all of Palestinian experience, but all of human experience in these exquisitely lovely and heartbreaking phrases.

Today, on the day that Colin Powell turned his back and walked away from us, Nadine celebrated her 8th birthday, and I read this passage again for the hundred thousandth time in eight years. We spent the day under curfew, unable even to buy her a piece of candy or an ice cream, but never mind. No balloons, no film for the camera, no presents, no friends, but never mind. We did the best we could. As the sounds of gunfire and tank shells echoed across the hills and snipers looked down on us from their positions above the neighborhood, I baked her what she requested, chocolate cupcakes with white icing. We even had some sprinkles left over from Christmas, so I was able to add some red, green, white, and chocolate decorations. The colors of the Palestinian flag.

Nadine is a Palestinian. And she is a human being, with human needs and wishes and dreams, though neither Colin Powell nor George Bush is willing to acknowledge her humanity. Though Ariel Sharon and Shaul Mofaz have brutalized her humanity in every way that it is possible to brutalize it. Tanks and Apaches have attacked our neighborhood. Soldiers have shot at us. They have prevented us from going where we need and want to go. They have denied Nadine's father his livelihood and threatened his safety. They have impoverished us and humiliated us and besieged us every day for the last eighteen months. They have held us hostage in our own town, and then, in our own house. They have withheld water from us, and bread and electricity and medicine. They have prevented her from attending school. They have denied her past and taken away her future.

Eight candles for eight years. Every minute of her life has been spent under occupation. Every minute of her life has been determined by curfews and checkpoints and invasions and negotiations, with nothing at all to show for it except more curfews and checkpoints and invasions and negotiations. Like children everywhere, she wants to learn. She wants to run. She wants to laugh. She wants to be free. But as far as the world is concerned, she is not human enough to deserve these things. As far as the world is concerned, she is to blame for her own misery. As far as the world is concerned, her suffering counts for nothing.

Today, we lit candles for Nadine. Tonight, candles will be lit throughout the Occupied Territories for all the children just like her who have been killed, who have suffered injuries, all the children who have been made homeless, who have been made orphans, who have been made poor, who have struggled to assert their humanity despite the misery and injustice of daily life under occupation. Whether Colin Powell wants to acknowledge it or not, the bodies being pulled out from the rubble in the camps are the bodies of human beings, the houses that have been destroyed were the houses of human beings, the cities that have been besieged are cities where human beings live. Our humanity will transcend all inhumane attempts to strangle and suffocate it, to kill and maim it, to deny and degrade it. Our right to live in the world as human beings will never be relinquished and the prayers for a better life which burn in the hearts of our children will never be extinguished.

Surely God will hear.

15 June 2002

Yesterday morning I took Nadine for her annual appointment with the cardiologist. Usually she should be checked around the time of her birthday in April. This year, of course, we were under invasion and the appointment had to be delayed. It had to be postponed a second time when we were invaded yet again the last week of May. I hesitated to reschedule it a third time because of the persistent rumors warning of yet another reinvasion, but fortunately those have proven to be false, at least for the time being. Early Friday morning, I woke up and flipped on the local channel, half-expecting as always to see the invasion/curfew announcement in red and black at the bottom of the screen. No announcement. So I had my cup of coffee, woke Nadine, and we headed off. Our first stop was Caritas Baby Hospital, where Phoebe was hospitalized last year for pneumonia and where George's sister Amal works. It is the only place in Bethlehem with a machine to measure the level of oxygen saturation in the blood, a test routinely used to monitor the stability of Nadine's post-operative cardiac efficiency. The next nearest machine is at Mukassed Hospital in East Jerusalem, a 15-minute trip which can take two hours or more if you're lucky enough to get out straight through the checkpoint, and four hours or more sneaking around through Wadi Nar ("The Valley of Fire") if no spontaneous roadblocks have been erected to turn you back.

We met Amal, and while we were waiting for the technician to arrive, she asked if I wanted to see Hind. Hind is three now, and I first heard her story last year during Phoebe's hospitalization. She was brought to Caritas via ambulance from Gaza at six months of age, suffering from malnutrition and a metabolic imbalance. She hasn't seen her mother or father since her arrival two and a half years ago because they can't get permission to come. They regularly call her on the phone. Because of her metabolic imbalance and her need for special foods and medications, she would probably die if she were sent back to Gaza. Caritas is full of kids like her, rendered orphans by the political situation and the unique needs of their medical conditions. We met Muhammed last year too, a sweet little red-faced boy about Phoebe's age who is from a village south of Hebron. Muhammed suffers from such acute asthma that to discharge him to his home village would be like passing a death sentence. Even a brief delay at a checkpoint could lead to full respiratory arrest. Imagine being a parent in such a situation and having to make such an appalling choice. If you can't bear to part with them, you would most likely be condemning them to death. And if you want them to live, give up hope of ever seeing them again—also a kind of death. I ask myself what I would do if I was Hind's or Muhammed's mother, and the answer is, I really don't know.

The technician came, and we climbed the stairs to the premature ward on the second floor. I greeted nurses and nuns whom I remembered from last year, and they asked about Phoebe and cooed over Nadine's healthy appearance and lovely little face. While she sat quietly with the clip taped over her fingernail, Amal asked about the premie in the middle ward whose incubator was now vacant. "He died last night around 3:30." The young mother, who was rooming in the mother's ward upstairs, wanted someone from the family to come and help her carry the tiny corpse back to their home village near Hebron for burial. The hospital had been in contact with the family and had tried to arrange for an ambulance transport but was told that it would be very difficult. They were working on it.

On our way out of the hospital, saturation reading in hand (86%), we ran into Dr. Ehling, the Swiss hospital administrator. When Nadine was born, Dr. Ehling did not predict that she would live, and so she has always taken a special interest in the fact that she did and in the procedures that allowed her to do so. After admiring Nadine's height and color ("but she needs to eat more!"), she shrugged her shoulders and wondered how long the situation would be allowed to continue like this. According to her, the hospital is frequently understaffed because of the closure, and there are recurrent shortages of medicines and supplies. Mothers regularly arrive in hysterics holding children whose conditions are critical because it took so long for them to get there. Doctors are routinely hindered from entering Bethlehem, and so some have simply had to start sleeping on the premises.

The same is often true at the Greek Catholic Convent Clinic in Beit Sahour, where Nadine's appointment was scheduled. Her cardiologist, Dr. Mahmoud Nashashibi, is a Palestinian from Jerusalem who comes once a week to the Beit Sahour clinic to serve patients who are no longer able to come to Jerusalem. On Friday morning, he should have been there at 8:30 but was held up at the checkpoint for more than an hour and a half, average for the checkpoint these days. He walked in at 10:15.

While we waited for him, I spoke to my gynecologist, Dr. Ghada Kandalaft, a beautiful, intelligent, and articulate woman of mixed Syrian-Palestinian background. Every Monday through Thursday and Saturday, Dr. Ghada participates in a mobile clinic funded by the Australian government that serves the rural villages surrounding Bethlehem. She told me that the last year and a half has been hell for her and the other nurses and physicians participating in the clinic because of the ever-increasing restrictions on movement and the out-of-control belligerence of the soldiers.

Medical personnel are not supposed to be subject to such treatment, but they are, even the ones who are simply trying to serve their own populations and have no interest in entering or even passing through Israel. These days there is only one way in and out of Bethlehem, and that is the Rachel's Tomb checkpoint that leads into Jerusalem/Israel. All other roads have been blocked by mounds of dirt, boulders, trenches, and barbed wire and are occasionally guarded by soldiers. So the mobile clinic staff now has to drive up to one of these barriers, park, and unload all of the equipment, medicines, and supplies, including a mobile ultrasound machine, across the barrier into a yellow-plated van (blue-plated Palestinian cars are no longer permitted to drive on the main Bethlehem/ Hebron highway) waiting on the other side. This is the vehicle which takes them on their rounds.

But, she said, even the yellow plates don't give them free access to the villages they need to enter, even though many of them are Area C, and they are often stopped by army jeeps or border police and made to stand on the side of the road while the van and equipment are searched. Frequently the driver is issued a fine for transporting people holding West Bank ID cards, and more than once doctors have been arrested and taken for questioning to the Gush Etzion security compound. Five days a week they have to do this, and if they can't get out, then the villagers are simply deprived of treatment. Dr. Ghada told me that the incidence of miscarriages, premature deliveries, and birth complications of various kinds had risen dramatically in the last year. Village mothers do not have adequate access to nutritious food, milk, medicines, or even clean supplies of water, and poverty among these populations has also increased drastically. Most people, if they are aware of these things at all, only know them in the form of sterile statistical percentages. For Dr. Ghada, there is nothing sterile about it.

As we spoke, an ambulance arrived transporting a middle-aged man who seemed to be unconscious and in respiratory distress, and I could hear the attendants discussing his status. He was a resident of Artas, the next village over to the south from Bethlehem, who had displayed signs of possible cardiac arrest early in the morning. The family had called the ambulance crew at 7:30. It had taken them approximately three hours to enter the village and get him back to the clinic, negotiating checkpoints in both directions, during which time he had continued to deteriorate. They rushed him into a back room shouting pulse rates and adrenaline dosages, while an elderly female relative trailed helplessly after them, wheezing and murmuring prayers. Despite all the attempts to deprive her of her humanity, the tears still dropped from her eyes.

Nadine's turn finally came, and she had her annual echography and clinical exam. As I held her hand and watched the shadowy images writhe fluidly across the screen, I remembered a time not too long ago when it could have been me rushing hysterically into the hospital entrance carrying her limp little body. How would I have coped if she had been born in 2001? Would she have had the same chances for survival? The thought gave me chills. She had received the care she needed to thrive. How many people nowadays do not get the care they need, simply because they are Palestinian, and will not survive, much less thrive, because of it?

This is what it means to be sick in Palestine.

17 July 2002

George has been stuck for a week in Jerusalem. He went back to work last Thursday morning, and when the curfew was lifted on Saturday, he had hoped to come back home. When I spoke to him on Saturday morning, I told him that the announcement indicated 9 a.m. to 5 p.m. and he said he'd work until around 3 p.m. and then leave. But around midday, they changed it from 5 p.m. to 3 p.m. and I went into a panic worrying that I wouldn't be able to catch him. I called but his mobile was turned off to save the battery. So I alerted his entire family who tried continually to phone him, and Daoud finally reached him. So he had to remain at work. On Tuesday the curfew was lifted for four hours, but I warned him that if he came home, he could be stuck here for several days and lose the remainder of the week, so he stayed. Now it seems they won't lift the curfew again until Saturday or Sunday at the earliest. In the evenings he has long conversations with each of his daughters, and they tell him in minute detail everything that has taken place during the long days. Tonight Phoebe became weepy and said to me, "Daddy's never going to come back."

In the fall of 2002, another military action loomed on the horizon: war with Iraq. On September 12, President Bush addressed the United Nations asking for support against Iraq. Earlier the U.S. administration had signaled that the Palestinian-Israeli conflict was to be put on hold. What did this mean for Palestinians? A group of Israeli academics warned that the Sharon government would use the distraction of Iraq to wreck havoc on the Palestinians, even perhaps to carry out transfer from Palestinian lands. In the meantime, there were memories of the first Gulf War when Iraq launched scud missiles at Haifa and Tel Aviv. What if there were more missiles? What if there were chemical weapon attacks? What if Israel fought back? With Americans leaving the Middle East, what should Alison and her family do?

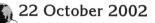

22 October 2002

A Day in Jerusalem, A Day in America

Most Palestinians these days are like deer caught in the headlights of an oncoming car, so terrified are they at the thought of impending doom as to be virtually paralyzed. The oncoming car is a U.S. strike on Iraq, and although they are hoping against all hope that the car will manage to swerve at the last second, Congress' overwhelming vote of support for Bush to use unilateral force without international backing makes that prospect highly unlikely. And all we can do is watch it come at us.

It is difficult even to think about imminent disaster, much less prepare for it. I know that when the conversation rolls around to "*su biddo yisir*" (what will happen) as it invariably always does, my mind simply shuts down. Not that my imagination has trouble conjuring up doomsday scenarios, and the rumors that are circulating range from wild to apocalyptic. Given the last two years, however, none of them can be considered completely implausible.

The word on the street both among Palestinians and Israelis is that Sharon plans to take the opportunity to launch a campaign of mass transfer in one form or another. How many forms can there be? Cattle cars? Flight on foot? I try to imagine myself running to Jordan with my children in my arms. Massacre? Thanks to Jenin, that doesn't require too much imagination. Carpet bombing? Or worse? Will Sharon use chemical weapons on us and blame it on Saddam? Will he nuke Iraq at the first provocation as he has intimated more than once? Will he liquidate Arafat and take over the *Haram Al-Sharif*? Will the American Evangelicals finally get their Battle of Armageddon?

These are events that an ordinary sane person like myself cannot reasonably contemplate. We are trying to prepare in our pitiful little ways. People are stocking up on food and supplies and medicines. They are emptying their bank accounts. They are organizing their important papers, their land titles and birth certificates and marriage licenses. They are renewing their travel documents.

And so it was with considerable shock that I realized one day not too long ago that Mathilda and Nadine's U.S. passports were due to expire at the end of December. The end of December! My initial reaction was to lapse into a coma. The options—submitting the applications now, which would necessitate handing the old passports in with them and thus being without for three weeks, versus waiting until the last minute—seemed too fraught with unseen risk. The weight of the decision caused me to overload on anxiety, actually hyperventilating if I thought about it too hard. A couple of weeks ago an article in *HaAretz* announced that the U.S. strike would most likely begin around mid-to-end November. Time—and timing—seemed of the essence. What to do? How to know?

If, between my frequent episodes of narcolepsy, I could be said to have any sort of plan, I guess it would look something like this: as long as the situation remained more or less like it has been, we would just hunker down and ride it out. Curfew is routine for us now, as is shelling, strafing, tank assaults, and arbitrary gunfire. But the minute it escalates or deteriorates or deviates in any way from the horizontal of known experience, we would resort to plan B. Plan B is to evacuate the girls.

Evacuate the girls. That brings all kinds of weird images to my mind, like putting them into a basket and sending them floating off down a river. Actually, what we planned do is to send them with friends who have already agreed to escort them to Virginia in the event of a general evacuation. So the matter is settled. Renew the passports now.

Which is why, last Tuesday, I found myself heading to Jerusalem with George. We parked at the top of Beit Jala, in the same spot where I had delivered the girls to Sherry almost three months before, and walked across the spike-encrusted border to catch a transport van. At the checkpoint at the entrance to the tunnel road, we were stopped and the reserve soldier glanced at my passport. "Now it's safer to be here than in Maryland," he commented, and I just smiled and nodded, realizing he was trying to be sympathetic. "We hope for better times for everyone." Did that include my husband?

As soon as we arrived at Damascus Gate, we headed straight for the American Consulate, where we found polite mobs of people waiting in the Immigrant Visa and Non-Immigrant Visa lines. Black-garbed families of Ultra-Orthodox Jews stood beside traditionally robed and veiled Muslims, united for once in their mutual desire to flee before it got any worse. In contrast, the American Citizens line was relatively short—I believe the vast majority of "non-essential" Americans have probably already left—so we assumed our places and waited. It didn't take long for us to get inside, complete our paperwork, and commence the wait for our number to be called.

When you've got time on your hands, the American Consulate in East Jerusalem is a great place to observe people and eavesdrop on conversations.

Everyone in the lower waiting room is, in theory, united by the fact that they all hold American citizenship (the packed Visa Section is on the second floor). However, it's not hard to see that the divisions which govern the city of Jerusalem continue to apply within the walls of the consulate and that they are subtly (and sometimes not so subtly) upheld by the consulate personnel. This fact never struck me quite like it did this time, and I don't know how much of it is a result of 9/11. Nevertheless, it is undeniable.

One of the people whose stories we were able to learn was that of a silver-haired Palestinian man sitting beside George who currently resides in Ramallah. Tall, erect, and distinguished-looking, he resembled one of our honorable congressmen. Across from him sat his two lovely black-haired teenage daughters. According to him, he had married an American woman and lived for 13 years in the tranquil Pennsylvania countryside. They had returned to live in Palestine in 1996 but had subsequently divorced. Because of the new regulations governing U.S. passport renewals for minors, he had had to present himself that day in the consulate to fill out some forms on behalf of his daughters (somewhere in his story I recall a detail about the divorce never having been legally finalized). He, like us, wanted his children's travel documents to be ready "in case." This man reminisced fondly and at length about his years in America and spoke in hushed whispers about the horrors he had witnessed over the past two years in Ramallah. When it came to speculating about what would be, we all fell silent.

The woman sitting across from me chattered nervously to everyone around her, and we soon understood what her predicament was about. She was Palestinian, originally from Taybeh (north of Ramallah), but had resided for the last ten years in Chicago with her American husband. Although she had a West Bank identity card number, she had lost her card three years ago and had not bothered to follow up on it since she no longer considered herself beholden to this system or its rules. She was an American citizen. Two weeks earlier she had flown to Israel, leaving her husband and children behind, to pay a brief visit to her sick mother who had remained in Taybeh. Upon her arrival at Ben Gurion, instead of being issued a standard visitor's visa, the airport authorities had stamped the number of her West Bank ID card in her passport.

On the day of her return flight to Chicago, she had been prevented from exiting the country the way she had entered, as an American citizen. Instead, the authorities had insisted that she depart on a Palestinian passport. She didn't have one and her ID card was lost. She had tried to exit through Jordan and been told the same thing. She had returned to Taybeh to apply for a replacement ID and had been told she could not be issued one without a police report documenting the loss of the original. And a passport cannot be issued in the absence of a valid ID. Imagine being trapped in such a surreal situation. Imagine her sense of panic. As a last resort, she had come to the consulate for help.

Her number was called and she stepped up to the window. It soon became evident that the clerk to whom she was speaking was not willing to help. We all sat there listening to the argument which lasted quite a while and increased steadily in volume. Finally the woman, by that time in tears, demanded to speak with the consul in person, and the clerk's rude reply rang out in the hushed waiting room. "You may not speak to him. We cannot help you." The woman came back, collapsed in a chair, and began crying loudly. The Palestinian-Americans surrounding her immediately went into a huddle, brainstorming on how she should proceed. I said to her, "If it were me, I'd stay right here until the consul agreed to speak to me." Someone else chimed in with: "We'll bring you a pillow and a blanket!" George told the story of his friend David Jallo, to whom the exact same thing had happened a few years back. David had promptly declared his passport "lost," replaced it with a clean one, and departed the country without further incident. Was she sure a replacement ID could not be issued? Yes, and besides: "I am an American citizen. I will leave Israel like an American citizen." So it was finally concluded that she should either replace the stamped passport or get herself a lawyer. When we finally finished with our own business and were ready to go, she was still sitting there, her face streaked with tears, fingering a photo of her three small children. I have thought of her many times since.

Our number was called and we approached the window with all our paperwork ready. It was a fairly straightforward procedure, and I felt relieved when the clerk, who had thus far been very helpful and friendly ("Lovely children!"), handed me the receipt and told me the passports would be ready in three weeks' time.

As we prepared to vacate the window, George nudged me and I turned back to her. "I have a kind of unrelated question." She indicated that she'd help if she could.

They must have been getting loads of worst-case-scenario questions recently, because when I launched into "If the situation should get worse . . ." she nodded her head toward the girls' applications in an understanding way and smiled. She knew why we were renewing them now. I continued: "Well, we all have American passports except for my husband. So I was wondering if there's any kind of special family evacuation arrangement that could apply to him in this circumstance."

Although neither her voice nor her manner turned cold, I suddenly felt her gaze flatten as if she could no longer see us. Without looking at George, she told me: "He will have to stay here."

I held her eyes for a second, wanting to direct her attention one last time to the photos of our "lovely children." "He's their father," I wanted to say, but instead I simply thanked her and turned away.

If they were unwilling to help the woman from Taybeh, a citizen of the United States for ten years, then why would I think they'd be willing to help George, the father of my girls?

The return journey was uneventful. The passage back into Palestine was the same only in reverse. The soldier's words came back to me from the morning: "We hope for better times for everyone."

And my own unspoken reply: Does that include my husband? As I walked around the barbed wire barrier at the top of Beit Jala and headed back to the car, I realized that the consulate clerk had answered that question for me.

Only certain people are entitled to "better times." If worse comes to worst, we will evacuate the girls to Virginia. But as for me, I am ready to forfeit my privilege as an American. I will stay.

*B*y *January the Bush administration was announcing that the decision for war with Iraq was a matter of weeks rather than months.*

28 January, 2003

In another few minutes I will tuck Mathilda into bed. An hour or so later, she will emerge from her bedroom crying and wanting to curl up in my lap. She does it almost every night. At the age of ten, she has enough awareness to tune into what the adults around her are saying and she has experienced enough to know what it means. She doesn't have to imagine "war." She already has intimate knowledge of what it feels like to be crouched down in the dark with tank shells raining down on the houses to the right and left. She knows what it is like to have attack helicopters hovering in the night sky above and shooting down on the rooftops. Her gut has experienced the bone-shaking thunder of heavy machine guns at close range and the roar of tanks prowling the neighborhood streets. On the infrequent days when a curfew lifting allows her to attend school, she comes home breathlessly repeating some rumor circulating among the children, who gladly clutch at them—even when the predictions are for their own impending doom—because it gives them some small sense of control in a situation spinning into chaos and insanity.

The most recent one was, "World War III is going to start next month and all the Palestinians are going to be killed!" That was the night she revealed a secret to me. "I read so much so I can forget that I'm so scared."

Now, whenever I see her reclining on her bed with Harry Potter, I know she is doing her ten-year-old best to fight off the terror of real life. And I can't even resort to the usual bland reassurances that are the common prerogative of parenthood, because she knows, and I know she knows, that things are not "going to be all right."

Nadine's appointment with the cardiologist was postponed four times since the end of December before she could finally be seen, three times because of curfews and once because, even though curfew had been lifted, the doctor was not being allowed into Bethlehem. This is a state of affairs that I imagine would give any mother pause, and especially mothers of children with congenital heart conditions. It's not a comfortable feeling to know that your child won't necessarily be able to have access to treatment when it's needed. This was not an urgent appointment, but what if it had been? Last Friday morning, as I looked around the waiting room of the clinic at all the anxious mothers of small babies awaiting cardiology exams, I experienced such an intense rush of memory that I felt dizzy. The face of one young mother in particular broke what was left of my heart. Amidst the clatter and roar of a full waiting room, she couldn't seem to stop gazing with an expression of inexpressible sorrow at her pale and bluish baby daughter, from whose skull protruded the yellow plastic tube for an intravenous port. Clearly the baby's condition was serious, and when she reemerged into the waiting room after the exam, her moist eyes told me all I needed to know. The baby needs surgery to survive. The other mothers immediately crowded around her, offering reassurances and false optimism. "Don't be afraid." "She'll be fine." But no amount of reassurance could change the fear she surely feels. Because no amount of reassurance will make this terrible situation any less terrible. She is right to feel afraid.

Eight years ago that was me. And I am so immensely thankful that Nadine was able to get the treatment she needed. What we went through was bad enough, but it was nothing like this. God help that young mother.

Although Nadine's status is stable and her health is good for someone with her condition, she still needs one more procedure to close a hole in her heart. On 23 December we received a fax from her hospital in New Jersey asking us to bring her back for that procedure. For this reason we had wanted to consult her cardiologist; we were hoping he would make our decision for us. The arrival of the fax has created an atmosphere of upheaval in the house and I have filled a notebook with charts and columns labeled "stay" versus "go." Above all, we want to do the right thing for Nadine. And with so many peripheral factors converging so ominously, many people might consider our conclusion to be obvious. But I can't explain it. There is something deep within me that is resisting the obvious conclusions and telling me that, somehow, here is where we ought to be, as crushing, as terrifying as it is. I don't know what it is but I caught a glimpse of it in that young mother's face. Or rather, I glimpsed it in the thing that unites me with her, my children with her children. The wish we all have to do the right thing for our families, to keep them safe and protect them from the dangers that are threatening them from every direction.

And what do we do when we can't do that? Tell us. What do we do?

This is what it feels like to stand, naked and alone before the onslaught. No one should have to live like this.

It has been estimated that during the first Intifada 35% of the school days were lost for Palestinian children. The fall of the 2002-2003 academic year began with the hope that schools would return to normal. By October, however, the situation of school closures was so serious that Pierre Poupard of UNICEF expressed strong criticism of the Israeli government. "Right now the Israeli military is preventing thousands of Palestinian children and teachers from attending school," Mr. Poupard said. "A generation of Palestinian children is being denied their right to an education." There are nearly one million Palestinian children of school age. According to UNICEF estimates, more than 226,000 children and 9,300 teachers have been unable to reach their classrooms on a regular basis. Five hundred eighty schools have been completely closed.

In response, teachers and parents sought various solutions, including home-schooling and underground schools. Some called for parents to defy curfews and to transport their children to schools in a communal act of non-violent resistance. Parents and teachers held public demonstrations calling for freedom to educate their children. In Hebron, a bomb exploded in a school yard wounding eight children. In Ramallah, two children were killed by Israeli soldiers walking home from school.

15 March 2003 • Saturday

A hush of expectant dread has descended on Bethlehem over the past couple of weeks and the tension is so thick and malignant that you could slice it with a knife. From sunset to daybreak the streets are unnaturally still and silent, and televisions stay tuned to the local stations for news bulletins from 6 a.m. to well past midnight. Although curfew has been lifted since 20 February, the army presence in town has increased dramatically since the 1st of March, and soldiers are wreaking nightly havoc in selected neighborhoods. In the early morning hours of Thursday the 6th, they dragged a local activist (a.k.a. "wanted terrorist") out of his house in downtown Bethlehem, bound his hands and feet, forced him to lie down in the street, and executed him at close range. Although compared to the daily carnage in Gaza this incident is pretty mild, it's still sobering for a civilian population with no police force and no means whatsoever of protecting itself. It is Israel who defines who are the civilians and determines are who the "terrorists." It is Israel who passes the verdict of guilt and the sentence of death. And if the definitions of who is the former and who is the latter are getting a bit blurry as of late—a bit messy to be precise—well, no one is really paying too much attention anyway. The "most moral army in the world" does not need to justify its messes.

The bombing in Haifa just intensified this feeling, as far as that is possible, and proved that our systematic transformation into lab rats is nearly complete. Like abused spouses, we flinch at every shadow and subconsciously feel deserving of punishment regardless of the provocation, regardless of the imbalance of power which renders our attempts to liberate ourselves pathetically impotent. We struggle under the weight of a power beyond our meager strength and await the sting of the slap.

If it's not enough having gangs of armed twenty-year-olds prowling the neighborhoods and conducting summary executions in full view of the neighbors at 2 a.m., there is the relentless build-up to the U.S. confrontation with Iraq, which in itself constitutes a uniquely sadistic form of torture I feel barely capable of withstanding. And it's not just me. The week before last we received a strange questionnaire from the school administration, although in the context of our daily lives it was not strange at all. The questions, all relating to curfews and states of emergency, were surreal. Do we agree to send our children to school during curfew? I reread it numerous times, wondering what the real meaning could be. Do we agree to send them out in defiance of military orders to face unknown possibilities? To confront armed soldiers? To inhale tear gas? To become another statistic? I have defied curfew myself, and I often wish the residents of Bethlehem would organize collective acts of defiance, even though I know the memory of the October 2001 invasion, when 23 people were shot to death for moving outside of their homes, is still too raw for most people. But my kids? No. Do we agree to send the children to an alternate location for classes if the school facilities are closed by the military or damaged in warfare? Oh boy, I don't even want to think about that one. Many schools have been closed by default where the military is "too active" during daylight hours, and schools in Al-Khader, the next village over from Bethlehem, were formally closed by the army, so the former is certainly not out of the realm of possibility. For that matter, neither is the latter, which is why I don't even want to think about it. No, no, no, no, no.

Nadine's teacher called a parents' meeting last week to discuss the fact that the children are completely out of control in the classroom. One parent made the observation that the entire society is in need of trauma counseling following the last two years, and it's difficult for them to help their children when they don't know how to help themselves. I think that if we can't do anything else, we can at least be gentle and patient with them and try to let them know that we understand because we are feeling it, too. Mathilda missed three days last week due to a mysterious virus that I'm not convinced was not at least partially psychological in nature. Her most prominent symptom was—guess what?—tiredness. But I for one am ready to testify that I have awakened every morning for the last week feeling as if I never went to sleep. It's a feeling of profound exhaustion that is not a result of sleep-deprivation, but pure, breathless, edge-of-the-chair tension. For five months now we have lived in a state of ugly suspension, never knowing what was around the next corner. At the very least we had the randomly imposed, randomly lifted, randomly amended curfews that made every minute of every day a guessing game contingent on the will of the army command. Every time a pattern of predictability began to emerge, the rules were abruptly changed. Every time we began to relax, something would happen to jerk us back onto the edge of the chair. Five months of this has wrecked any surviving mechanism we may have had to maintain our sense of internal balance and perspective and generosity toward one another. So even the very simple acts of being gentle and patient and understanding with others challenge us almost beyond what we are capable of. People don't know where else to direct their feelings of exquisite frustration and anger and exhaustion, so they fling it at one another. Arguments and misunderstandings have been erupting all week. The tension is almost literally too much to bear.

Nadine had a school trip last Wednesday, and for several days preceding the trip she was so excited she could barely sleep. You would have thought she was going somewhere new, distant, and thrilling, that she was going to do something she had never before experienced. In fact, the trip took them to the Nativity Church and the Milk Grotto, both located in downtown Bethlehem and both sites that we have visited before and that we pass every day. But it was just the thought of breaking out of the grinding hunkered-down routine of the past five months and doing something different! She was so worried that curfew would be imposed, and the rumors have been flying since the first of the month about punishing curfews in advance of the war. We are so used to being suffocated that we can't believe it when, for a moment, we can just breathe in the fresh air. Instead of enjoying the refreshing breeze, we hysterically try to gulp down supplies of air that can somehow be saved for later when it is too stale and we are too crazy to appreciate it.

Mathilda is tired, Phoebe has headaches, and Nadine's stomach hurts. Mom works too much and Dad glares silently at the television. None of us sleep well. None of us can concentrate. Our tempers are short and explosive. Our words are inadequate. This is the scene being played out in homes all over Bethlehem as we contemplate our future, crushed by wars and imprisoned by walls. And we are lucky compared to Gaza, Jenin, Nablus, and Tul Karm. For them, what is to come will only be a continuation of what already is. For them the nightmare is ongoing. Ours is about to begin.

23 March 2003

Last Friday was Mother's Day here in Palestine. A little over a year ago the little girl in the black ski cap watched her mother die on the floor at the entrance to their home in Aida Camp, and I have thought of her literally almost every day since then. It's not quite accurate to say I wonder how she is, because how else could a little girl be after losing her mother in such a horrific way. I look at my own daughters and realize what terribly fragile things little children are, and how something as big as the loss of one's mother can never really heal. It's a hole that will always and forever ache to be filled, and for her it never will be; for me this is a source of awesome sadness. Look, everyone, at what we have done to her. And here we are a year later, still killing parents, still killing children, and it doesn't make any more sense now than it did then, and it can never really make sense because there is no sense in it. Yesterday we saw footage of little Iraqi kids with their skulls destroyed, and parents holding trembling children in front of bombed homes. Today we saw the bodies of U.S. soldiers whose families will soon be in mourning. How can it be that yet another war has been launched? How many wars and how much killing will the world tolerate before it finally is enough? No matter how many trivialized images of torn bodies and ripped flesh and spilled blood I see, the realization always pierces my heart: what a terrible, terrible thing it is that we have done.

It is a great temptation these days to go to sleep and stay asleep as long as possible, hoping that when you finally wake up it will have all been a bad nightmare. These days I am ready to collapse into bed by 8:30, and no matter how much sleep I get, I always wake up feeling the exhaustion of profound grief. And I think that what I am feeling is actually a kind of grief, real physical grief on the visceral level of actual personal loss. Annie Lamott recently wrote that salvation is identification with other people, but I wonder. In this world that we have made, it feels more like damnation than salvation. The accumulated weight of all this killing and misery and sorrow that we have witnessed over the last two plus years feels like a yoke too heavy to bear, and still it goes on. On and on and on. I no longer seem able to distinguish between the pleasures of life and the sorrows, because even the pleasures seem saturated with the blood we so carelessly, so casually, so needlessly spill. Tears spring as easily to my eyes at the sight of the blue dome of a sunny morning as at the evening's summary of carnage on Al Jezeera, and I go through my days with a crushing weight poised on my chest. There is a simple reality here that cannot be escaped: you cannot redeem the loss of life, least of all by taking more life. Period. As much as·we want to sleep, we do not deserve it. We deserve only to be haunted unto eternity by the faces of the orphans whose parents we killed, and the parents whose children we have buried, by the sickening finality of dead eyes whose lights we are responsible for extinguishing. No amount of rhetoric can shift the blame elsewhere. This hell is of our own making.

On Tuesday, 25 March 2003, on the streets of Bethlehem, Israeli undercover agents opened fire on a vehicle driven by George Sa'ada, principle of the Greek Orthodox School in Beit Sahour. It was an ordinary family on an everyday errand, in a heavily populated area of town. The undercover agents were in the process of apprehending two men suspected of Hamas ties when they panicked and turned their weapons on the Sa'ada family car hitting all four—father, mother, and two daughters. It was not a stray bullet. Thirty rounds were emptied into the vehicle coming up the street. The three eldest were wounded seriously. The youngest—10-year old Christine—did not survive the trip to the hospital.

In normal times such an incident would have been the lead story on the nightly news and displayed prominently in the morning paper back in the United States. But the Iraqi war was underway and the story of Christine was not news for Americans. An AP story merely mentioned that the Israeli agents who saw the approaching Sa'ada vehicle feared that they were coming under attack and that one Palestinian was killed. There was nothing to suggest that this was an ordinary family, nothing about the cross dangling from the rearview mirror, nothing that the victim was a ten-year old girl who loved pizza, who had spent the afternoon studying for a math test, and who dreamed of becoming a lawyer when she grew up.

Yet for mothers in Bethlehem, Christine Sa'ada's death was a reminder of their own children's vulnerability.

Christine Sa'ada was the 406th child killed in this conflict two and half years old.

🌍 3 April 2003

On Thursday 27 March, two days after the Sa'ada family car was fired upon by Israeli soldiers in downtown Bethlehem, Nadine asked me if she could go with Miriam Abu Laban to their friend Majd's house in Aida Camp after school. There was no curfew that day, the weather was warm, and I couldn't think of a good reason why not. Nadine and her two best friends call themselves the "powertuff girls" and I am happy to encourage their friendship, especially since Majd and Miriam are Muslims. So I agreed. At sunset, as I drove up through Bethlehem to pick them up from Majd's home, I suddenly realized that Christine Sa'ada had died of gunshot wounds around dusk, and I started looking nervously around for army jeeps cruising the area.

The Aida Camp neighborhood has suffered incredibly over the last two years from army "operations" in all their varied forms (invasions, assassinations, house-to-house searches, tank fire, helicopter attacks) and, being a refugee camp, it is a favorite army target. The mother of the little girl in the black ski cap was killed as the result of a house-to-house search during the March 2002 invasion, and Majd's own house had been hit by tank shells during the October 2001 invasion, though the family had thankfully been evacuated to the home of a relative at the time. One of Bethlehem's first victims of the current Intifada was the little Jawarish boy, shot in the head while walking home from school. He was pronounced dead with his school backpack still on his back. Bethlehem's most recent victims apart from Christine, the two intended victims of the "operation" which killed her, were both from Aida Camp. So the camp has buried many martyrs and will no doubt endure much more suffering before it is all over.

The hair stood up on the back of my neck as I sped up the hill in the fading light toward Majd's house. I could imagine a similar headline: "Four-year-old girl killed during Israeli military operation" or alternatively "Mother of three dies of head wounds following operation in Aida Camp." As with Christine, the army would call it a "regrettable accident," and that would be the end of the story. The next day there would be other news to attend to, and the world would quickly move on, leaving the family members to mourn and wonder what it is that differentiates this senseless act from an Act of Terror.

I begged off the obligatory invitation for coffee from Majd's mom and quickly drove Miriam back to her home in Doha, another favorite haunt of soldiers looking for trouble. As I returned in the thickening darkness to Beit Sahour, I continued to keep an eye peeled for jeep convoys flashing lights and honking horns, and it wasn't until my kids were safely back in their own bedroom that I felt a sense of relief. There, you see, I told myself, nothing happened. And I was determined not to allow these fears, reasonable as they perhaps are considering our circumstances, to dominate and oppress our already too dominated and oppressed lives.

There have been many demonstrations of solidarity with Iraq in town since the war was launched, and we have participated in several of them. On the afternoon of Saturday 29 March, the Holy Land Trust organized a solidarity event for Palestinian children that I was planning to take the girls to, even though my mother-in-law, who has already succumbed to the paranoia, begged me not to. It'll be broad daylight, I reminded her, and in an attempt to convince myself I added, nothing's going to happen. It was to take place in Manger Square after school, and there would be balloons, music, and scout troops. Since there are very few activities for children in Bethlehem these days, I wanted to take advantage of it, and the girls were eager to do something different.

The square was relatively full of parents and children, and the program got underway on schedule at 1:00 p.m. with the audience facing toward the Ministry of Tourism building under the Millennium clock, which had counted down the seconds to midnight before the packed square on that rain-soaked night three and a half years ago. Half an hour into the program, the familiar sound of an army jeep penetrated the noise, and everyone turned toward the Peace Center to see a single jeep idling beside it, its yellow light revolving ominously. It sat there, its engine revving, and the crowd froze. Each side waited for the other to act, and nobody moved or breathed. Suddenly two of the organizers sprinted toward the jeep and asked the soldiers to please leave the square before the boys started to throw stones. Instead of leaving, the jeep advanced into the square and the young boys in the audience quickly made the transition from peaceful demonstrators to angry rock-throwers. Within

seconds the jeep was being pelted with stones. It roared out of the square in reverse, the boys chasing it as far down as the Terra Santa school. As it neared the bottom of the hill, it halted abruptly and one of the soldiers leaned out of his door just long enough to launch a percussion bomb
before taking off again. The organizers implored everyone to return to the square, where the program resumed after a few more minutes.

After perhaps another half hour, two jeeps roared back into the square, plowing right into the crowd and causing total pandemonium. The young boys immediately mobilized for a second stone-throwing assault, while panicked parents fled in every direction with their small children, screaming in fear. These are the same parents who, two years ago, were being accused of intentionally sending their children to become martyrs. Anyone watching this scene would immediately recognize two truths: that parents here are compelled by the same loving instinct to protect their children from harm as parents anywhere, and that the soldiers are seeking to deliberately provoke violent confrontations in order to justify "retaliation." And the more scenes you witness in Palestine, the more you would realize the consistency of these two truths. The West has got it all backwards.

Yesterday evening at 6:45 George arrived back from Jerusalem on public transportation and called me to collect him at Bab Iskag near Rachel's Tomb, about seven or eight minutes from our house. As usual, Phoebe wanted to come. We left the house and found him waiting by the side of the road in the deepening gloom, and on the way back decided to pick up some vegetables at Shady Market near the Paradise Hotel, opposite Azza Camp. I pulled up to the curb and George got out. A second later, a single army jeep, yellow light flashing, cruised slowly down the street. The evening was very warm and plenty of people were out, shopping, strolling, and enjoying the close night air. As the jeep made its way down the street, the very same thing happened. All eyes focused on it in breathless anticipation and all movement froze. At the intersection, it made a U-turn and slowly headed back toward us, passing directly in front of the market. My heart thudding, I told Phoebe to come and lay her head in my lap. Again the jeep made a U-turn and cruised slowly down the street a second time, and again it returned. I was convinced a shoot-out was on the verge of erupting. The jeep passed just out of sight around a corner, though we could tell it was still there because of the flashing yellow light sweeping along the shop front on the opposite side of the street. No one moved. No one spoke above a murmur. Necks craned. And then suddenly, from around the corner, one of the soldiers launched a sound bomb, and again chaos descended and families fled in terror. A mother crossing the street directly in front of our car was so startled by the noise that she dragged the toddler gripping her hand along the ground for several meters before regaining her senses enough to pick him up and run. The jeep backed up and drove off, and you could almost see the soldiers laughing as they watched the people scramble for safety in their rearview mirrors.

As a mother who loves her three daughters and husband, I can only say that life is getting harder and harder.

The Land

*T*here's a Palestinian saying, "A man without land is a man without honor." One can easily understand how many Palestinians today feel shame at the loss of land. George and Alison rent their apartment in Beit Sahour, just as they did in Beit Jala. The same goes for George's brothers. Their honor is in a piece of farmland south of Bethlehem. In the same way, the residents of Bethlehem have experienced both shame and economic loss because their ancestral land has been confiscated for Israeli housing settlements at Gilo and Abu Ghaneim, so the Nassars are feeling the same crunch in the south.

When discussing land, it is common to throw out figures and percentages to show how land ownership has changed. When the UN partition plan was approved on 29 November, 1947, Palestinians owned 93% of all the lands that have become Israel and the Occupied Territories. The partition plan, however, granted 53% of the territory to the new state of Israel. In the war of 1947-49, Israel gained another 24% so Palestinian land ownership had been reduced to 23% of their ancestral lands. This is the West Bank and Gaza. In the war of 1967, Israel gained political control of these lands as well, although United Nations resolutions and the U.S. State Department position has been united that Israel must withdraw. The government of Israel also has been in agreement at least in a partial sense. This is what the Oslo agreements were all about.

However, in the 35 years of occupation, Israel has had a massive program of settling these territories as a way of retaining the economic benefit of prime land and water resources as well as strategic control of the entire West Bank. The man responsible for settlement expansion over the past 35 years has been Ariel Sharon, the current Prime Minister. In fact, Israel's Peace Now organization announced that 34 new Israeli settlements were built on Palestinian land in the year since Sharon took office as Prime Minister. The Nassars' misfortune is that their ancestral land lies within reach of one of Israel's largest settlement blocs. In fact, it was scheduled for appropriation to the settlements according to the maps presented by Prime Minister Ehud Barak at Camp David in July 2000.

George often talks about the days when the farm flourished with vineyards and olive groves in the 1930s and 1940s—debunking the myth that the land was all undeveloped desert prior to the establishment of Israel. The family sold grapes to local wineries and even exported grapes to Europe. That changed after 1967 when water from the underground aquifer was diverted for the settlements and when building permits were denied. In 1991 Israel declared that it was confiscating the land. Pastor Mitri Raheb has compared this situation with the biblical story of Naboth's vineyard in I Am a Palestinian Christian (Fortress Press: Minneapolis, 1995), pages 47-52 [see also Fred Strickert, "A Farm in Palestine: In the Shadow of the Settlements," Christian Century (April 9, 1997), 356-357].

For Alison's husband, George, this is not merely a question of livelihood and economic loss. It is a question of personal honor and identity.

18 October 2001

On the tenth of next month, George and I will celebrate our ten-year anniversary. This also means that it will have been ten years (the same week we were married) since the Israeli government—in collusion with the surrounding settlements—first tried to declare parts of George's family farm as "state land." For those of you who are unfamiliar with this issue, George's grandfather acquired this land (a total of more than 100 acres which covers an entire mountain top in what is now "Area C" of the Bethlehem region of the West Bank between the settlements of Neve Daniel, Efrat, Betar Illit, and Eli'ezer) in two separate parcels in 1924 and 1925. Both George's grandfather and father earned their livelihoods primarily from the land, and most of George's recollections of his childhood and his father are framed within the context of the farm. George's sense of himself and his place in the universe are also deeply and inextricably rooted within this land, and so the entire duration of our marriage has been haunted by the specter of confiscation. Our anniversaries are always bittersweet.

This past Tuesday, 16 October, George was required to represent the family in the military court at Beit El near Ramallah, for a summons issued by border police 13 days previously out at the farm. George's brother Daoud has, since August 2000, been overseeing basic infrastructural development of the land as part of an integrated project whose ultimate objectives include a youth exchange camping facility, an agricultural model school promoting alternative farming strategies and environment-friendly technologies like water recycling and solar energy systems, and a center for alternative tourism and Palestinian cultural heritage.

Since October 2000, of course, it has been both difficult and dangerous to attempt going to the land. Ordinarily, it should not take more than ten minutes to reach the area by car. Now it can take between 30 and 45 minutes, involve as many as four military checkpoints, and require changing taxis three or more times. The army physically blocked their main access road with mounds of dirt and tore up the pavement on both sides of the blockade for extra measure. In addition, they routinely declare the main highway leading south from

Bethlehem to Hebron off-limits to Palestinian traffic, obliging people like George's family to travel miles out of their way along rocky tracks to reach their destination.

If all this weren't enough, the residents of the four surrounding settlements are heavily-armed thugs who come around regularly toting their guns and interfering with any and all attempts to work the land. They have prevented family members—at gunpoint—from clearing, planting, and harvesting. They have trespassed, vandalized, and intimidated, all with the implicit support of the soldiers who passively turn their faces while settlers act extra-judicially or actively accompany them and stand armed guard.

Legally, the Nassar land cannot be declared "state land" because the family is in possession of all the necessary private ownership documents. Confronted with this inconvenience, the Israeli government has opted instead for a policy of continuous low-level harassment. The military administration claims that, because the land is under litigation, it is unlawful to do any kind of work out there. But for ten years they have deliberately delayed a resolution of the case—which would clearly have to favor private family ownership—with endless postponements and meaningless legal strategies. In the meantime, virtually every attempt to do work there (i.e. plowing with a tractor, repairing the fences surrounding the property, or collecting the ripened grapes) has been frustrated by the appearance of soldiers (notified by the settlers, who have a clear vantage point overlooking the land) who are dispatched in order to deliberately interfere with the work. Last summer, George's brother Daher was hauled off to jail in full view of a team of American volunteer workers armed with a video camera. His crime was operating a tractor.

On 3 October, Daoud was supervising some workers who were covering an old well with a concrete cover. Previously the well had been covered by wooden planks, which had rotted from constant exposure to sunlight. The workers did not dig a new well, which Palestinians are prohibited from doing without a permit (settlers, needless to say, are not required to request permits for similar work, and settlement construction and expansion occurs non-stop). Nor did they construct any sort of edifice or building, which is also prohibited for Palestinians. They just covered the well with cement. At the court appearance, George was told by the judge (a settler) that if he did not succeed in getting a permit for the work within two weeks, the whole structure including the cover AND the well itself, as well as the drainage pipes, would be demolished. Guess what—they are about as likely to issue a permit for this work as they are to rule in the family's favor regarding the ownership.

Now, if instead of "Israelis" and "Palestinians," we described the above episode using the terms "whites" and "blacks," what would you be inclined to call it? If it is not racism, then I do not know what is.

*F*ollowing *the typical pattern of delays, the case was postponed another six months.*

12 March 2002
The Courts and the Family Farm

On Wednesday 6 March 2002, the lawyer representing the Nassar family received a response from the Israeli military court in Beit El regarding the confiscation of the family farm. In a half-page response, the court tersely rejected the family's objection to the confiscation, repeating the original claims that a) the land was not privately owned property, and b) the land was not being actively cultivated and could therefore be expropriated by the state of Israel. The response made no mention of the ten years of legal deliberations, no mention of the legal arguments made on behalf of the family, no mention of the ownership documents in the family's possession, no mention of the dozens of witnesses whose personal testimonies confirmed the family's ownership and activities on the land for the last seventy-five years (for a summary of the facts of the case, please refer to the update attached below).

Since the case is unable to go further in the lower court, the family is obliged to take any further objections to the high court. Palestinian lawyers from the occupied West Bank are legally prohibited from submitting petitions to the high court, so the family is obliged to hire and pay another lawyer. Jonathan Kuttab, of Jerusalem, was immediately contacted as a replacement for Ousameh Oudeh, the family's previous legal representative, and the relevant documents had to be rushed to his office in East Jerusalem despite the exaggerated dangers of attempting to cross the borders at this time, when F-16s were conducting nightly strikes against targets in Bethlehem and occupation troops were preparing for another massive invasion of the town.

Upon examination of the documents, Jonathan declared that the Nassar case is very strong in legal terms for several reasons. First, the court rejected one of the four borders as described in the two original land registers as imprecise and declared that this was a violation of Turkish law (which was in effect at the time of the original purchases), which they claim demands the articulation of four distinct borders. According to Jonathan, Turkish law in fact demands the precise articulation of two distinct borders only, so rejection of ownership based on this law is invalid.

The two original land registers corroborate each other 100% on three of the borders, and the "problematic" fourth border varies only in the transliteration from Arabic to English of the areas being used as border references. Even a casual examination of the two documents reveals that the two registers are, in fact, referring to the same exact area.

In fact, the family has thoroughly fulfilled all of its legal responsibilities in demonstrating ownership as well as active cultivation (as far as the circumstances allow) by providing all the necessary documentation and corroboration of witnesses, so rejection of the claim of ownership is in itself legally invalid. If these documents were truly inadequate in legal terms, the case would have been concluded long ago. It is obvious that the court is simply taking advantage of the deterioration in the overall situation and hoping that international supporters are too preoccupied with the "War on Terror."

The military judge is either ignorant of the precise dictations of Turkish as well as Israeli law or counting on the ignorance of our lawyer, or else simply hoping that we do not have the resources or stamina to continue with the case. We do. Jonathan submitted his objections to the high court on the following day, and we are awaiting a response.

According to Israeli civil legal procedure, this case cannot be permitted to extend beyond a one-year time period. We want to strenuously encourage everyone familiar with this case to keep updated on these procedures and to take action at the appropriate time. Such actions could include writing letters to Israeli and international authorities, contacting local political representatives and human rights organizations, contributing funds to pay legal fees, and publicizing the facts of this case in the media.

As the case proceeds, we will be in touch regarding what to do and who to contact. Many people feel a sense of powerlessness with regard to the injustices taking place in Palestine and wonder, "What can I do to help?" With this case, we are providing you with a very powerful opportunity to take action and make your stand for justice count in an important way. For ten years we have been fighting this confiscation alone. Now more than ever, we need your help. Please take the time to acquaint yourself with this case and let your voice be heard. It is time to say NO to Israel. NO more land confiscations. NO more oppression. NO more occupation. Your support will make a difference.

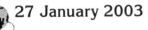

27 January 2003

Dear Friends,

The date for the final decision regarding the Nassar land case is fast approaching. On 5 February 2003, the Israeli Supreme Court will hand down a final ruling regarding the legal ownership of the property belonging to the Nassar family. According to lawyer Jonathan Kuttab, "*previously the Court has shown great reluctance to interfere in any decision regard-*

ing the rights of Palestinians to their land (see the attached legal statement)."

For those who are unfamiliar with this case, the Nassar family of Bethlehem has owned and cultivated 420 dunums (a little over 100 acres) of farmland just south of Bethlehem since 1924. They possess all the necessary private ownership documents, and the land has been properly registered in the official "*Tabu*" or land registry over the course of four successive occupations (Turkish, British Mandate, Jordanian, and Israeli). Property taxes have been paid on the land continuously since 1924. The Nassar farm is located on a hilltop south of Bethlehem. It is surrounded by four continuously expanding settlements (Efrat, Neve Daniel, Maalot Betar, and Eli'ezer), the closest of which is Neve Daniel.

In November 1991, the Israeli government declared the land "state land." This has been one of several standard methods the Israeli government has used to "legally" confiscate land owned by Palestinians in the Occupied West Bank. The majority of Palestinian farmers are unable to provide the necessary documentation in order to challenge these declarations because most never resorted to official land registration. Prior to the advent of Israel's aggressive land settlement enterprise, it was enough for property to be either communally owned or for ownership to be informally acknowledged according to an "honor" system. In the era of Zionist land colonization, "honor" ceased to be an operative term.

In any case, the Nassar family did challenge the declaration on the basis of its ownership documents and thus began a twelve-year legal battle. The family hired a lawyer, consulted a variety of experts including a team of land surveyors, provided numerous witnesses, submitted all the required documents and corroborative statements, and navigated checkpoints, closures, and curfews on hundreds of occasions in order to attend hearings at the regional military court at Beit El, near Ramallah.

On 29 January 2002, the lawyer representing the Nassar family received a response from the Israeli military court in Beit El regarding the confiscation of a part of the family land. In a half-page response, the court tersely rejected the family's objection to the confiscation, repeating the original claims that

a) the land was not privately owned property, and b) the land was not being actively cultivated and could therefore be expropriated by the State of Israel.

The response made no mention of the twelve years of legal deliberations, no mention of the legal arguments made on behalf of the family, no mention of the ownership documents in the family's possession, no mention of the dozens of witnesses whose personal testimonies confirmed the family's ownership and activities on the land for the last seventy-five years. The military court, without articulating any legal basis for its decision, rejected the Nassar family claim to ownership of the property.

The family, convinced of the legal strength and moral justice of its cause, responded by hiring a new lawyer and resubmitting the case for consideration to the Israeli Supreme Court. According to the attached legal statement, "*it is hoped that international pressure will have a positive influence on the final decision of the court.*" Therefore we strenuously encourage everyone committed to peace with justice in the Middle East to become involved and take immediate and prolonged action.

The next two weeks may prove crucial to the outcome of this case, so please let your voices be heard. We urge you to educate others about the facts of this issue by promptly forwarding this bulletin and to be in repeated contact with members of your local, state, and national governments; with church bodies; with international human rights organizations; and with representatives of the media.

Many people feel a sense of powerlessness with regard to the injustices taking place in Palestine and wonder, "What can I do to help?" With this case, we are providing you with a very powerful opportunity to take action and make your stand for justice count in an important way. For more than twelve years we have been fighting this confiscation. Now more than ever, we need your help and support.

Make a difference today. Tomorrow will be too late.
Sincerely,
The Nassar family, Bethlehem

Statement by legal advisor Jonathan Kuttab

In 1991 the military authorities in the West Bank declared part of the land comprising of 300 dunums belonging to the Nassar family in the Bethlehem area as "State Land" in order to transfer them to the Israeli settlement of Neve Daniel. The Nassar family appealed this decision to an Appeals Committee designated by the military authorities as an advisory committee of a judicial nature that discusses petitions against the decisions of the military authorities to declare land as belonging to the State. The Appeals Committee decided on 29 January 2002 to reject the appeal by the owners, the Nassar family, against the decision of the military authorities to declare a part of their land comprising of 300 dunums as "State Land". The rejection of the appeal was made in spite of the fact that the owners possessed land registration documents ("Tabu") proving the land was theirs, and in spite of the fact that they had been using the land for generations. The appellants presented conclusive evidence of ownership to the committee. However, it rejected their appeal, completely ignoring the facts and the law. The Nassar family has appealed to the Supreme Court of Israel against this decision, and the appeal with be heard on 5 February 2003. Previously the court has shown great reluctance to interfere in any decision regarding the rights of Palestinians to their land. It is hoped that international pressure will have a positive influence on the final decision of the court. The Nassar family is one of the few Christian families left in the Bethlehem area that owns hundreds of dunums of land. The transfer of their land to nearby Israelis settlements in contradiction to international law would deal a great blow to the dwindling Christian population in the Bethlehem area in these already very difficult times.

*I*n October and November, there was an organized effort by the Israeli peace camp to participate in the olive harvest for Palestinians who are farming in the shadow of the settlements. Chuck Lutz also led a group of fourteen, mainly from Minnesota, to take part. He wrote, "The particular campaign we were to join had focused since mid-October on presence with Palestinian olive harvesters in the West Bank. The campaign was organized because many of the groves located near Israeli colonies (settlements) had suffered harassment by settlers. Some trees had been uprooted, others were picked by Israeli colonists, and in still other groves, the Israelis tried to prevent Palestinians from harvesting, saying the land from the sea to the Jordan River and all its fruit had been promised forever by God to Jews, the descendants of the original Chosen People. The Israeli military, supposedly present to keep the Israelis and the Palestinians from confrontation, more often than not sided with the colonists and told the rightful harvesters to leave their fields. We internationals were to be a kind of buffer between the contending parties and, at times, to negotiate with the Israeli Occupying Force."

The situation facing the Nassar family concerning their farm is experienced by Palestinians on a regular basis throughout the West Bank.

28 January 2003

I have been sitting here on my couch over the last several days, stuck in my house under curfew since Saturday, with a feeling of fear and dread unlike any I have ever felt before. I have the feeling that the very existence of my own family is under threat from every direction and I am absolutely powerless to do anything about it. It's not an abstract threat, like what people in Montana might have felt following the attacks on 9/11 half a continent away. It's not a threat I need to switch my television on to feel. It's concrete in every sense of the word. It's an assault on our bodies and minds and wills, and it's only a taste of what is to come if Sharon gets reelected today and if Bush goes through with his war in another couple of weeks. In fact, there is so much to be afraid of now that, as the deep pit of anxiety in my stomach grows, I almost don't even know which fear to give first priority. All I know is that no one should have to live like this. And that we are still, incredibly, better off than many others. If there is any consolation in that, which there isn't.

As I write this, my husband is out making a last stand to defend his farm. He rushed out there on Sunday afternoon, risking arrest or worse by moving under curfew, after receiving a phone call from his brother that settlers from nearby Neve Daniel were using bulldozers to cut a road into the property. It was anticipated that by the following morning, they would have reached the top of the family property and planted a caravan or two, just enough for it to qualify as a new settlement and create the necessary "facts on the ground" to preempt a legal reversal. He told me over the phone today that he and five or six others had been involved in a confrontation with dozens of settlers armed with machine guns and snarling dogs, and as dramatic as that may sound, I was able to easily verify it through several other participants as well as a Danish pastor who had gone to act as an observer and take photographs. They literally had to stand in front of the bulldozers in order to stop the intrusion, and in fact, their lawyer was actually knocked to the ground by one before the police finally arrived and ordered the settlers to remove their machinery and go home. CNN wasn't around, and there were no journalists to record the scene for the evening news, but their bravery was heroic nonetheless. Yet another unreported act of courage in Palestine. As night falls, I am deeply fearful for George's very life. Like spoiled toddlers, these settlers do not accept interference gracefully, and they are never held accountable for their acts of intimidation and violence.

And even if George's family has won today's battle, the overwhelming odds are that they will lose the war in another two weeks when the Israeli Supreme Court hands down its final ruling on the confiscation of the land. How can an ordinary person live with such an extraordinary experience of injustice? What comfort can there be when the very foundation of your existence has been taken from you against your will and without further recourse? And when Israelis are not willing to play by the rules, how is it that Palestinians have to? Where is the brave soul who can admit that every suicide bomber is reacting to a profound and profoundly intimate experience of injustice and that every bombing can at the very least be understood within this context if not justified? I ask myself whether George will ever be able to fully recover from this, and the answer, I know, is probably no. I ask myself whether my sixty-year-old mother-in-law, whom I dearly love, will survive, and I am afraid to consider the answer. I know she is too frail to withstand such a crushing weight, and my tears of mourning are already tumbling down.

4 February 2003 • Tuesday

I would like to update you on the events of the past ten days regarding the Nassar Land Case. The family, with the support of a variety of individuals and organizations, has accomplished a number of positive steps. We want to encourage you to keep up-to-date on the situation during the very crucial weeks to come, and continue to do what you can to educate others and let your voices be heard. Your support is appreciated and is making a difference!

On Sunday, 26 January 2003, members of the Nassar family were informed that settlers from Neve Daniel had trespassed onto the property with bulldozers and were cutting a new road. Although curfew was imposed on Bethlehem that day, several family members managed to get to the land and began mobilizing resources to put an immediate stop to the intrusion.

On Tuesday, 28 January, family members accompanied by legal representative Jonathan Kuttab, Pastor Alex Awad, and Danish Pastor Arne Simonsen physically blocked passage of the bulldozers into the property. Israeli police were summoned and compelled the settlers to leave the area in order to avert further confrontation.

On Wednesday, 29 January 2003, the Israeli High Court issued an injunction instructing the settlers to cease all activity in the area. This is a definite victory for the Nassar family.

According to Jonathan Kuttab, the military appeal committee requested an indefinite postponement of the scheduled court date of 5 February 2003. This was agreed upon after receiving the injunction from the high court to prevent further work. No date has been set for the subsequent hearing, but an extension date of up to 60 days is permissible.

Our family is looking at a number of pro-active steps.

A tree-planting solidarity activity is being planned for Friday morning, 7 February 2003, at 9:00 a.m. Rabbis for Human Rights will be providing 1000 saplings, and we hope to involve as many concerned groups and individuals as possible in this event.

Lawyer Jonathan Kuttab is preparing a legal suit against the settlers to collect damages for the violations of trespassing and destruction of private property. This suit will proceed regardless of the eventual Supreme Court ruling, since the area where the settlers were attempting to cut the road is located in an area of the property which is not under dispute.

Since August 2000, the Nassar family agreed to commit a part of their property for development of the Tent of Nations Project—People Building Bridges—for the benefit of local and international youth. The long-term objective of this project is to bring Jewish, Christian, and Muslim youth together with youth from a variety of different backgrounds and cultures in international camps in order to facilitate mutual understanding, tolerance, and respect. This is the first step on the way to achieving peace with justice. Since its establishment, Tent of Nations, with the support of partner organizations in Switzerland and Germany, has been involved in developing the project's foundation, preparing the infrastructure of the site to accommodate groups, establishing contacts, and raising funds. As the struggle for ownership of the land continues, the project continues to move forward with plans and projects.

Sincere thanks for your continued contact and support,

The Nassar Family

10 February 2003

Friday, 7 February was the date we set for the first tree-planting activity out at the land, and when we woke up that morning, the weather seemed to indicate that it would be a perfect day. The sky was a clear blue and the sun was shining, despite the forecast for stormy weather. We immediately started calling people to confirm the time and place for the meeting and everyone seemed ready and eager to get started. It was about 8:30 when I rang Rev. Sandra Olewine, who broke the news: "The jeeps just passed my house announcing curfew. They're chasing all the people out of the intersection." I couldn't believe it and asked if she was sure. "I just talked to a friend of mine living near Manger Square, and jeeps are passing through there too."

The night before, around 2 a.m., we had been awakened from sleep by explosions nearby, which had continued for about an hour, accompanied by the sounds of sporadic shooting. So the fact is that we had expected to see the curfew announcement when we woke up and had considered it an auspicious sign to find nothing written at the bottom of the TV screen the next morning. I started calling back all the people I had called and we discussed what to do. The final conclusion was to proceed with our original plans and see how far we could get. So we finished dressing and preparing supplies and were out the door by five after nine. We had to drive slowly in anticipation of encountering army jeeps head-on, but in fact we made it all the way up to the top of Beit Jala without seeing or hearing any. We parked beside the huge mound of dirt and rubble which has blocked the road leading out of Beit Jala since early 2001 and climbed over to the other side. Step one accomplished.

Step two was to get the group out to the land. We were thirteen: George, me, and the girls; my friend Elaine Myers from the Albright and two of her friends, Franak Hilloowala and Chris MacEvitt; Bob May; Ed Nyce of the Central Mennonite Committee; Johannes Zanger, a German teacher of music at Dar Al-Kalimah school; George's brother Tony and his sister Amal. Tony had arranged for a twelve-seat transport van to take us the six kilometers from Beit Jala to the turn-off to the farm, so we piled in. The driver was nervous because we were one person too many and the short stretch of road leading to the land is heavily patrolled by soldiers and border police. But we managed to avoid being stopped and took the familiar pothole-riddled turn-off adjacent to the settlement of Neve Daniel.

It has probably been two years since the girls and I went out to the land, so we were excited. Our tense "escape" from Bethlehem had heightened the sense of adventure. And as the van crested the hill and the land came into view with the clear dome of blue sky overhead, I felt the old sense of breathless gratitude that I have always felt about this place. There is a poem by Wendell Berry, I think, called "The Cure of the Ground," which captures the inexpressible beauty and the primordial healing capacity of landscape. I don't pretend to understand the profound way in which Palestinian farmers are attached, bone and tendon, to their land, or how the soil seems to flow through their very veins. But I have seen how the moment he plants a foot it transforms my husband into who he really is, the person God seemingly meant him to be. I suspect that not too many people in this world know exactly where they want to be and are in that place. The simplicity of this is a pure gift of grace, and grace is what you feel all around you out there. But if land can cure, what can the result of its being taking away be other than brokenness and despair?

Once there, we were joined by seven more: George's brothers Daher and Daoud; his mom; our friends Sherry and Vernon; Dror Etkes of Peace Now; and Efrat Ben Ze'ev of Ta'Ayush. Following some introductory chat, we got to work planting olive trees in two fields on the northern slope. If you've never planted a tree, there is something about it that, like bread-making, feels not merely therapeutic but holy, especially in this specific location. Our task was regenerative, reparative, redemptive in a place where the last two years have been devoted to the single purpose of destruction and devastation and extinction. After the suffocation of months of curfew and confinement in Bethlehem, I felt something in me miraculously reviving: the possibility of hope.

By 1:00 we had planted sixty trees and were ready to stop for food. That's when we were joined by three more: a settler and two armed police.

According to local residents, Hanania has succeeded in taking land all over the area surrounding Nahallin. Maybe it is his official job. In any case, he seems to have plenty of time and energy to devote to the enterprise of land theft on behalf of the State of Israel, and he must be good at it, judging by the expanding settlements obscenely visible from every direction. I don't know if he's a good person or a bad person. Maybe he sincerely believes that all this land is unowned. What I do know is that he has been single-handedly harassing George's family for years and that he is causing them a great amount of grief. If his intentions are truly benign and if he genuinely believes in the legitimacy of his claim to the land, why doesn't he wait for the outcome of the case to be determined by the court?

Hanania charged straight over to the two plots of land we had just finished planting with the armed policemen in tow and commenced taking photographs. Point: He must be keeping the area under constant surveillance to have known. Point: While it was fine for him to photograph whatever he pleased, the policeman made it clear in no uncertain terms that we were not to take photographs. Point: The land where we had planted the trees is not even included in the area under dispute. Point: A

Palestinian would never be able to get away with charging into the middle of a settlement to take photographs of land he claimed as his. Point: Even if we win this case, it is clear that the low-level harassment will continue. If the decision is in their favor, it will be enforced. If it is in our favor, it will not be. They have the resources and the time and the energy and the money to make us miserable for as long as it takes.

The policeman kept insisting that "this can end well or it can end badly" and that it was "up to us not to resort to violence." But from the beginning his language was very belligerent, never mind the guns. He threatened Bob about photographing any of them. He told Vernon to shut up. He spoke rudely to all three of George's brothers. And according to Sherry and Vernon, both Hebrew speakers, he had actually intended to arrest George and take him to the detention cell in Gush Etzion, although he claimed only to want a "private word" with him down by the jeep. The entire group proceeded to follow them down to the road, Nadine clinging to me on the verge of tears because they were going to take her daddy. Mathilda held his arm and refused to let go, her first real act of civil disobedience. On the way down the hillside, Sherry overheard a phone call to the policeman instructing him not to detain George. And standing beside the jeep, she heard the him tell Hanania (in Hebrew) that "the owner is in the right." Nevertheless, he wrote George up. In the end, however, it was they who left and we who remained. Another victory for the Nassar family.

We went back to our lunch and tea. Dror, who had left before the arrival of Hanania, came back to find out the details of the exchange and share a plate of food. We had a few more rounds of tea. The air was scented with the smell of the wood fire. The sun started going down and it was curfew in Bethlehem. We had to get back. We called the same driver who had brought us out and he met us at the end of the road. As the van slowly picked its way back up the pothole-riddled track to the main highway, I looked over to the settlement, feeling sure Hanania was watching us depart and devising his schemes for the next disruption.

We climbed back over the mound of rubble into Beit Jala and navigated slowly back down towards Bethlehem in the fading light. As we neared the main road, a driver heading toward us indicated that soldiers were stopping cars up ahead, so we turned back and detoured through Al-Madbasah, narrowly avoiding another jeep convoy coming up from Manger Square. We dropped off our final passengers and headed for home.

Despite everything, the land is a testimony to coexistence. Despite everything, there is hope for a cure.

17 April 2003

In the last few weeks the Nassar family has been anxiously preparing for the scheduled high court hearing that was supposed to take place on 27 April 2003 (Orthodox Easter Sunday). The Israeli military representative was originally supposed to submit his final arguments to the Nassar family's legal representative by 1 April. The first week of April, we were informed that the final arguments would not be submitted until the eve of the Jewish festival of Passover on 16 April, just 11 days prior to the day of the expected final decision. Then, on the afternoon of 16 April, a postponement of the final decision was once again requested by the Israeli military representative, which has been granted. No new date has been scheduled.

Although the family's lawyer has previously indicated that the high court displays a historical reluctance to overturn lower court rulings in cases involving land ownership disputes, this second postponement would seem to confirm the impression of many people and organizations that have been consulted on this case: that the Nassar family has an exceptionally strong case for legal ownership and that a landmark ruling, which would be detrimental to existing Israeli land acquisition policies, could result. As we await a new date for the high court ruling, we ask that you continue to pray and advocate for a just outcome.

We will inform you as soon as we have a new date for the final decision by the high court. In the meantime, thank you for your continued interest and support!

The Nassar family

Suicide Bombers

Suicide bomb attacks against innocent civilians have become one of the predominant images of the second Intifada. This is partly due to the sheer horror of these attacks. It is partly due to the high number of children whose lives have been thus cut short. The Passover Seder. The Bat Mitzvah celebration. The mall shopping spree. The daily travel by Egged bus. In fact, four times as many suicide bomb attacks have been documented during Ariel Sharon's two years as Prime Minister (78 contrast to a total of 20 under the four previous Prime Ministers together: Rabin, 4; Peres, 8; Netanyahu, 4, Barak, 4). And yet, suicide bomb attacks were not that common during the first eight months of the Intifada.

Yet the situation changed during the summer of 2001. On June 1, a Palestinian blew himself up outside the Dolphinarium Disco in Tel Aviv, killing twelve teenagers. On August 9, a Palestinian blew himself up at the Sbarro restaurant in a busy shopping section of Jerusalem. Among the dead were seven children, ranging in age from two to 16.

Alison and her three girls could easily have been among them.

10 August 2001

On Thursday the 9th at 2:00 p.m., the estimated time of the explosion, I was at the Zeytoonah swimming pool with the girls. Directly overlooking the Zeytoonah is the settler bypass tunnel road and the Jerusalem neighborhood of Gilo, as well as the tanks "guarding" them. It's unnerving, to say the least, swimming down there in their sights, knowing that exchanges could start at any time without warning, as they so often have done in the past. But you get used to it. We did and we swam. At 5:00 p.m. one of the lifeguards came out and announced over a bullhorn that the pool was closing. Ordinarily they remain open until dark at least, if not later. Something's happened, was what I thought.

A few minutes later, I looked at my mobile, and saw that my mother-in-law had tried to call me seven times. The hairs stood up on the back of my neck. I dialed and she answered, breathless and nearly hysterical. "Call George, let him come home now, there's an explosion, 14 people dead in Jaffa Road, they're stopping Arab taxis and beating people up, let him come, no, let him stay there. Tell him to sleep there, why didn't you answer your phone, I was scared to death, you don't know what happened? It's terrible! They're going to start attacking soon! George doesn't answer his phone, why won't he answer? Are the girls with you? Get out of Beit Jala!"

I hung up and called George, who answered quickly. I asked where he was.

"We are about to leave. Brother Sebastian has agreed to drive me to the checkpoint."

"We'll pick you up as soon as you're in."

Waiting for George to be delivered back to Bethlehem, my mind went into "batten down the hatches" mode. We needed to put gas in the car because the Israelis would probably prevent gasoline deliveries for a while. We needed to buy some things from the grocery store, just in case, because who knew what would happen, and also pick up a full gas bottle. Luckily, George had picked up his month's pay the day before, because it might be some time before he could get back into Jerusalem. I would skip the two weeks' vacation that I had coming up, and be paid instead. How long before he would be able to go back to work? Months? Were the phones paid? When was the last time we'd checked the mailbox? Had I backed up my files at work? Will Phoebe's birthday be another occasion for shelling, as Mathilda's and Nadine's birthdays were?

Then I began to consider the list of friends and acquaintances who could conceivably have been at or near the scene of the explosion. Sherry and her gang, Jay and his family, Albright people, Elaine, HUC folks, David Ilan and his family, Uri the bookstore owner around the corner who always plays with Phoebe . . . I read the list of casualties with relief the next day. No one I knew. But still, they were all people that someone knew, they were all related to people, they all had friends and acquaintances of their own. Obviously, it is not any less of a tragedy because the people involved were not people I knew.

I do know many Palestinians on a personal level, and I know how many tragedies and hardships they have experienced, not just since October either, but long-term. And we have noticed that no world leaders have been tripping over themselves to acknowledge those tragedies or to sympathize with those victims.

It is not that Palestinians don't empathize with Jewish grief. They don't dance at the sight of Israelis splattered across the sidewalk, contrary to what many choose to believe. Despite the constant attempts to dehumanize them, they still react with heartfelt sorrow at this senseless carnage. Despite the certain knowledge that life will become that much harder for them as a result of these acts, they still shake their heads and mutter, "*Haram.*" Pity.

How many people do the same at the sight of shelled Palestinian houses?   How many have mourned the hundreds of young people who have been killed within the last ten months, or shared the pain of their loved ones? How many have tried to imagine how it must feel to plead with an 18-year-old holding a gun, whose orders are to prevent you from passing, whatever the reason?

My office colleague Brenda asked me, "But what if your kids had been in Sbarro?" And I have been thinking hard about that. It's a question I have asked myself many times, in the wake of the many explosions that have taken place in the last ten-plus years I have lived here. So it's not the first time I have imagined that possibility, and no doubt it will not be the last. I guess my answer would be similar to my comment about the two little boys in Nablus—I'd be on my way somewhere, wanting to kill someone, to make someone pay. But at least the world had the grace and generosity of heart to grieve with Sbarro's victims, whereas the two little boys in Nablus, as well as the hundreds of other dead Palestinian children, never even got that much.

As if death itself was not a heavy enough burden to bear, Palestinians also have to bear the horrendous weight of worldwide indifference to their suffering. But despite the killing double standard which routinely elevates and personalizes Jewish suffering while simultaneously diminishing and depersonalizing Palestinian suffering, Palestinian pain is just as human and hurts just as much. I often wonder how they can stand to go on.

13 August 2001 • Monday

The last time I walked past the front windows of the Sbarro restaurant on the corner of Jaffa Road and King George was the last time I was in Jerusalem, about three months ago. I haven't been able to get into Jerusalem since, because of the situation. But there are a couple of fabric stores just across the street from Sbarro that I visit on my periodic fabric hunts, and when I heard of the explosion, I could envision myself quite clearly passing in front of its curved plate glass window fronts.

According to Friday's papers, the family in which five members were killed in that explosion lived in a West Bank settlement, and had come into Jerusalem that day to "get away from the war zone." My first thought was, at least they have that option, unlike Palestinians living in the same war zone and enduring much harder conditions.

In fact, the last time I was able to get to Jerusalem, it made me almost physically sick for that very reason. The soldiers waved me through that day, while ahead of me a

Palestinian bus full of people wanting to get to Jerusalem was turned back. To my right, on the sidewalk, soldiers stopped a woman wearing a head wrap and carrying numerous bags, trailed by several small children. She was arguing, and I could hear the soldier in a raised voice telling her, "*Ruhi a dar!*" Go back home. Apparently, she was a big security risk. To my left on the opposite sidewalk, two soldiers flanked a group of twenty-something men in shabby work clothes. They were probably caught sneaking into Jerusalem to work without permits. The soldiers trained their guns in the direction of the group, all the while laughing and acting rowdy, like the 18-year-olds they are. Through them all, I was passed, waving my American passport, passport of the collaborators in this whole sick scenario. I was one of the privileged, though not anymore.

So I went on into Jerusalem, going about my business. But unlike other times, this time I couldn't stop looking around me and feeling sick at what I saw. What did I see? Israelis going about their business. Driving their cars without being stopped and harassed by police. Couples walking freely, families with children, eating ice cream in a leisurely way, completely unaware of the nightmare taking place just meters away behind the checkpoints. Eating, buying, shopping, money to spare, while Palestinian workers are prohibited from getting to their measly underpaid jobs and households struggle by on $400 a month, if they're lucky (and this was three months ago, mind you, so things were not even as desperate then as they are now). I saw kids wearing chic little outfits and sunglasses and sandals I know probably cost 150 shekels ($40) or more, while my sister-in-law's kids dress in their raggedy clothes and stay at home all summer long because they don't have the money to go anywhere or do anything because their dad was laid off, because the company where he works trades with Ramallah, but no one can get to Ramallah these days because it necessitates crossing Jerusalem. Almost the entire staff was let go, and my sister-in-law works in a sweat shop next to their house making 30 shekels, or $7.50, per eight hours, and that's all they have to live on for the time being. Imagine it.

People talking on their mobile phones. People wearing sophisticated outfits sitting in coffee shops reading newspapers.

What were they reading about? Stock prices? The latest movie at the Cinematheque? All these images struck me with great force and made me feel physically nauseous, not in isolation but in juxtaposition to the scenes from which I had just passed, and those I witness and experience every day. I looked into peoples' faces thinking, will you be next? And will your loved ones cry and wonder "why?"

I got out of there fast.

The plain truth is that, as long as Israelis are willing to indulge their own pursuit of "normal life" at the expense of even the most basic definitions of "normal life" for Palestinians—work, income, food, freedom of movement—there can never be peace. There can never be peace. There can only be endless reruns of the Dolphinarium and Sbarro, no less nauseating but no more so either. In any case, we on this side of the check-points do not wonder "why."

16 August 2001 • Thursday

Every morning, as I open my computer and prepare to do another day's work, I read the words I have pasted to the corner of my terminal: "I come to say to you . . . however difficult the moment, however frustrating the hour, it will not be long, be-cause truth pressed to the earth will rise again. How long? Not long, because no lie can live forever. How long? Not long, because you still reap what you sow. How long? Not long, because the arm of the moral universe is long, but it bends toward justice." Those words were spoken by Martin Luther King, Jr. not long before he was assassinated, but they are by no means inappropriate to the situation facing the Palestinians today. Although Israelis are quick to point out that Arafat is by no means M.L.K, Jr., Palestinian self-determination is neverthe-less a just cause, and Palestinian suffering can be reasonably compared to the suffering which lead to the American Civil Rights Movement. No one now would dare to deny the truth of that cause. I am convinced that some day, people will also know the truth behind the conflict here and bow their heads in shame in the knowledge of what their ignorance justified. I have to believe the day is coming.

Things are going too fast these days. I am still trying to think about Sbarro, but since then we have had an explosion in Haifa, the brief reoccupation of Jenin, Tuesday morning's shootout in Beit Jala and Bethlehem, and Tuesday night, when we apparently came within a hair's breadth of being reoccupied ourselves. Three days ago a seven-year-old girl was shot dead in Hebron, and yesterday a twenty-three-year-old. So my thoughts have necessarily shifted from "What if my kids had been in Sbarro?" to "What if that seven-year-old girl had been Nadine?" and "How bad will reoccupation be?"

Last night Mathilda couldn't sleep. She came shuffling into the kitchen crying, and when I asked her what the problem was (thinking it was the pain in her ear), she said, "I'm afraid to go back to Talitha Kumi. I'm afraid we'll be there when the shooting will start. What will happen to us? How will you know where to find us?" The same thoughts occur to me frequently, but we are made powerless by our inability to know or answer. I don't know what I can tell her that will calm her fears, because she is of course right to be afraid. All of this seems to be lead-ing inexorably in the direction of some unthinkable action, some ultimate response. A Final Solution? "Expulsion" is articulated with increasing frequency in the Hebrew dailies. "Massacre" is the term used in the Arabic dailies. The more I think about it, the more I think that, in the absence of any willingness to make peace with justice, this is finally what the Israelis will have to do: mass expulsion or mass murder, pret-tied up, of course, using the right language and properly justi-fied with the appropriate mental gymnastics. Because nothing less than peace with justice will do now. Palestinians will not return to passively sit in their little enclaves while their land and their houses and their possessions and their jobs and their incomes and their young people's futures and their right to move from A to B are taken from them one by one. Nor should they.

The four-hour middle-of-the-night reoccupation of Jenin supposedly had the goal of "decreasing terrorist activity in that area." What a joke! They demolished an evacuated police station and left. Do they—does anybody—really think that such a pitifully impotent action could have accomplished that objective? It was the act of a bully, strutting in front of the crowd. If Israelis really want to end the suicide bombings, if they really want to put an end to "the cycle of terrorism," if they want to achieve total separation from Palestinians, there is one ridiculously easy way to do it. Dismantle the settlements, get out of the West Bank, slam and lock the door. They stay there. We stay here. Just do it.

But the truth is that they don't really want any of these things. Or rather, they want the best of all worlds—for themselves. They don't want Palestinians in their midst doing damage, but they insist on Israeli soldiers and settlers remaining in our midst doing damage. You can have both, or you can have neither. They go together.

18 August 2001 • Saturday

Watching Israel's English newscast is always a challenging experience. Since English-speaking Jews are disproportionately represented in the settlements, the perspective is even more myopic than the Hebrew broadcasts. Night before last, there were two items worth comment.

First, the grandmother of the three settler children killed in Sbarro (along with their parents) was interviewed. Much was made of the fact that she was a Holocaust survivor. With a straight face she told the camera, "I survived the Holocaust and came to Israel to escape the nightmare, but the nightmare is not over . . ." Conveniently declining to mention that, thanks to her presence and the presence of her children and grandchildren in the West Bank, that same nightmare has now been imported to Israel and is being perpetuated by Holocaust survivors like herself? I listened to her and asked myself, can it be that she really believes that, or is this solely for the benefit of the English-speaking audience? She is either appallingly self-deluded or appallingly cynical.

The second item had to do with a car accident on the Jericho highway that was originally reported to be "an act of Palestinian terrorism" directed at a car full of Israeli passengers. Once it was determined that it was actually the opposite—that is, it was an Israeli who threw a rock at an oncoming transport van full of Palestinians which then lost control and crashed—the language magically metamorphosed into a much more cautious and skeptical commentary, full of words like "supposed" and "alleged" and "may have been," delivered in the passive tense (i.e. "passengers sustained injuries" as opposed to "A Palestinian injured passengers . . ."), and ending with "Police are investigating the incident."

I neglected to mention one small detail in my 16 August update: the takeover of Orient House. As provocative as that was (and was no doubt intended to be), the silver lining has been that we have had many opportunities in the last several days to hear Hanan Ashrawi's commentaries delivered into the microphone, and this is and will always be a pleasure. Both in English and in Arabic, the woman is a devastating speaker. The Israelis can't touch her on the basis of her arguments, which is why they always resort to personal attacks. She makes Dore Gold (Sharon's spokesman) look like the obnoxious simpleton that he is. I pointed her out to the girls a few days ago and told them, be like her, she's a hero!

The Zionism = Racism issue was recently placed on the table once again, and once again tossed out! And people wonder why the Palestinians insist that nothing ever changes. . . Ten years ago, this issue brought about my very first turning point. As a typical (dumb) American, my response was a reflexive "No, it can't be." I was working at Hebrew Union College at the time, among Israelis and American Jews, and I recall the discussions we had. Zionism does NOT equal Racism! But then I recall asking myself very quietly, but what if it really does? And that was the crack through which all the light started to flood in. The more I thought about it, the more I gave consideration to possibilities that I had previously been unable to consider, the more things started falling into place and making sense. When people shake their heads in bewilderment (or grief) and ask, "Why? Why?" it reminds me that, from that perspective, it truly does not make sense. Because that perspective does not take in the entire frame, and it omits numerous details necessary to a full comprehension of the situation. Zionism does not equal Racism if and only if we subtract the people from the landscape. The only glitch is that, the very act of "subtracting" the people from their landscape is in itself racism in its purest form. Otherwise known as expulsion, ethnic cleansing, or the "E" word. So folks, if you haven't already figured it out, YES, Zionism DOES equal Racism. But don't take it from me. Think about it.

The skies over Bethlehem are filled with kites these days. Parents are so strapped because of the closure, and the situation is so scary and uncertain, that there is nowhere for kids to go and nothing for them to do. So they're building and flying kites. It's such an obvious metaphor for the freedom they are being denied that it's almost a cliché. And yet there they are, all over the place, hundreds of them. Hand-constructed kites made out of bits of wood and newspaper with scrap tails. You can also see red kites for George Habash, green kites for Hamas, black kites for Fatah, but my favorite are the kites in the combined colors of the Palestinian flag, flying over the shelled houses of the refugee camps where the combined household salary is less than $300. These people are not about to give up!

*O*n 27 March, a Palestinian blew himself up in Netanya, killing 19 and wounding 100. This was the week when the Christian and Jewish calendars come together, Holy Week for Christians, with Maundy Thursday and Good Friday, Passover for Jews. The bombing took place not on a bus or a street corner, but at a Passover Seder.

 28 March 2002 • Thursday

1:00 a.m.

Sometimes the clouds part for a brief moment and I realize with sudden and painful clarity that in writing statements such as "I do not feel inclined to seem apologetic." I have willed myself to feel a kind of numbness which keeps it all from overwhelming me.

It's a mechanism, like my husband's free laughter, that protects me from the awful, immediate, and wrenching sorrow of all this death, all around us, and our awful and wrenching powerlessness to do anything about it.

Looking at tonight's rain-soaked footage in Netanya through tear-soaked eyes, I feel profoundly sorry if anything I have said or written contributed in any way to an atmosphere in which its realization was made possible, either psychologically or emotionally or ideologically or actually. My intention was to penetrate the numbness, not to increase it. I am profoundly sorry for all of it.

This is not what we want for anyone, this death, this loss, this unbearable grief or the even more unbearable rage and hatred that precede and succeed it like ocean waves in an endless black sea. It is all too much.

The little girl in the black ski cap cries and her tears mingle with those of the mother of the soldier and the father of the teenager at the mall and the family of the suicide bomber and the husband of the lost mother and her lost baby, and mine. And it is a flood, and we are all drowning.

And we save ourselves by numbing ourselves to "them." And I can understand that, in the same way and for the same reason, they numb themselves to "us." To the assaults in the camps, to the deaths of pregnant women, to the decades of misery, to the homelessness, to the assassinations, to the tears of little girls. And it is something we have all succumbed to, in order not to be drowned. And I can forgive it because I have done it. But now I know that I mustn't succumb because even though I am saved from drowning, something has died after all.

And our numbness will not bring anyone back, no, the mother from Aida camp will not be brought back through our numbness toward this soldier, that civilian. It just makes them all seem somehow more dead, more gone. The living memory of one can be evoked only when they are all granted this same connective force, which is the force of our collective humanity. And when we acknowledge this for all, we cease to understand whatever meaning any of it had in the first place.

What meaning could all this death possibly have?

The lack of an answer will soon overwhelm us all.

Cease.

Fire.

*P*rime Minister Sharon responded to the Passover Seder bombing with the most brutal incursions into the West Bank that had been seen since Oslo. Death and destruction was all around. A strict curfew and closure had confined Palestinians to their homes for over three weeks. Nevertheless this show of power did nothing to stop the suicide bombings.

March 30—suicide bomber wounded 32 in Tel Aviv.

March 31—suicide bomber killed 14 in Haifa.

April 10—suicide bomber killed 13 in bus attack in northern Israel.

April 11—suicide bomber killed 8 in bus attack in Haifa.

April 12—suicide bomber killed 6 in Jerusalem.

April 17—suicide bomber attacked Gaza checkpoint.

Several months earlier, the first woman suicide bomber, Wafa Idris, from the Dheishah camp near Bethlehem, blew herself up along with an Israeli girl, wounding 100 in downtown Jerusalem. With her photo on the cover of news magazines, people wondered, "Who were these suicide bombers?"

22 April 2002 • Monday

It must be great to have such an uncomplicated world-view. In a world where everything is black and white, you get rid of so many inconvenient layers of subtlety. In fact, you can just forego depth and profundity altogether. You don't have to ask questions and you don't have to search for connections, because all the important stuff is all laid out there right on the surface. A martyr is a murderer, yes. But that's not all he (or she) is.

Martyrs are also sons (and daughters), devoted brothers and loving husbands and fathers of children. Very often they are second- or third- or fourth-generation refugees. Very often they have lived their entire lives in refugee camps, surviving well below "the poverty line" in any conventional sense of the term. Very often they have been imprisoned, or are related to someone who was, sometimes more than one. Very often they have experienced excruciating torture. Very often they come from a family of a martyr, sometimes more than one. Very often, they come from a family in which a small child has been needlessly shot and killed, or crippled for life, sometimes more than one. Very often, they come from the family of someone chronically ill whose treatment is routinely hindered or pre-vented. Very often they have stood and watched as bulldozers knocked their house down, or their grove of trees, or their grape vineyard. Very often their family has had land confiscated, and has been forced to watch helplessly as settlers develop the land that once belonged to them. Very often they experience regular humiliation at some checkpoint or other. Very often they have had to endure, again and again, the rude speech and behavior of gum-chewing, sunglasses-wearing eighteen-year-old sol-diers. Very often they are unemployed because of the Occupa-tion. Very often education has been made difficult or impossible for them because of the Occupation. Very often all opportuni-ties for a meaningful future have been taken from them be-cause of the Occupation.

Martyrdom is a form of suicide, and suicide is an act of absolute desperation and utter hopelessness. It is the one thing left when everything else has been taken away. And so martyrs are, above all, people with nothing left but the final act of martyrdom. Their lives have been rendered unlivable. Their pasts are filled with pain. Their futures are a blank void. Their final act takes all this and flings it back into the faces of the people responsible.

Time and time again, America has failed to demonstrate compassion for the living death that constitutes existence for Palestinians. It has failed at even the relatively modest act of simply acknowledging the pain and despair invested in these acts, of acknowledging the truth that Palestinians need to forgive as well as be forgiven. How then does it have the outrageous audacity to demand of Palestinians the infinitely more difficult act of not giving in to hopelessness? When tomorrow promises only more of the same pain, frustration, hopelessness, and despair that yesterday and today held? The waste of life embodied in these acts is only a fraction of the life and humanity and potential that has been crushed by decades of Occupation. Only forgiveness can lead to hope, and only hope can lead to the choice of life over death. It is time to forgive the Palestinian martyrs and also to ask for their forgiveness. They—we all—want to live.

T he second lengthy curfew of 2002 brought another reflection concerning suicide bombs and non-violent resistance. Again the twelve days of curfew had been imposed when a Hamas bus bombing killed the bomber and 18 others, including one child, and injured 54 near a Jerusalem settlement.

1 July 2002 • Day Twelve

"Refuse to be occupied," exhorts one article we recently received, riding the noble wave of the latest fashionable idea, Non-Violent Resistance, as if it has never been thought of before. "Palestinians should start publicly burning identity cards and peacefully marching through checkpoints and 'closed

military zones'—even when they come under sustained fire . . .
[T]here should be a massive campaign of 'illegal' home construction and land development . . . [T]here are thousands [of
Palestinians] in Israeli prisons. Let's flood those same prisons by
the tens of thousands . . ." My favorite part is "Let's . . ." How
easy to speak in first-person plural when you are many thousands of comfortable miles away and have not already been
living this nightmare for decades. I have been sitting on this
couch wondering who would be insane enough to try any of
these acts, given the ferocious brutality of the last two years
and the virtual certainty of being mowed down and then spun
away into some easily digestible and quickly forgotten War-on-
Terror sound bite? These are just ordinary people. It is a
gargantuan effort for them just to keep getting up each morning. Their simple determination to keep existing against all
odds, to stay and to endure, to witness and to testify, is all the
heroics they are capable of. That is more than can be said for
many. And it should be more than enough.

The first Intifada of 1987-92 was largely a nonviolent
movement, and it was largely ignored by the champions of
Non-Violence. Thus our present deterioration into violence.
For five years, Palestinians armed only with rocks, slingshots,
and Molotov cocktails were shot, beaten, jailed, tortured, dis-
possessed, and humiliated with virtual impunity. Been there,
done that. We are personally acquainted with people who lost
everything as a result of their refusal to pay taxes to Israel—
trained pharmacists, merchants, and factory owners who had
to start again from zero when everything they owned was
confiscated as punishment for their acts of civil disobedience.
The man who owns the supermarket down the road was jailed
for his participation in the Beit Sahour tax revolt. Are you
saying these folks should risk it all again because you were not
paying attention? In any case, the dead will not be resurrected
for the replay.

One person wrote yearning for more strategies (like the
Starbucks boycott) reminiscent of the non-violent leadership of
Martin Luther King, Jr. "The peaceful demonstrations of those
involved in the war against the racists in the States was much
more effective than any violence." And yet, the Civil Rights
Movement also deteriorated into violence and factionalism

because frustration and hopelessness was allowed to build up for too long. Brown vs. The Board of Education was ruled upon in 1954 (which is not to say that African Americans did not suffer a history of oppression much longer in duration) and only slightly more than a decade later, King was vying for leadership alongside Eldridge Cleaver, Malcolm X, and Jesse Jackson among many others, and violence was raging across the U.S. And of course the assassination of King himself went a long way to discourage the strategies he so eloquently promoted. Only Black Americans themselves can say how much King's leadership really achieved and how much is superficial. In any case, the Palestinians, too, have a Dream which has been allowed to simmer for more than fifty years, and if it is now beginning to implode in a gory and senseless bloodbath, then where does responsibility truly lay? With the powerless, voiceless, wretched miserable people whose only demand, after all these lousy years, is plain freedom? Or with the wealthy, armed, and self-righteous wielders of power that take their sweet time and dole out rights like favors for "good behavior?"

The suicide bombings are "not endearing the Palestinians to the free world." I think it can safely be said that the feeling is mutual. The "free world" has not "endeared itself" to the Palestinians by standing obliviously by and allowing this military onslaught to go on and on. If the world wants the Palestinians to be more passive, then it is obvious that it will have to reciprocate by being more active. People have to be given some reason to believe that they are not totally on their own in this, and that there is hope for justice. Don't stonewall the investigating committee on Jenin and then whine that Palestinian tactics are not acceptable. In South Africa, blacks accused of collaborating with the white regime were "necklaced"—that is, they were bound at the wrists, rubber tires soaked in gasoline were placed around their necks and set alight. The desperate savagery of acts like this did not distract ANC supporters from the basic injustice of Apartheid, and we surpassed Apartheid long ago. The current emphasis on Non-Violence has less to do with strategic purity than with the "free world's" need to exonerate itself somehow for its outrageous failure to act in the face of ongoing systematic atrocity.

There was one miraculous day just following the Gilo bombing (in which the brother of someone I used to work with was killed), in which Ted Turner, Cherie Blair, and Jack Straw all made strikingly similar comments about the lack of hope which must fuel the motives of the suicide bombers. But of course they were all later forced to apologize for their "insensitivity towards the victims" of those bombings. When will the "free world" understand that it is not "insensitivity" but independent thought that is the enemy of Sharon's cleansing policies? It doesn't take a genius to figure out that these acts are not occurring within a vacuum, and recognizing that fact is not equivalent to condoning them.

It's a standard Israeli tactic to make things seem equivalent which are not so. Understanding is condoning. Condoning is celebrating. Boycotting Starbucks is the same as spray-painting a swastika on the entrance to a synagogue. Throwing rocks is the same as blowing yourself up in downtown Jerusalem, which is the same as sniping soldiers at a checkpoint or attacking a settlement. The end result is that, when it comes to resisting the Occupation, nothing should be considered legitimate. But if everything is equivalent, then there's no basis, moral or otherwise, for choosing boycotting over suicide bombing. Distinctions need to be made every minute, and until they are, the violence will not abate and the "free world" will bear a heavy burden of guilt for perpetuating it.

It already does.

*A*fter five weeks under strict curfew and closures, it appeared at last in the summer of 2002 that the Palestinian leadership had reached an agreement to end suicide bomb attacks against Israeli civilians. There was hope that a great chasm between Palestinians and Israelis might be bridged. Yet as Alison notes, the political will to end the violence is necessary on both sides.

23 July 2002

My feelings of disgust today are complete. Last night, when we saw the item on Al Jazeera about the Hamas offer, I told George that Israel was going to do something really spectacular, and last night in Gaza, they did. None of you will probably ever see the footage from the immediate aftermath of their little "operation"—all the kids being brought into the emergency room in obvious states of shock, the body parts everywhere, the medical personnel rushing around with hysterical parents, an infant being given CPR. They F-16 bombed five apartment buildings full of sleeping families at midnight in order to get their man. They got him, along with many others. I don't think it is known at this point how many are dead, how many wounded. And buildings in the surrounding area continue to collapse. But they don't target civilians, and they definitely do want peace. The following short statement says it all, I think. Now, who can say what will happen?

The Israeli peace group Gush Shalom gave the details:

> Less than twenty-four hours ago, the Hamas leader Sheikh Ahamad Yassin made an unprecedented public call for a cease-fire with Israel. That call was the culmination of long, patient negotiations between the Palestinian Authority and the Hamas leadership, aimed at achieving a ceasefire between the Palestinians and Israel, putting an end to suicide bombings and paving the way to a resumption of some kind of political process. Saudi Arabia, too, is known to have made direct approaches to the Hamas leaders in order to achieve the same result.

> A government of Israel caring even a little bit for the well-being of its own citizens would have welcomed the opening. Not so the Sharon Government, whose response was to send an F-16 fighter plane on a bombing spree in Gaza. The effect of attempting to assassinate a senior Hamas leader was a carnage whose victims included many women and children. Now, instead of offers of ceasefire, the Hamas leadership is coming out with calls for revenge, which seems to suit Sharon much better. It is the Prime Minister, with his endless string of provocations, who bears the responsibility for this missed opportunity of ending the cycle of bloodshed.

Deputy Defence Minister Dalia Rabin-Pelosof resigned this evening, charging the Sharon government with destroying the life work of the late Yitzchak Rabin, her father.

*T*he situation reverted back to the way it had been for over two years. The cycle of violence between suicide bombs and Israeli assassinations continued throughout the fall. On 21 November 2002, a suicide bomber killed 11 passengers and wounded 48 on a bus in Jerusalem's Kiryat Menachem neighborhood during rush hour. On the following day, for the fourth time in 12 months, more than 30 Israeli tanks and 70 armored personnel carriers, bulldozers and helicopters reoccupied the towns of Bethlehem, Beit Jala, Beit Sahour and the villages of Irtas and Al-Khader, and re-imposed a curfew on an estimated 80,000 inhabitants. With troops in Bethlehem, Israeli forces reoccupied all of the major Palestinian population centers in the West Bank except for Jericho.

21 November 2002

At 9:17 a.m. the bomber was identified as being from Bethlehem. By 9:30 the town was in chaos. Children are being sent home early from most schools. The market is swamped with shoppers purchasing food supplies and trying to prepare for an invasion. The banks are swamped. Mobile phones are ringing constantly with the latest information. We are preparing for the worst.

28 November 2002

Very quick note! We are under curfew. Today is the first time they lifted it since they came in last Thursday night. Only four hours. The town is a madhouse. I am running quickly in and out of work. Things are quiet where we are— we have only seen the jeeps once. But we can hear the houses being blown up over the hill in Jabal Hindazi. George is in Jerusalem. The girls are okay, just bored. Looks like this is going to screw up the school year for them. The rest of the family's okay. We speak on the phone a lot. We heard they will be in until AFTER Christmas. Why am I not surprised?

*I*n late April 2003, with the Iraq war winding down, several events signaled the possibility of a new day in Israeli-Palestinian discussions. Abu Mazen, a man who had consistently spoken out against armed struggle in general and suicide bombings in particular, was named Prime Minister of the Palestinian Authority. The Palestinian Legislative Council gave official approval for the Prime Minister and his cabinet on 29 April. Almost immediately, the United States announced the long-anticipated release for the Quartet's "Road Map to a Permanent Two-State Solution to the Israeli-Palestinian Conflict."

Yet teh glimmers of hope came amidst violence. On that same Tuesday morning, 29 April, in Bethlehem, Israeli forces assassinated two people and demolished a home, bringing tanks into the city streets for the first time in a while. Later that day in Gaza, another target assassination was carried out using an Apache helicopter, killing one person in a car and a bystander. Within four hours of the "Road Map" release, a suicide bombing in Tel Aviv killed three Israelis. Over the next days, another four suicide bombs led many to question whether the "Road Map" had any chance of success. The new Palestinian prime minister went to work negotiating with various Palestinian groups concerning an end to suicide bombs.

Messages for Americans

*T*he entire world was shocked on September 11 when a group of al-Qaeda terrorists hijacked four domestic passenger planes to attack New York's World Trade Center and the Pentagon in Washington D.C., killing thousands. Palestinians were likewise stunned and, for the most part, expressed concern to a wounded America. Yasser Arafat donated blood and made public remarks of condolence and support. A group of Muslim teenagers held a candlelight vigil outside the U.S. Consulate in East Jerusalem. One American church worker visited the West Jerusalem American Consulate to discover that fax machines and computers had been running non-stop with messages from concerned Palestinians that had accumulated to a stack several feet high. Nevertheless, the single image portrayed by U.S. media was a scene of Palestinians celebrating over American loss.

In subsequent weeks and months, there would be dual efforts to understand the issue of American innocence and to link the Palestinian resistance to Israeli occupation with al-Qaeda attacks on America. From her perspective as an American living in the West Bank, Alison provides a unique reflection on issues confronting all Americans.

12 September 2001 • Wednesday

As we stood transfixed in front of the television yesterday, watching the breaking news (about 5 p.m. local time), Nadine was busy coloring. As we gripped our knuckles, gasping in disbelief, she handed me what she had drawn. At a single glance, I could see she had absorbed the magnitude of what had happened without anyone saying a word. The picture was streaked with orange and red. Flames zigzagged off the tops and sides of two tall buildings, the peaked roofs tilting off at an angle, stick people tumbling down. Fire everywhere. In the sky above the buildings, Nadine transposed her own experience of cataclysm in an effort to understand the role of the airplanes in the disaster. For her, the hijacked airplane was transformed into a helicopter firing missiles down at the buildings and people.

All day long at work today and on the walk home, people were coming up to ask if I had relatives in the New York area. "We are so sorry for those people." People would look at me and shake their heads. "We don't know what to say. We don't have the words for this." This from people who have been living under military siege for the past year. I was reminded of the villagers I lived with in Senegal, explaining to me their reason for observing Ramadan: "So we can appreciate the suffering of those who are hungry and go without." Even though they themselves lived in straw huts and were impoverished beyond words. It is this generosity of spirit that I have come to know here in Palestine.

For those of you who saw the stills and footage of Palestinians passing out sweets and celebrating, I say that for every one who did that, there were hundreds more who reacted with stunned shock and sorrow. Never mind the many Palestinians living in NYC, even recently returning to the U.S. to escape the shelling and closures of the West Bank. In fact, this confirms the dismal conclusion that most Palestinians had already come to over the past year: "Nowhere and no one is safe." And as one Palestinian acquaintance very wisely observed, "What happened to you yesterday is what we have been going through for 50 years, only in very slow motion. Believe me, we know how it feels."

Of course, many Israelis and Americans are exaggerating the images of celebration in the West Bank and using the occasion to indulge prejudices of their own. A bumper sticker has recently been seen around Jerusalem which says, "No Arabs = No Terror." At the risk of seeming as if I in any way condone or justify this, which I DO NOT, I feel obliged to consider the uncomfortable parallels. It can't be denied that many Americans, whether or not they are even consciously aware of it, would be inclined to agree with that bumper sticker, and American policy certainly leans in that direction. Americans must come to terms with this, as Israelis must. These things do not happen in isolation. Today I heard many different theories for why such a horrendous event should happen precisely when and where it did.

"Durban. They turned their backs on the whole world when they walked out."

"They always side with Israel against us, they give them weapons to kill us."

"They hate Muslims. Their politics, their culture, is saturated with it."

"Iraq. Look at what they did to the innocent people there."

"They start accusing us without even knowing. Look at Oklahoma City."

It needs to be kept in mind that Palestinians have over 50 years of first-hand experience with the American double standard that brands their acts of resistance as "terror" while justifying Israeli acts of aggression as "retaliation" or "self-defense." For a year we have been crying at the tops of our lungs that this infuriating double standard does not promote American interests. Indeed, it does not promote anything except hatred and division. Yesterday's horrific tragedy gives us the best proof of this that we will ever have.

Later on Tuesday night, the girls went to sleep to the sound of gunfire and exploding shells. As I was about to turn out the light, Nadine said she was afraid of having a bad dream. "Why should you have a bad dream, sweetie?"

"Because everywhere feels scary."

Ten Palestinians were shot to death on Tuesday, including a little girl. Innocent people everywhere suffer and die as a result of man's cruelty and indifference to their fellow man. If only Tuesday's dreadful event could succeed in convincing us all of this simple fact, I would not declare it a total disaster.

25 September 2001

I must get this out of my system: From Operation Desert Storm to Operation Infinite Justice

The attacks in the United States on the 11th quickly deteriorated into an issue of who occupies the high moral ground, because this issue will not only determine what response, if any, can be considered truly appropriate, but more importantly, who will be invited to join in the response and who, by virtue of exclusion, will stand to face the wrath of this so-called "infinite justice." Those of us in Palestine, at least, were not surprised at the haste of the transition. We are well-acquainted with the familiar phenomenon of how, within hours of mercilessly shelling or strafing some West Bank village or other, Israel can be instantly and miraculously transformed (by a bombing or shooting directed at them rather than perpetrated by them) into "the poor defenseless victim" whose "terrorist" tormentors deserve (and invariably receive) immediate universal condemnation and punishment. However, the sheer incongruity of the term "victim" from the perspective of those who have been on the receiving end of the shelling or strafing is seldom acknowledged, much less considered within any sort of legitimate context. Funny how that works.

Having spent the last two weeks brooding about the "celebrating Palestinians," I finally realize that the issue is not about confirming or denying the existence or authenticity of these incidents. I don't doubt that isolated incidents did take place here. I don't doubt that isolated incidents took place all over the world (and I am by no means restricting myself to the Muslim world) and that, within the context of real life and *Realpolitik*, they could at the very least be understood, if not condoned. The real issue is how these images (whether they are recent or 10 years old, whether they were spontaneous or bought and paid for) were used—maliciously manipulated is the phrase I want—to establish moral superiority and a clear distinction between who is "us" ("the forces of good") and who is "them" ("the forces of evil").

When I first got married in 1991 (the year of Operation Desert Storm), the first Intifada was beginning to wind down and the most prevalent phenomenon seemed to be that of "collaborator killings," the brutal killing of Palestinians by fellow Palestinians for their suspected collaboration with Israel. I can clearly recall the great number of graphic and blood-curdling images appearing on the front pages of the Hebrew dailies, always accompanied by commentaries wondering why they (the Israelis) should be agonizing over their "alleged" abuses of Palestinian civil and human rights when it was clear (look at the photo!) that people who were capable of such primitive and animalistic acts toward their own people did not deserve any better. After a while, however, I began to wonder about the conspicuous number and nature of these highly candid images. How is it that these cameramen managed, time after time, to be so precisely in the right place at the right moment? That thought might not have occurred to me were it not for the fact that Israel clearly took such exquisite advantage of the opportunity these images presented to justify their own moral position. As far as they were concerned, these photographs made it as clear as it needed to be who the "good guys" were and who the "bad guys" were. Later, the Israeli human rights group B'tselem issued a thoroughly documented report accusing Israeli undercover units of being guilty of up to one third of these so-called "collaborator killings." Click. Question: If reality is on your side, why manipulate it?

Please note that my point here is not to deny or justify the two out of three, if indeed that is an accurate figure. As far as I'm concerned, the numbers don't even matter. What mattered in this particular instance was the revelation that information can be manufactured or manipulated, revealed or concealed in a selective manner, juxtaposed or framed to artificially illustrate moral distinctions which in reality simply do not exist. When both Palestinians and Israelis are doing the killing, all talk of "moral distinctions" becomes not merely silly, but hypocritical and self-righteous. And when Israelis are doing the killing dressed as Palestinians with the deliberate intention of manipulating public conclusions, what we end with is nothing less than a total cynical and malicious corruption of the very concepts that were supposed to be the standards of the discourse.

Which brings us back to the "celebrating Palestinians." I no longer consider the authenticity of those images the point. After weeks I have pretty much come to the conclusion that Palestinians should not really be apologetic for what Americans do or do not think about them, after all this time. And I have become somewhat impatient with those who consider all of them or some of them or a few or even a handful as "bad," "immoral," "inhuman," or any of the many other labels that have been so freely and generously applied over the last two weeks. Because unless you have been under siege for a year, you frankly are in no position to judge what constitutes "appropriate" from the perspective of those who have. In fact, the more I think of it, the more I think it should be considered a miracle that the majority of these people feel anything other than blind rage and resentment with the country that has been directly and indirectly responsible for their endless misery. And yet most of them did, but guess what? No one took any particular notice because the damage had already been done. The media made sure of that.

If Palestinians—after everything they have been through—have finally managed to show up on the screens of America's emotional radar, then it is as much a reflection on Americans as Palestinians. Americans have, as a nation, steadfastly refused to acknowledge the common humanity of Palestinians for years, for decades, despite the wealth of images and words which confirmed it beyond question (as if such a thing needs confirmation). For years their suffering did not even register on the American scale of emotions, it did not even qualify for so complicated a response as "happiness" or "satisfaction." For most, it was routinely and repeatedly dismissed with the blink of an eye, the rustled turning of the page to the next article, the click of the remote to another channel. What essentially is the moral distinction between "happiness," "satisfaction," and "indifference"? Because in the end the result is the same: abstraction of pain and dehumanization of suffering. And a great many more Americans are guilty of this to a much greater degree than Palestinians ever were.

However, the real point about these images is how they were so obscenely juxtaposed, to the exclusion of all other possible images, with the fresh coverage of the attacks in the atmosphere of acute vulnerability and pain which characterized the immediate 48 hours that followed, to deliberately manipulate public conclusions about the nature of who the "good guys" are and who the "bad guys" are. Had they been shown as one Palestinian response of many, or as one "celebration" of many around the world, or as the concluding image from 50 years' worth of images depicting the reality of Palestinian experience under occupation, then the overall interpretation would, as we all know, have been vastly different. This is the real point. In a way, I consider the cheap opportunism of this "media triumph" to be the ugliest, the most violent, and the most dehumanizing act ever committed against the Palestinians. Or just another blip on the screen, depending on your perspective.

Two weeks after the attacks, American rhetoric only has room for two perspectives, "the forces of Light" versus "the forces of Darkness," the "good guys" versus the "bad guys," "us" versus "them." But I reckon that the sooner "the forces of Light" dispose of such absolute terms as "goodness," "morality," and "innocence," the better. Because they risk being measured by their own sanctimonious yardsticks and winding up down in the mud with the rest of "humanity." And it's ugly down here.

24 October 2001

In our state of enforced inactivity, we have been sitting here for six straight days watching the same things again and again, simultaneously exhilarated and horrified by the events seizing the area. Every few hours, we get the Arabic newscasts from Al-Jezeera (in Qatar) plus local news footage from the Bethlehem station Al-Mahed. Bulletins are flashed up at the bottom of the screen every half hour or so on a quiet day, much more frequently as the situation intensifies (and I finally have the proper motivation to progress with my reading!). And in between the news updates, they play classic Palestinian liberation songs accompanied by scenes of the Occupation from 1948 to one hour ago. It is one long unbroken narrative of injustice and human suffering rolling on and on without end, just like the real thing. The songs are all rousingly familiar: Marcel Khalifeh's "I Call You (to be Steadfast)"; Fairouz's mournful rendition of "Jerusalem (How Long Will You Weep?)"; "Arabian Dream", a group effort of popular Arabic singers in the style of "We Are The World"; and Phoebe's favorite, Julia Boutrous's "Our Arab Brothers, Where Are They?".

Occasionally we switch over to the Israel channels, but it is sickening to watch. Either they are lying outright about the situation here, or they are trumpeting their self-righteous rhetoric ("If Yasser Arafat cannot bring order to his house, then we have no choice but to do so"), or they are confiscating American rhetoric about Afghanistan for their own purposes ("We are not against the Palestinian people"). That is, when they even bother to interrupt regular programming. I literally cannot stand to watch.

And so we sit and watch the same scenes repeated dozens of times each day. A military jeep plowing into the body of a stone thrower. A boy of maybe fourteen shinnying up a pole to pull down an Israeli flag. A concrete block house being demolished by an army bulldozer. A young couple holding their screaming children and crying themselves, against the background of their destroyed home. Mohammed Al-Dura being shielded in the crook of his father's arm. The same boy, his dead body draped with a Palestinian flag and being borne aloft through a crowd of thousands of raised fists. A soldier roughly gripping a boy of perhaps ten by the shoulder and suddenly whacking him across the back of the head with a stick. A soldier savagely shoving a woman in a head scarf and knocking her to the ground. A hazy shot of five or six soldiers surrounding a man on the ground and holding his arm out straight while one of them takes a massive rock and slams it repeatedly against the man's elbow. A crying man being forcibly pulled off the dead body of his teenage son. A dead three-month old baby girl, her perfect little mouth slightly open. The camera pans out and the gaping wound in her abdomen comes into view. A solitary boy heaving a stone at a tank, its turret pointed at him (he was shot dead the next day). A soldier shoving a man with a bloodied face against another soldier, as the man holds his hands out in a pleading gesture and the second soldier grabs the man by the hair and rams his head into the metal door behind them. Soldiers firing. Missiles hitting the Kassassfiyeh building in Beit Jala. Funeral after funeral. Women crying. Men crying. Soldiers dragging a dead body roughly along the ground. Police clubbing people with sticks. Helicopters launching missiles mid-air. A soldier screaming into the face of a woman, his nose five centimeters from hers. Sharon in sunglasses at Al-Aqsa, surrounded by police in riot gear. Women in mourning, their faces streaming with tears and holding up the V sign. A man tearing his hair at the sight of his son's body. A group of soldiers surrounding a man on the ground, kicking him in a vicious frenzy. An old woman in a head wrap, throwing a stone. A small boy on a respirator, his forehead obscured by a bloody bandage and his mouth slack. A little girl lying on a hospital bed with a black patch over her eye. A woman gently wiping tears from an old man's face. The view from behind the shoulder of a soldier as he fires on and hits a stone thrower. Demonstration after demonstration. Stone after stone. Young boys collapsing in clouds of tear gas. A crying woman holding a crying baby and a photo of her newly martyred husband.

Ironically, the bulletins and newscasts are substantially the same as the scenes from 50 years ago, and 30 years ago, and three years ago. In other words, nothing has changed for these people. Imagine the sense of utter hopelessness arising out of that. I keep thinking, if Americans could just see these scenes, surely they would begin to understand. Surely they would begin finally to see just how misled they have been. I think to myself that I would force them to watch, that no matter how difficult I would not allow them to turn away. Because as hard as these scenes are to watch (even after seeing them hundreds of times), watching them is nothing compared to living them, and this is what needs to be understood. And once

Americans really begin to understand, then real change will finally become possible.

But watching and listening to America these days, I have come to the chilling realization that we are farther away than ever from being understood. Israel's spin campaign has successfully tapped into the similarities between America's destructive crusade against Afghanistan and Israel's relentless drive to crush the collective Palestinian will to be free.

There are differences, of course, and the dynamic between the U.S. and Afghanistan ultimately cannot be compared to the day-to-day brutality of Israel's fifty-plus-year-long occupation and dispossession of the Palestinians. But Israel knows that America cannot condemn Israeli slaughter and destruction in Palestine without drawing parallel criticism of its own "campaign against terrorism," and they are not about to become self-critical at this stage. In fact, their behavior has been nothing if not sickeningly reminiscent of Israel in response to this or that suicide bombing. They have reflexively resorted to military strength despite indications testifying to its futility and counter-productivity, and without even demonstrating compelling evidence for who "the enemy" is. They have developed a lexicon that invests their retaliation with archetypal qualities of goodness, righteousness, and chosenness while resorting to every conceivable strategy to demonize and dehumanize that "enemy." Their citizens have become ridiculously patriotic and intolerant of criticism or self-reflection even in its mildest forms. They have expressed willingness to compromise the civil rights of some groups in order to protect the security of other groups. They have gone deeply into denial regarding obvious facts of their own historical role in creating the context within which the hostility against them was crystallized. Their politicians, and especially their journalists, have reverted to a form of rhetoric whose ultimate objective is the appearance of a uniform and unified display of support, in which all perceived expressions of opposition fade into oblivion.

I am beginning to realize with nauseating finality that ordinary American decency and honesty will never come to our rescue, and the sooner we abandon this foolish hope, the better. Perhaps America and Israel are indeed soul mates, though this does not, as Israel imagines, elevate them to the lofty moral heights of the USA. Rather it lowers the U.S. down into the gutter with Israel. And this is a thought—moral equivalence with Ariel Sharon—that should give Americans great pause. Either way, we are screwed. True, there is no South Lebanese Army now to do Israel's dirty work, as in 1982 at Sabra and Shatilla. But with cunning, a good dose of spin, and the help of American naïveté and self-absorption, they will find a way. And afterward will be too late for "now we understand."

*O*ver the previous year, there were numerous calls for both sides to return to the peace table. Ariel Sharon had a consistent response. There must be seven full days without violence before talks can resume. The focus of diplomatic efforts was thus on a cease fire. With violence begetting violence this became an almost impossible task. December and January provided a unique opportunity for progress toward the resumption of negotiations. Over a period of three and a half weeks beginning December 13, there was only a single Israeli death. Much of this was due to Yasser Arafat's appeal on December 16 to end all the violence. Three days later, Hamas and other militant Palestinian factions agreed not to strike against Israel within its pre-1967 borders. In that same period, however, there were thirty-one Palestinian deaths at the hands of the Israeli army, most of them unarmed civilians, including eleven children.

The situation was so hopeful to the United States that Anthony Zinni was sent back to the region on January 3 to seek a resumption of peace talks. However, that same day Israel seized in international waters the ship Karine-A carrying 50 tons of weapons. Ariel Sharon responded by blaming Yasser Arafat and by suspending relations with the Palestinian Authority. One week later the Israeli army destroyed 58 homes in Rafah refugee camp leaving 700 homeless.

17 January 2002

Where to begin? Events pile up so fast here that a few days can seem like a month or more elsewhere. In three weeks, total lunacy can descend, and that is exactly what happened during my self-imposed absence from the news over the Christmas/New Year break. I had barely had a chance on Monday to start sifting through the numerous awful—some of them truly blood-curdling—reports of what has transpired here (particularly in Gaza) since 22 December and begin making sense of them within the framework of some sort of commentary, when it began spinning out of control yet again. Just like that. An assassination followed by an ambush followed by two drive-by shootings.

On Tuesday evening, as I sat on this couch still struggling to understand the sadistic torture and murder of the three teenage boys in Gaza in December, word came that an Israeli had been killed—where else?—in Beit Sahour. Just up the street. A 72-year-old man with a bad leg, who apparently had lived near the Beit Jala checkpoint for many years and often did his errands—fixing the car, buying vegetables, socializing—in Bethlehem. Seventy-two years old. Why? Was there a reason, beyond killing for the sake of killing? I wondered the same thing about the three boys in Gaza. Just 15, 16, and 17. Young kids. Why? Their bodies were mutilated beyond description by someone possessed by unspeakable hatred and cruelty. Why? Why? Why?

The violence has gone way beyond logic or justification or ideology or rhetoric. It has entered the realm of the truly obscene. It is entirely visceral and utterly sickening. What has to happen for it to stop?

Don't we have enough sorrow and misery and ugliness in our lives, just navigating the random events that assault us from every direction? Aren't we at the mercy of enough nastiness within the course of our natural lives, and do we not suffer enough without having to inflict additional meanness on each other just for the sake of inflicting meanness?

"All-out war" was a phrase repeated countless times on the Hebrew news programs of the last week, which just goes to show the vast disparity between their experience and ours. Are they only just arriving at this point? We knew a year ago that this was "all-out war," regardless of whatever euphemistic term they chose to apply, for what else could it be called when people are dying on a daily basis and tank shells and Apache missiles are being fired at houses? In truth, their experience is still not a quarter of what ours has been and continues to be. Even bare statistics can attest to that. How many deaths have they mourned over the last sixteen months? How many children? How many are permanently disabled? How many families have been made homeless by tank shells or bulldozers, or anything else for that matter? How many have been forced to survive on next to nothing, deprived of their land, their livelihood, their most basic right to feed themselves? How many are physically prevented from getting to work or school or, God forbid, from getting to a hospital? How many are being tortured or detained indefinitely? How many have been assassinated (for those of you who do not know the precise numbers, the ratio is one to eighty-two, not including the assassinations over the past week, of which I have lost count)? There is just no comparison between experiences. None.

Whatever can be said about Israeli suffering is four times as true for Palestinians, five times as true, ten times. And if the Hadera shooting, or Sbarro, or the Dolphinarium gives testimony to Palestinian cruelty and barbarity, to their murderous intentions and subhuman lack of compassion and sensitivity, then Israel's acts speak volumes. Ask yourself how a soldier could aim down his sights at a twelve-year-old rock thrower and pull the trigger. Ask yourself how they could bulldoze not one home, not dozens, but hundreds. Ask yourself how they could torture and mutilate three teenagers, how they could refuse passage to a woman in labor. The fact that they can get away with it should be beside the point, for morality is an internal mechanism. But two weeks ago, Israel's Defense Minister declared that they would suspend house demolitions, not because it is a thoroughly evil practice, but because of the bad press. How cynical can you get? (In any case, the practice was resumed the same day in East Jerusalem.) This is all the proof we need that they will not do the right thing unless forced to do it. It will not happen without pressure from outside. Come on, folks, wake up!

With all this in mind, it is simply not logical to dump all the responsibility on Arafat for the despicable state in which we now find ourselves, and it makes even less sense now that he has been placed under house arrest in Ramallah, surrounded by tanks on all sides. It should never, ever have been allowed to get this far, and I can think of many people to blame for the fact that it did, but Arafat is not one of them. I am no particular fan of his, but from our perspective it is obvious who the real aggressor is, with or without legal proceedings at the Hague (and Sharon is apparently so nervous about the outcome that he has threatened to suspend diplomatic ties with Belgium rather than trusting the legal procedure to exonerate him. What does that tell you?) Word from the latest bulletin is that he just fingered the Lebanese Phalangist officer who was scheduled to testify against him in Belgium.

I can't decide what disgusts me more, Sharon's self-righteous routine of feigned innocence and restraint or the Bush administration's gullible willingness to swallow it whole. The deliberate linguistic manipulations and misrepresentations of the Palestinian perspective in the U.S. press or the deliberate and systematic omissions of any face, name, detail, relationship, or experience that would accord them some reality or dignity or simple human substance. Where are the stories of the twice-homeless in Rafah? Where are the parents of the three mutilated boys? Could it be that the media is all too aware of how these stories would shift public opinion? It might even render comprehensible the suicide bombings and shooting attacks, the shipments of arms and the stubborn refusal against all odds to surrender on bended knees. And we wouldn't want that.

So, it's finally "all-out war." In that case, spare us the expressions of outrage and indignation at every Israeli death. That's what war is. They kill us, we kill them. Sharon asked for it. Now, it seems, he's going to get it. And the rest of the world, as usual, will just stand around and watch.

20 February 2002

When I was younger, I would sometimes become gripped with some trivial obsession like ice hockey or drama or some movie or book, and I would pester people with it until it became an embarrassment for both them and me. Lately, I confess that I often feel guilty about what I write (updates) and send (forwards), especially when they are received with deafening silence. I ask myself why anyone else should care about any of this, and if I would care if I lived there instead of here. I wonder if I have lost my perspective. Every place, after all, has its own problems and every person his own concerns. Is it selfish of me to presume that my concerns take precedence over others? Am I just imposing my own private obsession on people who can't be reasonably expected to share it? Am I burdening others with my anger? Sometimes I worry that I am. Would I care that much if I didn't live here? Sometimes I worry that I would not.

At times I feel like I am being devoured bit by bit. Or suffocated slowly. Buried alive by all this. Right now I feel more exhausted than I ever have, and I wish like hell I could walk away from it, just for one day. I wish that for me it meant nothing more than a couple of lines in the "international" section of the paper. I wish I could just turn the page and move on to something that interests me more. Movies. Travel. The crossword. Anything.

Then I walk to work.

Every morning I walk down the narrow alleyway connecting Manger Square with Star Street. It is now so heavily plastered with posters of local "Intifada martyrs" that it is like a gauntlet of death. Ironically, all the posters are of smiling faces, images carefully chosen to memorialize these people as their happier selves, before the Occupation killed them. Whereas the faces of the living people among whom I walk reflect only terrible hardship, fear, and exhaustion. Between the dead and the living, there is nowhere to look, no turning away. And I admit that one part of me wants others to have this same sense of being unable to turn away.

Not long ago I saw a photo in the paper of Germans being forced (by Americans no less) to parade past the mass graves of Jews murdered in the concentration camps of World War II. In a way, I feel that Americans should now be forced to do the same thing. Especially after September 11. No American should be able to utter the words "Why do they hate us?" until they have paraded past the scenes of Iraq and Lebanon, Vietnam and Cambodia, Guatemala and El Salvador, and been forced to see and smell and hear and touch the suffering that has been perpetrated there on their behalf.

I forgot to mention Palestine. I know that Palestine is only one of many places experiencing suffering and injustice. And I hope that Americans in all those other places are disturbing the comfort and complacency of their friends back home with updates and forwards of their own. Perhaps they sometimes feel burdensome, as I sometimes do. But then I think of all the people we know here, enduring in silence, powerless to change their fate. Powerless to walk away. Voiceless. I think of how Mathilda expressed the thoughts and fears of so many kids just like herself, who are never even asked how it has been for them to live through this past year. The ones who lived through it, that is.

Then I begin to feel the opposite. I feel guilty for not writing more, not sending more. I know that, however uncomfortable I feel, I am in a unique position and I have a moral responsibility to speak about what it is my privilege to see and experience. It is often exhausting and occasionally demoralizing to have to be so continuously vigilant. But walking away at this point is just not an option and neither is keeping quiet.

Intellectually, I am striving to cultivate the same attitude that I feel all Palestinians should exhibit, that is, completely unapologetic and in-your-face.

Simply, they are and continue to be victims of Christian Western conceit. Europe and America deliberately sacrificed them on the altar of history in order to exonerate themselves for the Holocaust, an event which had nothing whatsoever to do with them. And out-of-the-way Palestine was ideal, because it allowed the West to support Zionism without actually having to live next door to Jews. Israelis could vent the aggression which resulted from their collective trauma on the local population with minimal publicity or interference, but they'll never heal unless they move beyond this. And they'll never move beyond this unless there is healing. But now the most convenient thing for everyone would be for Palestinians to just give in, shut up, and accept their "fate." This would save the West from having to admit the truth and accept responsibility for this 53-year-old tragedy.

Ultimately our comfort is always a relative thing, and always bought at the expense of others. Americans have been comfortable for too long, and Palestinians have been paying for too long.

So at the risk of seeming obsessive or obnoxious, I guess I will continue to write and send, not for myself but for my husband and my kids and everyone else for whom walking away is neither possible nor right. At least in my middle age I am obsessed with something worthwhile.

12 March 2002 • Tuesday

The atmosphere in the town is a palpable mix of exhaustion and dread in equal parts. People are exhausted from being besieged, and they dread the fact that it is not over and that we have probably not seen the worst. They are exhausted by all the senseless death and all the horrible destruction, and they dread the more senseless and more horrible death and destruction still to come, as we know it will. They are exhausted from wondering where the income will come from for the next month and they dread not even having enough to get them from day to day. It is exhausting to read and hear and see the continuous news updates of what is taking place, and yet we dread not knowing what is happening and where this is leading, though we already know that as well.

If Zinni had done his job properly the last time he was here, all these people would not be dead. And if Sharon had abided by any one of the numerous cease-fires announced within the last six months, all these people would not be dead. And if the U.S. government had had an ounce of backbone and withdrawn its support for this filthy occupation, all these people

would not be dead. Now George Bush wants Zinni to come?
Now, after it has already gone on weeks and months and years
and decades longer than it should have? And will he have
something more creative to say than "Arafat needs to reign in
the violence"? If not then he shouldn't bother wasting our time.
We are much too busy being exterminated. What can be said
that hasn't already been said hundreds of thousands of times?
What more evidence is needed that all the guns and tanks and
Apaches and F-16s in the world will not solve this situation?

There is only one weapon capable of effectively opposing
the Palestinians cause for freedom. Justice. There can only be
one outcome for all this siege and destruction, all this murder
and humiliation, all this bloody mayhem and wretched suffering. Justice. They haven't endured all this just to fall on their
knees now, and Sharon is sorely mistaken if he thinks this
"heavy blow" will bring a solution. The only solution is justice.
The only solution is justice.

19 March 2002

There is a fragment of a poem by Yeats that is beating a
drum in my head:

> Turning and turning in the widening gyre
> The falconer cannot hear the falcon
> The best lack all conviction,
> While the worst are full of passionate intensity . . .

And now the real fear and disgust sink in as we wander
around town for the first time surveying the devastation and
gathering all the bloody details of what went on. As we down-
load our mail and read the horrific accounts from the other
towns and villages. As we listen to the lies churning in the
mouths of the killers (Sharon and Ben-Eliezer) and their collaborators (Cheney and Zinni). As we contemplate the next
invasion and the world's response—lack of response, I mean—
to it. Now we realize that Sharon will be permitted to get away
with all of it and that, in the end, no one will care very much.
We are on our own. In seven months, we have been invaded

three times. And each time has been more brutal than the time before. Each time the destruction has been more appalling, and each time the behavior of the soldiers more atrocious.

We have exhausted ourselves writing, continuing to labor under the tragic delusion that "if people really knew what was happening . . ." They know. It has all been spelled out. What part of "slaughtering innocent civilians" is unclear? What part of "60% unemployment" needs clarification? What part of "F-16 strikes in downtown Bethlehem" needs to be defined?

No one even has to bother straining their intellectual faculties wondering whether Sharon is really guilty of having committed war crimes in 1982. All the proof we need is right here under our noses; it is taking place right here and right now in the technicolor present tense. How much more obvious does it have to get? And yet, time after time after time, the world has failed to intervene. Hand-wringing does not help the tens of dead medical personnel or the hundreds of orphaned children or the thousands of homeless families. The Palestinian "celebrations" in the wake of 9/11 were nothing compared to the exponential indifference we have been and continue to be confronted with. And now we finally know that nothing we say will make a difference. The hair stands up on the back of my neck as I contemplate what is in store for us. Don't delude yourselves. Sharon is not about to implement Tenet or Mitchell or UN Resolutions 338 or 242. He is not about to allow the Palestinians to live in freedom or dignity. He is not about to let them live, period. He is buying time until circumstances become conducive (American strikes on Iraq) for a full-scale campaign, a "final solution." Who is the falconer and who is the falcon?

As terrified as I am for these people—and my hand trembles as I write this—my anger for them is greater. Anger that their children's blood counts for nothing, that their cries fall on deaf ears, that their tears are deemed unworthy of compassion. The time has come to act, if they are to be saved. The time has come when the only thing silence counts for is complicity. The woman in Aida camp who was killed by soldiers in front of her husband and five children was killed by a sword with a double edge. One edge was cruelty. The other was indifference. Both cut just as deeply and kill just as surely.

17 September 2002

September is a month of gloomy occasions and grim anniversaries. For years we have learned to dread the advent of September because of the numerous Jewish High Holidays. For us, even during "the Oslo years," it always meant closures and a creative variety of "increased security measures" intended to restrict our freedom so Israelis could enjoy theirs. For George it always meant missed workdays and extra transit hassles, valid permits abruptly invalidated and abbreviated incomes. I can recall times when the entire month consisted of nothing but closures and the end-of-the-month paycheck was not even enough to pay the rent. If non-Christian Americans were forcibly prevented from going about their daily lives on days which commemorate Christian holidays, the Anti-Defamation League and the A.C.L.U. would have a field day. But here the issue is always justified, without a murmur of challenge, within the ubiquitous terms of "security."

Now of course, closure to the point of metaphorical, if not literal, suffocation is the stuff of daily life, as are military invasions, comprehensive sieges of entire urban and rural populations, tank attacks, and Apache assaults. Sharon must have wracked his sadistic brains to come up with something above and beyond what has become the standard routine. But in fact, there has been nothing out of the ordinary. So far. Nothing apart from the usual buildings bombed in the dead of night, the usual family homes demolished on flimsy pretexts, and an inexorable swelling of the statistics in the dead and wounded categories, while the rhetoric of imminent escalation and bloodlust (veiled as self-sacrificing heroism) mimics itself at home and abroad.

Last week we held our collective breath and suppressed amorphous feelings of anxiety and foreboding as the first anniversary of 9/11 came and went. Intelligence predictions were apocalyptic (in the U.S. a flood of low-level attacks was anticipated while in Israel the forecast was for a "showcase" attack to coincide with Rosh Hashanah), but the week was in fact intensely mundane, characterized in the press as "relatively quiet" which can be translated to mean no Israeli or American deaths. For Palestinians, of course, this was not the case, but what happened to them before 9/11 never counted for much, and what happens to them in the wake of 9/11 counts for even less.

I read and reread what I wrote this time last year, feeling furious all over again at the appalling injustice of that hideous phony "celebrating" footage, convinced more than ever that somehow, some way, it was a thoroughly calculated maneuver. After all, look at all the horrendous torment and misery that that footage was used to justify. Refugee camps across the West Bank and Gaza were targeted, Rafah was razed, Jenin was laid to waste, the Church of the Nativity was besieged, Arafat's compound was reduced to rubble, entire cities were held hostage for weeks on end. And the only meaningful response Americans could come up with (when they could be bothered at all) was, "We haven't forgotten that footage . . ." even though there is absolutely nothing, not one single word uttered, that indicates that the people in that five-second film were celebrating mass destruction as opposed to somebody's engagement. Never mind. Although I personally feel as though I will never recover from Jenin, for Palestinians it is just one more tragic event in an endlessly long history of gross suffering and injustice. And on that subject they display a much more dignified sense of perspective than Americans ever will.

As a matter of fact, there is another anniversary following closely on the heels of 9/11 of which I'm willing to bet very few Americans are even remotely aware. Today marks the commemorative date of the massacres at Sabra and Shatilla twenty years ago, where more than 1700 Palestinian refugees were brutally murdered under the watchful gaze and indirect supervision of Ariel Sharon, then Minister of Defense. After twenty years, this ugly wound still festers in the collective Palestinian consciousness (as the attempt to try Sharon at the Hague demonstrates), and the American administration's warm embrace of Sharon as a "good friend" and "a man of peace," in the context of all the atrocities he has committed against Palestinians during his long and bloody lifetime, amounts to an offense which, in a world governed by a single, fair standard, would be ten times worse than those five seconds of bogus celebrating. Never mind. The month's not over yet.

September 29 will mark the end of the second year of the second Intifada, a year of misery beyond description. Roughly 2000 Palestinians have been killed and this figure does not even begin to summarize the whole catalogue of crimes that have been perpetrated against Palestinians in the last twenty-four months. In fact, mere death is perhaps the least of them. Much more outrageous has been the prolonged torture of confinement, the slow starvation of closure, the deliberate targeting of children, the relentlessly systematic denial of movement and work and medical care and schooling—how many times must it be said? The American administration had countless opportunities over the last two years to do the right thing. And it failed again and again. For Palestinians, September commemorates this failure more than anything else.

I desperately wish I could say that it stops there. But beyond September 29, Palestinians face yet another potential catastrophe beside which even the savagery of Sabra and Shatilla and the Al-Aqsa Intifada could pale in comparison. As we stand and watch helplessly as an American attack on Iraq looms ever nearer, I feel a paralyzing sense of fear and help-lessness for myself and everyone around me. Given everything Sharon has gotten away with so far, it's not likely that he will refrain from seizing the opportunity to "cleanse" the landscape once and for all. My heart feels unbearably heavy as I imagine the horrors to come. What grim anniversaries will we mark in October and November? Those of us who are still alive to mark them, that is.

24 September 2002

Yesterday I received a twelve-page (and that was after I condensed it!) newsletter from a former "mommy friend" whose husband (employed by CRS) is currently assigned to Jakarta, Indonesia. I read it in a mood of perverse fascination, awe-struck by the sheer volume of recent activity and future plans it described. Is it normal to be so energetic, so positively engaged with your surroundings? She seems so thoroughly captivated with the spectacle of Far East Asia, as I imagine I would be. Once upon a time, I had plans to travel there, and the period during which I taught English to Vietnamese immigrants during college only intensified my curious desire to encounter those faraway cultures. Probably if our family were living in Jakarta, I'd be writing twelve-page newsletters too. She writes of familiar things—school schedules and swim meets and library books—but she also writes of tantalizingly exotic things. A bird market in Yogyakarta. A ride in a horse-drawn carriage (known as a *dalman*). A visit to a temple. And just to assure us that the post 9/11 insanity has penetrated to every corner of the inhabited world, she mentions the ubiquitous issues of "security" and "specific and credible threats" (Indonesia being an acknowledged "hot spot of Terrorism" according to the State Department).

In Palestine we plan very little and we do even less. Maybe I have been here too long. Or maybe what we have endured in the last two years is equivalent to a lifetime of nightmares according to any normal scale of experience. The concepts of community productions and friendship clubs and scout activities are pretty much alien to us, not because we don't need or want such things but because to plan anything here is to set yourself up for frustration and disappointment and serious existential despair. Look at the last two years. In the first year of Intifada, when we were bracing ourselves for tank-shelling every afternoon from three o'clock onwards, anything extracurricular was pretty much out of the question. We awoke literally shell-shocked, made our groggy ways to school and work, and slouched back home to hunker down for another night. Period. The girls couldn't even arrange so much as an afternoon of play at a classmate's house, and I can recall many occasions when we did try to make a plan—pizza at Balloon's, a trip to the library (our options even under normal circumstances are pretty restricted)—only to be reminded of how little our pitiful plans counted for in this larger scheme of unfolding historical drama.

During the second year, even the concept of a "daily routine," as it had been reduced for us down to its skeletal remains, was degraded even further. In fact, we learned that "routine" is a wholly meaningless term when you are prohibited from leaving the house for days at a time. Even when you are allowed to leave, it is not "routine" in any normal sense that you resume, but a primitive mode of survival procedure that is much easier to get into than to get out of. And that is where we find ourselves now. We plan little and we do even less. In fact, we have cultivated a primordial ability for stillness, both literally and figuratively, both collectively and individually. We do it for protection, to deflect attention from ourselves as targets in a landscape which is completely saturated with violence. And we do it to maintain some sort of center of balance, to avoid being psychically overwhelmed by the raging sea of events over which we have no control and which threatens every minute of every day to take us down.

I have come to the conclusion that it is nearly impossible to describe the psychological effect our experiences of the last two years have had, and I have more or less given up even trying. It's pretty much something that you have to live through in order to understand its subtle and utterly destructive impact on the human spirit. We have ended up trivializing the content of almost every word and phrase in our repeated attempts to describe what is basically indescribable, and finally we are left speechless.

I feel myself in the presence of great mystery now, mystery which in any case cannot be articulated. I'm not referring to Bush's agenda or Sharon's motivations, because there's nothing mysterious about those. For me, they are ridiculously transparent manifestations of their crude, selfish, greedy, arrogant, bloodthirsty, and obscene campaigns for power and revenge at any cost. No-brainers. And I do not feel exactly blessed at the prospect of being at the center of the firestorm when all of this finally begins to unravel. The dreadful sense of heaviness I wake up with and go to bed with each and every day is sometimes almost unbearable. I search the faces of the young college students I work with, the radiant faces of Mathilda and Nadine's classmates, and wonder why? Why exactly do they have to go through this? What is the purpose and meaning of their past and present and future suffering? And the fact that I don't know the answer makes me feel heavier still.

But I also somehow feel a great sense of privilege in being where I am, way beyond the realm of logic. It's a privilege to witness how people have maintained their sense of humanity and generosity and hope despite everything they have been through. It's a privilege to give a voice to those who are voiceless and defend those who are defenseless, which I have tried in my own small way to do. It's a privilege to have a clarified sense of perspective and priorities, even though it is out of the shadow of looming disaster that they have emerged. And finally, it is a great privilege, in some absolutely inexpressible way, to share the burden instead of turning away. I don't know why, but I know I am thankful. With fear and trembling, I am thankful.

20 December 2002 • Friday

I'd like to be able to write something noble and uplifting, something which captures the true spirit of Christmas and transcends all the ugliness we live with every minute of every day. If that's the kind of thing you want to read, I suggest you take a look at Bob May's Christmas message or perhaps Sandra Olewine's or Alex Awad's. I'd like to be able to express the kind of simple thankfulness that I expressed back in May. I'd like to be able to say that we have been taking advantage of our confinement, listening to Christmas carols (*O Little Town of Bethlehem*) and making Christmas crafts and spending quality time together. And I know that would make everyone feel a lot better, wouldn't it?

But I am not going to try to make any of this acceptable for one simple reason. It is not acceptable. The struggle that most people are going through just to get from one day to the next is not inspiring. It's not admirable or heroic or victorious. It's ugly and nasty and hideous and exhausting, a perfect reflection of what's being done to them. Of what is being allowed by all the self-righteous champions of freedom, democracy, and civilization. All you folks who want to be assured of the triumph of the human spirit so you can sit down to your Christmas dinner, look elsewhere. You're not going to hear it from me.

We have been invaded six times in the last fifteen months. This is day 152 of curfew since last October, over five months' worth of suffocating house arrest. In the last six months we have been under curfew more often than not. Apart from an almost overwhelming sense of fatigue and nausea, I don't even know how I feel about that. Does anyone know or care that the most recent suicide bomber did not even come from Bethlehem? He didn't even live in Bethlehem, merely nearby. Shouldn't this small but significant detail have some weight, considering the severity of the punishment? You are asking me to care more about those Israelis who were killed on 21 November than I care about my own family and colleagues and neighbors, and the fact is that I don't. Their deaths were tragic and needless, but not more so than the 152 days of our lives that have been tragically and needlessly stolen from us. I am starting to take it very personally.

The army has very thoughtfully maintained a lower profile this invasion, albeit mostly for its own benefit. It's easier to lie with a straight face when the evidence is not so shockingly to the contrary. Yes, this invasion is somewhat more polite than the last five. Choirboys are not being assassinated in the Nativity Church, compound and historical sites are not being besieged, unless you count the town of Bethlehem itself, and we no longer do, thank goodness for that. But even though the savagery is more subtle, it is savagery nonetheless. As usual, it is the most powerless, the most voiceless, the most impoverished who are bearing the greatest burden, and some of the footage coming out of the refugee camps over the last month has been breathtakingly barbaric. I have sat here on my couch and listened to testimonies from women that chilled my blood, women whose entire lives have been lived as refugees, whose pathetic homes have been vandalized beyond recognition, and whose every male relative over the age of fourteen has been taken into custody. Their experiences can only be described as appalling beyond belief. Will you pause in your Christmas shopping long enough to consider the enormity of their suffering and loss?

As Christmas approaches, it is clear that the Christian world would feel more, well, comfortable if the army would withdraw from Bethlehem. Most church leaders have managed to mutter that request and thus ascend to the heights of cynicism. Do they imagine that such a hollow gesture could make a scrap of real difference in the lives of the people here, where every other household lives in a state of occupation-induced poverty? And would a withdrawal from Bethlehem mean anything to the citizens of Jenin or Nablus or Hebron? This is not about anything as easy or superficial as Christmas celebrations, because even if they do withdraw—and they have made it clear they won't—no one here will be celebrating. But it would allow the armchair activists to breathe a little easier, wouldn't it? If the last two years have taught us anything, it has taught us that the gesture, the occasional solidarity demonstration or letter to the editor or twenty-bucks donation is sufficient unto itself as far as most people are concerned. Like aid to the Third World, it convinces us of our own fundamental decency and assuages our enlightened Western consciences, all the while leaving the mechanisms of oppression securely in place. And when people write to us from their comfortable living rooms to say that, even under such difficult conditions, our religious faith can still give us hope and joy, I know that they are in fact simply using their religious faith as an excuse to remain passive and continue justifying this situation which allows them their comfortable living rooms while perpetuating our "difficult conditions." So long as the comfortable living rooms are there and the "difficult conditions" are here, praise the Lord!

As far as I know, Jesus called us to be His arms and legs and mouth, not His backside. If He expects those who are suffering to endure it with grace, it is only because He also expects those who are not suffering to bear witness to those who are and to act, to "remember those in prison as if you were their fellow prisoners, and those who are mistreated as if you yourselves were suffering." Anything else is pure hypocrisy. And only hypocrisy on the most massive scale could have gotten us to where we are now.

I just finished watching the most obscene piece of footage I have seen this month. In it, a monstrous ugly green army bulldozer slowly and patiently knocked over a pathetic little concrete block chicken coop—with all the chickens still inside—while a dozen fully armed soldiers surrounded the area standing guard. From a rooftop across the street, the camera recorded this scene while the neighbor from whose rooftop the scene was being filmed tearfully commented. It was not her chicken coop being demolished and the situation did not affect her personally. But as I listened to the comments of this nameless woman whom CNN will never interview, I knew that she, more than all the Christian leaders and politicians and media champions put together, had the moral clarity to know that what she was seeing was wrong and to say so. Without consulting the *New York Times* or the New Testament, she, and all of us who are here witnessing all of this, know that that chicken coop is not a threat to the security of the State of Israel and that its demolition is nothing but an act of pure malice committed by bullies whose intention is simply to further demoralize and impoverish its already demoralized and impoverished owners. For me this one little scene neatly summarized the entire purpose and meaning of the last two years and my tears have never tasted so sad or so bitter as they do today.

Merry Christmas from Occupied Palestine.

On 16 March 2003, Rachel Corrie, a 23-year-old college student from Olympia, Washington was killed in Gaza while trying to prevent an Israeli bulldozer from demolishing a house. The number of houses demolished in recent years has been in the hundreds. As a member of the International Solidarity Movement (the previous year, members of ISM had entered the besieged compound of Yasser Arafat and brought aid to the besieged Church of the Nativity in Bethlehem), Rachel had been in Gaza for two months and had participated in other demonstrations to prevent the destruction of homes. A month earlier she had sent an email to her family reporting on a similar action. "The internationals stood in the path of the bulldozer and were physically pushed with the shovel backwards, taking shelter in a house," wrote Rachel. "The bulldozer then proceeded on its course, demolishing one side of the house with the internationals inside."

On this particular Sunday afternoon the home marked for destruction belonged to a well-respected physician. His only crime was that his home happened to be in the way of Israeli plans to clear an open area on the southern edge of Rafah. According to the numerous reports of the event, Rachel was standing in the path of the bulldozer as it advanced towards her. When the bulldozer refused to stop or turn aside she climbed up onto the mound of dirt and rubble wearing a bright orange jacket and shouting through a megaphone. The bulldozer continued to advance so that she was pulled under the pile of dirt and rubble. After she had disappeared from view the driver kept advancing until the bulldozer was completely on top of her. The driver did not lift the bulldozer blade and so she was crushed beneath it. Then the driver backed up—effectively running over her again. The seven other ISM activists taking part in the action rushed to dig out her body. An ambulance rushed her to Al-Najar Hospital where she died.

Rachel's father Craig Corrie told an AP reporter, "Rachel was filled with a love and sense of duty to our fellow man, wherever they lived, and she gave her life trying to protect those that could not protect themselves."

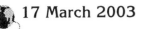 **17 March 2003**

Where does the Tragedy Lie?

Where does the tragedy of Rachel Corrie's death lie? Does it lie in the fact that she was American? No, because the life of an American is not more valuable and the death of an American is not more tragic.

Does it lie in the fact that she was only 23 years old? Not exactly. The lives of hundreds of children and young people have been cut short in Palestine over the last two years and the loss of each one is a tragedy. Rachel's death perhaps highlights their appalling vulnerability, but it is not any more or less heartbreaking because of that. To imagine the wrenching sense of anguish her parents must be feeling now is to imagine the inconsolable sorrow of parents throughout the Occupied West Bank and Gaza.

Does it lie in the fact that her death received unusual media exposure? No. In fact, the real tragedy is the faceless and nameless anonymity attributed to most Palestinian deaths.

Does it lie in the fact that she was resisting nonviolently? No, because the vast majority of Palestinians who have died were not engaging in resistance of any kind. They were simply trying to exist. Her terrible death under the treads of a bulldozer can perhaps be considered a kind of symbol for all the lives extinguished under the crushing weight of occupation.

Does it lie in the fact that the American administration refused to condemn her murder or the circumstances leading to it? No. The administration has only ever indicated a willingness to condemn the deaths of Israelis, Jewish Americans, and Americans living on the Israeli side. As far as I know, it has never condemned the killing of a single Palestinian since 29 September 2000. Rachel, though not Palestinian, was guilty by association and so her killing, by definition, fell into a category in which her guilt somehow contributed to her own "regrettable" death.

Does it lie in the courage she demonstrated? No. Palestine is full of courageous individuals confronting danger alone whose bravery is never acknowledged. In life they are dehumanized and in death they are "terrorists."

Does it lie in the pages of her beautifully articulated "Letter from Palestine"? Not really, because the beauty of that letter lies in her appreciation of the suffering of the people she came to stand with. Her focus was on them, not herself.

What was it about Rachel Corrie's death that was tragic? The tragedy is that individuals are obliged to come and make a stand for justice in Palestine because governments will not. The tragedy is that Rachel Corrie was left to face a bulldozer alone because her government, the most powerful government in the world, lacks the will to face the army whose orders killed her. The tragedy is that she did the right thing, and in both life and death, her own government chose not to defend her. She has put them all to shame.

Rachel, your convictions and your sacrifice have great meaning here in Palestine, and we are deeply thankful.

Israeli Friends

*P*eace is too often defined as an end to violence, hostility, and bloodshed. In the Middle East, the words for peace – Shalom and Salaam—mean much more than that. Peace is wholeness. It's based on relationships. It occurs when former enemies walk alongside each other as equals. It takes place when "the other" is valued as much as "the self." It blossoms when barriers of "us" and "them" are broken down.

The Nassar family for a long time has numbered Israelis among its friends and colleagues. Over the past two and a half years, there are countless stories of bridges burned and walls constructed that are a hindrance to the kind of relationships necessary for a true and lasting peace. Alison and family have managed to keep those friendships alive.

10 August 2001

My friend Jay called me week before last and told me he had reserve duty coming up, and he had been informed he would be in the Bethlehem area. Jay is an observant Jew (from Britain) who wears a kippa, and he's one of my very favorite people, not just here, but anywhere, a really nice guy (I worked with him at the Albright). Every time stuff gets bad here and I start getting into a "those %$#@* Israelis" mode, I think about Jay. Jay's girls Tal and Mirav have played on numerous occasions with our girls and are just about the same age and temperament. When the soldier got thrown out of the window of the police station in Ramallah last October, I reminded Mathilda and Nadine (who had brought home some "those %$#@* Israelis" comments from school) that that could have been Tal and Mirav's daddy, that it should not have happened and was a terrible thing, no matter what.

With Jay in mind, I read the excellent article from last Friday's *HaAretz* regarding the observant reserve duty soldier who was imprisoned for 13 days for refusing to serve in the Occupied Territories. Some of his remarks are definitely worth quoting extensively:

> My refusal to serve is the result of what I learned in Gaza and Tul Karm in the early 1990's. . . . It didn't come from theories; it came from what I saw. And after I saw what I did there, no one can tell me any stories. . . . I remember it as if it was this morning—tired, bleary-eyed Palestinians [like George] fixing you with a stare that is a mixture of panic, fear, and terrible hatred. People who are old enough to be your grandparents, who got out of bed at four in the morning, are standing there with their pitiful bundles; they're on their way to work in Israel; and the question of whether or not they will be allowed through hangs in the balance. . . . It all depends on who the commander is and how he got out of bed that morning, and whether or not he had already spoken to his girlfriend. . . This year, I asked myself: What am I doing there in the territories? And don't let them think they can tell me stories about how it is better that I, and not others who are less sensitive, am doing it.
>
> Sensitivity in this context is irrelevant: There is an occupier and an occupied; and we are there to maintain the occupation. . . . Rabbi Lichtenstein is my teacher and rabbi,

but when I read that he expects his students [to serve, but to do so in such a way that conveys an air of respect to the other side by] show[ing] smiling faces at a roadblock, I wonder where he is living - perhaps on Mars? What are we talking about here, about manners and good graces?

After all, the gross and real injustices aren't whether this or the other soldier smiles or doesn't. The real story is that there are people living there in the territories without any basic rights, and therefore, the smiling faces are irrelevant. . . . Over the past few months, we have somewhat forgotten that between every Tanzim and Hamas fighter, there are 10,000 peasants who have been closed off in their villages for a number of months now and can't bring home the bread, let alone the butter. They don't have water either—people literally on the brink of starvation. . . . And as for all those great men of authority and morals who say that my action was immoral, I wonder: When was the last time they went hungry? When last were they closed off in their villages? . . . Each time I come under a barrage of criticism, I . . . picture the images of the Palestinians and it bring[s] me back to my senses.

I almost wept when I read that. And the irony is that I should feel such profound gratitude, when the only thing he really is doing is acknowledging Palestinian humanity. That seems to be a lot to ask these days.

17 January 2002

Our friend Ornit Ilan was buried on January 6th. She died of cancer and has three boys, the youngest Nadine's age. Her funeral took place in the pouring rain, and George and I made the effort to attend because she was a nice decent person who had touched our lives in a number of meaningful ways. She liked George immensely and encouraged me to marry him. She was genuinely concerned for Nadine's medical saga and the emotional distress that it caused me. Countless times she welcomed us into their home for visits. We even house-sat for them. The fact that she was an Israeli Jew never entered into the relationship one way or another, except for the times when we needed to remind ourselves that, hey, that Jewish lady killed in the bus explosion could have been Ornit, that dead soldier could've been her husband David, the kid killed in the restaurant blast could've been one of theirs. These reminders always, thankfully, pull us back from the edge of insanity and inhumanity toward which we are constantly being drawn by this crazy, inhuman, killing place known as the Holy Land.

Ornit's death was tragic in its own way, certainly. Not a single day has passed since the funeral that I have not awakened thinking of her boys, her husband, her parents, their tremendous loss and profound grief. But at least it wasn't hatred or cruelty that killed her. It was sad and senseless enough without being gratuitously so.

Please, please, let it stop.

*N*ow under long-term curfew for the second time in 2002—beginning week five this time around—Alison still finds a way to stand in solidarity with Israeli friends.

17 July 2002

My sewing project of the last couple of weeks has been, ironically, my contribution to the Peace Quilt. The Peace Quilt is a group project involving Israelis and Palestinians, and the quilt itself, when it is complete, will be a series of interlocking hands, each embellished with some sort of Peace image. For my "hand," I am doing a mini version of the wall-hanging I finished last month, a Jerusalem cityscape in which a church, a mosque, and a synagogue are nestled alongside one another among other buildings, palm trees, steps, and arches. I like it as a Peace image because it doesn't make any falsely optimistic *We-Are-The-World* statements or assumptions. I think right now the most we can hope for is simple tolerance, mere acceptance of the Other's presence.

That's the Jerusalem I came to fifteen years ago, a vastly different place from what it is now. As a case in point, I have never actually been to a group meeting or met any of the participants. My guardian angel Kay Munayer brought my hand to Bethlehem, and she reports back to me about the meetings she attends. She said there have been meetings where the Palestinians complain viciously and the Israelis wonder out loud why they should sit there and listen to it. At least one of the women lost a child in a suicide bombing and others, though self-proclaimed lefties, manage to find ways to justify what is happening. Interestingly though, at the last meeting, Kay said it was the Israelis who ended up arguing with one another after one of them made a we-can't-go-on-living-like-this comment and another turned on her in a burst of impatience. "Like what?" And she proceeded to enumerate all of the things Israelis still have the freedom to do that Palestinians do not. I want to meet that woman. I need to meet her, because I have gotten to the point where I can't even listen to Hebrew being spoken on *Channel Two*.

Kay said there are women participating who belong to Gush Shalom, Yesh Guvul, Women in Black. Some do Checkpoint Watch and others have sons who have been imprisoned for refusing to serve in the Territories. So whenever I sit in my house under curfew and wonder why in hell I should bother contributing to the Peace Quilt, I remind myself that I am doing it for these women, whom I consider heroic. I hope I will one day have the privilege of meeting them. Now that International Solidarity volunteers are being either deported or turned back at the airport, and every major NGO and international aid organization has been intimidated into respectful silence, the Israeli Peace groups are our final hope.

I think of them and I pray for them and I wish for them, as I wish for myself and everyone I know, Peace.

31 July 2002 • Wednesday

Day Forty-Two of Curfew

Last Saturday Mathilda and Nadine were awake and dressed by 7:30 in the morning, sitting quietly on the couch with their hands primly folded in their laps, murmuring, "Is it 10:30 yet? Is it 10:30 yet?" You would have thought they were getting ready to board a plane to America. Or at the very least, going on an exciting trip to a beach, a pool, or an amusement park. In fact, they were heading off for a sleepover at the home of our Israeli friends, affectionately known around our house as "Sherry's gang": Sherry and Vernon; Debra and Daphna; Ariel, Efrat, and Eran; Art and Aviva.

The logistics of getting the girls from Beit Sahour to Sherry's moshav in Zafririm are not necessarily as straightforward as they should be. First of all, there are curfews. We had originally arranged for Friday, but the curfew lifting that had been announced for that day was abruptly cancelled and the girls were excruciatingly disappointed. So we tried again for Saturday, holding our breath for another arbitrary cancellation. How long 24 hours can be in the lives of expectant little girls. Saturday came and the lifting went according to schedule, nine to two. Sherry and I arranged to meet at 10:30 at the top of Beit Jala. This road used to lead out of Beit Jala toward the now-infamous tunnel road, which takes you north toward Jerusalem or south toward Hebron, depending on your destination. Now it doesn't lead anywhere, as the intersection is blocked off with a snarl of spiked barbed wire and a battalion of vertical concrete slabs. At 10:30 we drove up to the barrier, parked on "our" side, and unloaded all their stuff, including two bikes. There is an army base right there where the fence blocks the road, but no soldiers monitored the crossing. As we crossed on foot to the other side, plenty of other people crossed with us in full view of the camp. So much for "airtight" closures. Sherry's car promptly appeared, and we loaded the stuff and said goodbye. My throat closed up like I was sending them off to college. In two impossible years of Intifada, I have only been separated from them on one occasion, when George and I celebrated our ten-year anniversary with an overnight stay at Latrun Monastery last November. So I felt funny, though I knew without the slightest doubt that Sherry would take great care of them and they'd have a wonderful time.

"Now girls, remember that Sherry's family doesn't see things quite the way we do because their circumstances are different from ours. It's hard for them to understand exactly what we go through and it's hard for us to understand exactly what they go through. Don't stomp around saying 'Sharon this' and 'Sharon that.' They probably don't like Ariel Sharon any more than we do, but you have to remember that things are complicated. And if there's a bad attack—God forbid, but the chances are unfortunately very good after Gaza the other night—just try to see it through their eyes. Try to understand how scary it must be for Debra and Daphna. And while you're there, you can help Daphna with her Arabic."

On the previous afternoon, four Israeli settlers had been ambushed in their car near Hebron and shot to death. Friday night, every member of George's family including George himself called with warnings. Although Sherry's route would not take her anywhere near Hebron, she would have to travel along the settler highway bypassing the villages of Husan and Al-Khader before taking the turn up to Beit Jala.

"Don't let the girls go! It's too dangerous!" "Tell her to put a sign, 'Press,' 'TV,' 'Red Cross,' anything!" "Tell her to put a 'hatta' (a checked Palestinian scarf) on the dashboard!" In the end, I stuffed a scarf in the suitcase and told Sherry to use it at her own discretion. But the bitter irony of the situation was not lost on me. I would never have forgiven myself if something had happened to her on the way to picking up my girls. And I would never have survived if something had happened to them on the way back. I didn't want to admit it, but I let out an audible sigh of relief when she called to say they had arrived. They were safe.

All week long they have been calling, breathlessly describing their exciting adventures and assuring me that they're having a fantastic time (and being good). Tree houses, bike rides, videos, pizza, McDonalds, swimming, shopping. I'm so glad—so thankful—I could cry. When I think of how awful the year has been, and how lousy the summer was, all I can do is tell Sherry thank you, thank you, thank you. From the bottom of my heart, thank you. She and her family have given my girls a priceless gift: a week of normality. Never have I been so convinced as I have been this past week-a week of assassinations and settler ambushes, of one-ton bombs dropped in residential neighborhoods and suicide bombs at falafel stands— that our destinies are inextricably intertwined. That our futures are inseparable. That our graves will lie adjacent to one another if we don't do something fast.

The last thing we need are checkpoints or fences or walls or trenches. We don't need the punishment of separation. We need the punishment of inextricable togetherness. We need compulsory sleepovers. We need to be reminded every hour of every day that if I don't have peace, then you don't have peace, and if you don't have security, then I don't have security.

It's that simple. Israelis, would you send your precious children to sleep over in the miserable refugee camps, with motherless little girls in black ski caps? In the still and silent tank-patrolled towns? Palestinians, would you send your precious children down deathtrap roads, into the buses and falafel stands of downtown Jerusalem and Tel-Aviv? If kids, our and yours, walked hand in hand, what soldier would shoot? What bomber would bomb?

We must save each other from each other.

31 August 2002

At a time when most people are avoiding Jerusalem and Israel like the Black Plague, we received a miraculous offer to take a short vacation there and we accepted it without hesitation, for the sake of the girls if nothing else. Compared to the experience of living in Bethlehem over the last horrible year, Israel was a vacation for us in the truest sense of the word. We could move freely without giving thought to curfews, curfew liftings, and checkpoints. We could do what we wanted, when we wanted. We could be together as a family. And we even had the luxury of doing without news. But more than anything else, this vacation was a journey to the other side, and what we found there was transforming. Because the most insidious thing of all is the realization that the walls are going up within us just as surely as they are going up all around us and that, for the most part, we are unaware of the damage to our internal land-scapes, even though the external damage is so painfully obvi-ous and so hideously ugly. Each is a mirror reflection of the other, and together they are an appalling testament to the scourge laying waste to the land and everyone in it.

Toward the end of July, on a suffocatingly hot day (our third consecutive day of tank-enforced curfew in an invasion that would soon surpass the 40-day record set by the previous invasion), I was wondering whether to slash my wrists or blow my brains out when I received a phone call from my good friend Kay. She was calling to inform me that she and her husband Salim had decided ("You can't argue with me!") to pay for us to spend a week at the Scottish Hospice in Jerusalem. She was right, I couldn't argue, though I think I did sputter a bit out of sheer speechless gratitude. Refusing such a sanity-saving opportunity would have been like refusing the New Jersey hospital's all-expenses-paid offer in 1997 to perform the heart surgery that Nadine needed to survive. No thanks? No way. I hung up feeling deeply, inexpressibly thankful and, for the first time in six months, able to look forward to something besides checkpoints, tanks, and curfews. The mere thought that we would soon have a break gave me the sense of giddy optimism I needed to get through those last interminable weeks of summer. It was a feeling I had very nearly forgotten.

We left Bethlehem on Sunday the 11th of August, even though our reservations were technically for the 12th through the 19th. The curfew lifting that day, generously scheduled for 7:00 a.m. to 7:00 p.m., seemed like an auspicious sign for our departure, and in a world ruled by such sinister and unpredict-able forces, we perhaps could not help but regress to our primitive instincts, searching the heavens for favorable indica-tions in tacit acknowledgement of our own utter helplessness. In any case, we were afraid of the possibility that there would be no lifting at all the following day, and the thought that we might miss our chance was too awful to contemplate. We passed the dusty ruined Tantur checkpoint at precisely 1:09 p.m. with barely a second glance from the soldier, an older reserve officer who the girls immediately pronounced "very nice!" Not having been out of Bethlehem in more than six months (since before the March invasion) I can't accurately express how it felt to be driving down Hebron-Jerusalem Road toward the center of Jerusalem. Even the colors of the sky and trees seemed more vivid, a ridiculous hallucination for sure, born of a delirious sense of near-rapture. Like I said, prisons are as much a product of our minds as they are of any external circumstances, and we had just succeeded in busting out, in more ways than one. Sweet freedom.

And what about all the people we left behind, the ones who were not so fortunate? I'd like to say that they were in our thoughts the whole time. The first day Phoebe heard a sound similar to the nasal honk of a military jeep and she shrieked, "Mom, the soldiers are coming into the town! It's time for curfew!" Later that same evening, as we strolled across the Cinematheque overpass enjoying the sunset and the cool air, there was a moment (of which we had several more over the course of the week) in which we all stopped and looked at one another, realizing that this was the first time in many weeks in which strolling in the evening was even an option, and that meanwhile our friends and neighbors back in Bethlehem had, by that time, all been herded back inside their homes by tanks and jeeps. It was an intensely strange feeling, composed of equal measures of terrible relief and terrible guilt. But it was far more disturbing to realize just how easy it is in the end to walk away.

The week was perfectly mundane, and perfectly sacred. Isn't life really like that, when the future is eclipsed in menacing shadow? With our heightened awareness of the need to enjoy every minute, the time flew by. We knew that with the passage of each moment, we were being brought closer to our return to Bethlehem and to the ugly uncertainties looming on the political horizon in the fall. And yet there is a kind of grace which finally enables us to confront what is ahead and feel simple gratitude. Like the week of the sleepover, we did nothing but the most ordinary things. Walking around the Old City, swinging on the swings of the nearby parks, seeing a movie (*Lord of the Rings*), looking in the pet store at the mall, shopping in

Mahane Yehuda, spending a day at the Zova Fun Park, visiting old "mommy friends" whom we hadn't seen since the previous year. Jerusalem looks like a cursed city, empty of people and ringing with ambulance sirens, afflicted by the same doomed mentality that is oppressing the rest of the region. And yet, I felt genuine—and somewhat unexpected—compassion for the faces I saw there. I found myself constantly looking around and imagining us, my children, rocked by the sudden apocalypse of an explosion. And then I would recall all the people we knew, those imprisoned inside their houses and unsure of where the money would come from to get them and their families to the end of the month, and I felt haunted by a wrenching sense of defeat and despair. Although our fates seem to be manifesting themselves in different ways, they are fearfully symmetrical in their senselessness and tragedy. It is the senselessness of it, above all, that is most offensive because we know deep down that, if we just had the will, life would be so much better. For all of us.

It was the second week that afforded us a transcendent glimpse of what could be and which transformed my sense of despair into something like hope. On Monday, August 19th (the same day Ben-Eliezer announced the army withdrawal from Bethlehem, and absurdly, we read about it in the paper over breakfast just like everybody else!), we left Jerusalem for the Benedictine Monastery of Tabgha on the Sea of Galilee (the historic site of the miracle of the loaves and fishes), a three-and-a-half hour drive. The journey up the coast (we had elected not to take the Jordan Valley road because of the disproportionately high number of drive-by shootings that have recently occurred along there) was like a catalogue of the disasters of the past year, starting with Jerusalem, where so many terrible bombing incidents have taken place. On our way out of town we passed the tacky white Mt. Scopus sculpture, not far from which the most recent explosion at the Hebrew University cafeteria had killed and wounded many.

Rishon Lezion (the casino). Tel-Aviv (the Dolphinarium and others). Netanya (Passover and others). Hadera. Haifa. We passed Tul Karm and Qalqilya, both surpassing their 60th day of invasion and both experiencing killing curfews and breathtaking incidents of army brutality. How very shameful just to drive past such places, knowing what is taking place inside. In the distance we could see the cranes, used to erect the dreadful separation walls. On and on. Umm Al-Fahm. Megiddo junction. Afula junction. I could feel it all accumulating with sickening weight in the pit of my stomach, when suddenly, off to the right, I saw a sight which somehow seemed hauntingly familiar. A long level road lined with trees against a backdrop of hills. As we saw the sign indicating the turn-off to Jenin I had to pull over, because my sight was obscured by the memory of watching the Al-Jezeera coverage of the refrigerator trucks driving down that road in April to collect all the dead bodies (perhaps hundreds of them, otherwise why three trucks? In any case we will never know) that Israel would later deny ever existed. The image of those big white trucks and that tree-lined road was seared into my mind because of the horror of what had happened to the people there and the deep disillusionment I had felt in the wake of the cover-up. The worst is that it is still going on. Bethlehem was granted its freedom at the expense of all these other towns and villages, and to this day their nightmare has not ended. And here we were, on vacation, driving by.

How can I describe the small miracle that is Tabgha, especially in contrast to all the misery surrounding it? It is not just an oasis in the geographical sense, though it is without a doubt that. The church is a structure of simplistic beauty, where one can listen to the ethereal chants (in German) of the brothers five times a day. Through the center of the property runs a stream originating in the Golan Heights and emptying into the Sea of Galilee, and this stream has been captured to form a shallow elongated swimming pool, though the water continues to rush through the grates at either end. We shared the water with small fish, plenty of snails, and even a few crabs. The pool meanders under the trees and the fresh mountain water is blessedly cool and invigorating. Although we arrived after 6:00 p.m. that Monday night, we were able to swim in the dark, and it was not just therapeutic after such a long and agonizing drive, it was redemptive.

The following day, Mathilda made a swimming friend, a little girl nearly identical in age, appearance, and temperament who just happened to be Israeli. Her name was Ruth. By the end of the week, we were eating, drinking, cleaning up, conversing, and socializing with Ruth's family and the neighboring family that had accompanied them as if we had been friends for ages. Both families live in the progressive Galilee community of Alon HaGalil. Both were remarkable in their own unique ways. Mostly though, both families were just kind, decent, intelligent, thoughtful, compassionate, and loving in what I want to believe are very unremarkable ways. Ordinary folks like us. So many times during the week I felt almost like crying, to have been given the gift of these people, and when we left, I made sure they knew that meeting them had been the best thing about our vacation, if not the entire year.

But they were only part of the enchantment. All around us there were groups using the camping facilities which are directly adjacent to the pool. The first day there was a group of Palestinian workers from the Four Homes of Mercy, an institution for mentally and physically handicapped people in Al-Azariyyeh. The women would swim in the pool fully clothed, their headscarves ballooning out behind them, and one took a particular shine to Phoebe. There was also a small group of mentally handicapped people, young Israelis, supervised by three Israeli women, an Israeli man, and a Palestinian man. Mid-week more groups arrived, one composed of Messianic Jews, Christian Palestinians, and Romanian and Russian teenagers, and they actually performed a little song-and-dance show about being united by the love of Jesus. The troupe organizer flashed the song lyrics up in four languages on a small blackboard while pantomiming the gestures, and in between the numbers, Arab and Jewish kids would give little testimonies about how they had made friends with people who were "supposed" to be their enemies. If we hadn't been through the year we had just endured, I guess it might have seemed kind of hokey. But hokey or not, if we don't find some bridge to unite us, we are going to make each other's lives—and deaths—miserable for nothing, and as far as I am concerned, it doesn't matter what the bridge is. It can be Jesus or secular humanism or the Tabgha campground. The sight of everyone, just swimming together and eating together and cleaning up together and being together so effortlessly, is one I won't soon forget. It was like catching a glimpse of paradise after a year in hell.

Since we returned home, I have thought many times of Kobi, Tally, Shai, and Mathilda's friend Ruth, and of their friends. And of Tally's baby due to be born in January. When Tally said goodbye, she sincerely wished for better times for us, and I sincerely wished for them the same. And we made plans to meet again, same place next year. Unfortunately, a lot can happen between now and then, and too many people seem hell-bent on destroying our chances for redemption rather than rescuing them. But Tabgha made me believe in miracles, and I am ready to work for them. Who else is ready for miracles to happen?

Postscript

A Message from the Girls

4 February 2002

Update from Mathilda and Nadine

We would like to tell you about Palestine where we live.

We used to live in Beit Jala, but we had to move from there to Beit Sahour because of the Intifada. The Intifada started in September 2000 because Sharon went to the Al-Aqsa mosque, which is why it's called Intifada of Al-Aqsa. Sharon went there to make people mad, and they did get very mad and started throwing lots of stones at all the soldiers. The soldiers have guns, and they shot at the people throwing rocks, and this made them more mad.

Nobody likes Sharon because he killed lots of people in Lebanon, which is beside Israel, in a big war. And now he killed lots of people in Palestine, too.

The Intifada went on for 16 months, and that's a very long time, and it still hasn't stopped. And many towns got bombed with tanks and helicopters and jets, and they broke down lots of buildings and lots of people got killed.

In Beit Jala where we used to live, they broke down lots of houses, and our house almost got broken, too. And a bullet came in a window. We used to hide next to the bed on the floor in my mom's room, and once when we were hiding a missile came very close and it almost hit us. It sounded like a whistle. And sometimes we looked out our front window and saw the houses getting hit and blowing up.

One time our neighbor Dr. Harry Fisher was trying to help some people who were hurt. Instead of hiding in his house, he went out, and he was killed by a missile. His daughter Asanya who's in sixth grade goes to our school and also our Sunday School. And we felt very sorry for her because her dad died.

These are the kids in my class whose houses got hit by tanks: Rowan, Samih, Shireen, Jihan, Rami, Ramzi, Jamil, Amanda, Sophia, Yaqoub, and Irene. And some others, but I can't remember them all.

And these are some people who died: Abu Ali Moustapha, Rania Khouroufeh, Johnny Taljiyeh, Moussa Abu Eid, Muhammed Abayat, Jamal Abayat, Issa Abayat, and a lot more so I can't say all their names. About 1000 Palestinians died, and that's a lot. And the Israelis won't stop bombing us until we all get out of Palestine or until we're all dead.

Sometimes we hear shooting while we're at school. And everyone gets scared and they start to run around and scream. And also one time we were at my mom's work and we heard shooting, and we had to wait downstairs for a long time until it stopped, and everyone was scared.

My grandma is Nancy and she lives in Virginia in America, and she always sends us lots of presents because she's very worried about us. Sometimes she cries when we talk to her on the phone. Last year I couldn't have a birthday party because of all the shooting.

I have a friend called Nathan, and he's American. And the soldiers hit him on the leg because he was trying to help the Palestinians be free. And Brian is also our friend, and he was in a demonstration to free the people and the soldiers hit him, too. The Israelis like the Americans except the ones who want to help the Palestinians.

My dad has a big farm, and the Israelis want to take it from us and give it to the settlers. The settlers want everything and don't want the Palestinians to have anything.

Once we went to the checkpoint and the soldiers made us sit there for a whole hour and wouldn't let us go. Sometimes they tell my dad he can't go with us to Jerusalem because he's a Palestinian and Palestinians aren't allowed to go anywhere. Sometimes they want to make him get out of the car, and we get scared he'll get shot.

When he goes to his work in Jerusalem he has to take a taxi, and sometimes the soldiers won't let him. In the night he comes late, and we get worried that he got caught by soldiers. My mom is always worried and scared. If the soldiers catch the Palestinians, they make them stand in a line and they can't move or they'll shoot them. And they chase the Palestinians with their jeeps and put them in a jail for a long time.

We have some friends named Debra and Daphne, and they're Jewish. And we sometimes go to their house for Purim (which is like Halloween) and Hanukkah (which is like Christmas) and they come to our house for Christmas. And our friends are also Tal and Mirav. Some Israelis are nice and like the Palestinians and want peace. And the Palestinians also want peace, and they don't want to be bombed anymore or shot anymore.

In October, all the Israeli tanks came inside Bethlehem, and all the people had to stay inside their houses for ten days so they wouldn't get shot. Any person who went outside got killed. Our cousins stayed at our new house in Beit Sahour because they live in Beit Jala and lots of tanks were there. There was a tank right next to our old house in Beit Jala, and also there was lots of shooting and fighting. I was very worried about all my classmates and teachers and also worried about my school getting broken. Lots of houses and stores got broken down, and all the streets and streetlights got ruined. And a hotel called the Paradise Hotel got burned, and now it has to be fixed. Everyone was very sad about this and very mad, too. And we are scared it will happen again.

Palestinians don't have tanks or helicopters or jets, so we can't keep the Israelis from coming back to Bethlehem and wrecking everything and trying to kill all the people. If they want to do it again, they will just do it.

Bethlehem is where Jesus was born, and He is sad about all this fighting in His town. He wants people to get along and be fair. If the Israelis are fair to the Palestinians and give them their rights, then they won't be mad anymore and the Intifada will stop and there will be peace.

Timeline

May 14,	1948	Israel established as a nation.
June	1967	Six-Day War. Israel conquers West Bank including Bethlehem.
Dec.	1987	First Intifada begins
Sept.	1993	Oslo Accords
Dec. 22,	1995	Israel leaves Bethlehem to be an autonomous area.
July 25,	2000	Camp David negotiations break down.
Oct. 2,	2000	Battle at Joseph's Tomb in Nablus.
Oct. 12,	2000	Palestinian mob in Nablus kills 2 Israeli soldiers throwing bodies out of of window of police station.
Oct. 22,	2000	Israeli tanks attack the town of Beit Jala, where Alison, George and family live.
Nov. 29,	2000	Bethlehem officially cancels formal Jubilee year Christmas Celebrations.
Nov. 15,	2000	Israeli combat helicopters attack Beit Jala.
Feb. 6,	2000	Ariel Sharon elected Prime Minister.
May 6,	2001	Israel moved troops around Beit Jala, the deepest incursion since 1995.
July 17,	2001	Israel kills four Palestinians by guided missile in Bethlehem. Palestinians fire mortar at Gilo.
July 18,	2001	Israel stationed tanks north and south of Bethlehem.
Aug. 8,	2001	A Palestinian suicide bomber killed himself and injured three Israeli soldiers at a checkpoint and Israeli helicopter gunships launched two retaliatory missile strikes against Nablus.
Aug. 9,	2001	A Palestinian suicide bomber killed himself and 14 others in Jerusalem, injuring more than 100 people.

Aug. 27,	2001	Israel killed Mustafa Zibri, the ranking leader of PFLP, by firing missiles into his office. Israeli paratroopers backed by tanks, bulldozers, and helicopters moved into Beit Jala.
Aug. 28,	2001	Israeli tanks and paratroopers occupied Lutheran Church and orphanage in Beit Jala, using it as a base for heavy shelling.
Aug. 30,	2001	Israeli troops withdrew from Beit Jala.
Oct. 19,	2001	Israel occupied Bethlehem and Beit Jala, killing three Palestinians and wounding 27.
Oct. 21,	2001	Israeli sniper killed altar boy Johnny Taljieh leaving Church of the Nativity.
Oct. 28,	2001	Israel withdrew from Bethlehem and Beit Jala.
Dec. 24,	2001	Sharon denied Arafat permission to travel to Bethlehem for Christmas.
Mar. 8,	2002	Israeli tank and helicopter assaults killed 32 in various locations including five near Bethlehem. A Palestinian killed himself and wounded 10 Israelis in a settlement near Jerusalem.
Mar.11,	2002	Invading Israeli troops arrested over 500 Palestinian males between 15 and 45 in Dheisheh refugee camp in Bethlehem.
Mar. 14,	2002	Israeli tank fire damaged Church of the Nativity. Israel kills two members of al-Aqsa brigades. Palestinians bomb a Merkava tank killing three soldiers.
Mar. 17,	2002	Israeli troops launched a short tank-backed invasion of Bethlehem, killing one.
Mar. 19,	2002	Israel pulled tanks back from Bethlehem.
Mar. 27,	2002	Palestinian suicide bombers killed 19 and wound 100 at a Passover Seder in Netanya.
Mar. 29,	2002	Israeli tank and helicopter assaults kill 32 in various locations, five near Bethlehem.
April 1,	2002	Israel troops invade Ramallah, laying seige to Arafat's compound.
April 2,	2002	Siege of the Church of the Nativity began.
May 22,	2002	Siege of the Church of the Nativity ends.
May 25,	2002	Israel troops invaded Bethlehem.
May 27,	2002	Israeli troops in Bethlehem and the Dheisheh refugee camp imposed 24-hour curfew and kidnapped 15. Palestinian suicide bomber killed two and wounds 40 near Tel Aviv.

May 28,	2002	Israeli troops continue rounding up men in Bethlehem, Beit Jala, and other cities. Palestinian kills three in a settlement near Nablus.
May 30,	2002	Israeli troops withdraw from Bethlehem.
May 31,	2002	Israeli troops impose 24-hour curfews in other cities and arrest 100.
June 1,	2002	Israel invaded Nablus, Bethlehem, Tamoun, and Tulkarm, killing one Palestinian in Nablus and kidnapping at least 59.
June 11,	2002	Suicide bombs in Herzlyia and Hebron killed one and wounded 11 Israelis.
June 17,	2002	Israel kills Walid Sbeh near Bethlehem.
June 19,	2002	Israeli troops put several West Bank cities under 24-hour curfew including Bethlehem area. Six Palestinians killed in an Israeli attack.
July 22,	2002	Fatah, Tanzim, and Hamas agree to a halt in suicide bombings against Israeli civilians. An Israeli F-16 kills Hamas leader Salah Shehadeh in Gaza, killing 14 others including nine children and wounding 150.
Oct. 23,	2002	The "Quartet" (U.S., Russia, U.N., and European Union) presented new three-stage roadmap for peace.
Nov. 21,	2002	A suicide bomber killed 11 passengers and wounded 48 on a bus in Jerusalem's Kiryat Menachem neighborhood.
Nov. 22,	2002	Israeli tanks and troops reoccupied Bethlehem, Beit Sahour, and Beit Jala beginning curfew to continue in Bethlehem until Christmas. Israeli troops shot and killed UN worker Ian Hook in Jenin.
Jan. 28,	2003	Ariel Sharon reelected Prime Minister.
Feb. 15,	2003	Israel announced that it would build a 25-foot high wall splitting area around Rachel's tomb from the rest of Bethlehem.
Mar. 16,	2003	American ISM volunteer Rachel Corrie killed by bulldozer demolishing house.
Mar. 11,	2003	Mahmoud Abbas (Abu Mazen) named new Palestinian Prime Minister.
Mar. 19,	2003	Iraq war begins.
Mar. 25,	2003	Israeli undercover agents in attack on car in Bethlehem killed two Hamas members as well as ten-year old Christine Sa'ada.